MW00357113

American Universities and the
Birth of Modern Mormonism, 1867–1940

American Universities and the Birth of Modern Mormonism, 1867–1940

. . . .

THOMAS W. SIMPSON

The University of North Carolina Press Chapel Hill

This book was published with the assistance of the Anniversary Fund of the University of North Carolina Press.

© 2016 The University of North Carolina Press
All rights reserved
Set in Charis by Westchester Publishing Services
Manufactured in the United States of America

The University of North Carolina Press has been a member of the Green Press Initiative since 2003.

Cover illustration: Mormons from Utah and Idaho studying in Boston and Cambridge, 1893. Courtesy of the Church History Library, Salt Lake City, Utah.

Library of Congress Cataloging-in-Publication Data
Names: Simpson, Thomas Wendell, author.
Title: American universities and the birth of modern Mormonism, 1867-1940 / Thomas W. Simpson.
Description: Chapel Hill : The University of North Carolina Press, [2016] | Includes bibliographical references and index.
Identifiers: LCCN 2015038634| ISBN 9781469630229 (hardback: alk. paper) | ISBN 9781469628639 (pbk: alk. paper) | ISBN 9781469628646 (ebook)
Subjects: LCSH: Mormons—Education (Higher)—United States—History. | Education, Higher—United States—History. | Mormons—Intellectual life.
Classification: LCC BX8611 .S53 2016 | DDC 289.3/73—dc23 LC record available at http://lccn.loc.gov/2015038634

Chapter 1 is based on Thomas W. Simpson, "Mormons Study 'Abroad': Brigham Young's Romance with American Higher Education, 1867-1877," *Church History* 76.4 (December 2007): 778-798. © 2007 by Oxford University Press.

Chapter 2 is based on Thomas W. Simpson, "The Death of Mormon Separatism in American Universities, 1877-1896," *Religion and American Culture* 22.2 (Summer 2012): 163-201. © 2012 by the Regents of the University of California. Published by the University of California Press.

For Alex

Contents

Illustrations

Chronology

1886   Latter-day Saints' College (originally called the Salt Lake
        Academy, later called the Latter-day Saints University)
        opens in Salt Lake City

1887   Congressional Edmunds-Tucker Act intensifies federal
        pressure on Mormon polygamists and Mormon
        institutions

1888   The LDS First Presidency authorizes the formation of a
        General Board of Education and LDS "academies" in each
        stake to rival public schools; Agricultural College of Utah
        (later Utah State University) established as Utah's land-grant
        college

1890   Wilford Woodruff's Manifesto signals the church's official
        renunciation of polygamy; founding of the University of
        Chicago

1891   Joseph Marion Tanner leads group of Brigham Young
        College students to study at Harvard; founding of Stanford
        University

1892   Harvard president Charles Eliot visits Salt Lake City;
        widely publicized heresy trial of Presbyterian seminary
        professor Charles A. Briggs; popular and controversial New
        England minister and journalist Lyman Abbott publishes
        The Evolution of Christianity; Teachers College (affiliated
        with Columbia University by 1898) receives its permanent
        charter

1892–94 University of Michigan graduate and Brigham Young
        Academy president Benjamin Cluff brings famed educators
        to Provo for summer schools at the BYA

1896   Utah statehood; Martha Hughes Cannon, a graduate of the
        University of Michigan, becomes the first female state
        senator in the United States

1897   Clark University president and psychologist G. Stanley Hall
        lectures at the BYA summer school

1899, 1900 John A. Widtsoe (Goettingen, chemistry) and Joseph F.
        Merrill (Johns Hopkins, physics) become two of the first
        Mormons to earn the PhD; both would later serve at the
        head of the church educational system

1901   Joseph F. Smith becomes president of the church; John
        Dewey delivers summer school lectures at the Brigham
        Young Academy

1902   W. E. B. Du Bois publishes "On the Training of Black Men," an influential argument for higher education and critique of Booker T. Washington's conceptions of practical and vocational education

1903   Joseph Marion Tanner, superintendent of the church educational system, institutes the Education Fund to help Mormons study "abroad"

1904   Evidence of polygamy's persistence emerges in the context of controversy surrounding the seating of LDS apostle Reed Smoot in the U.S. Senate, prompting a "Second Manifesto" that denounces polygamy and forces prominent but unrepentant polygamist educators Joseph Marion Tanner and Benjamin Cluff Jr. into the shadows of Mormon intellectual life

1907   Pope Pius X condemns Catholic modernism; proponent of the Protestant Social Gospel movement Walter Rauschenbusch publishes *Christianity and the Social Crisis*

1908   John A. Widtsoe publishes *Joseph Smith as Scientist*

1909   The church centralizes its teacher training and all other college-level work at BYU; LDS First Presidency issues "The Origin of Man," criticizing scientific evolution

1911   Evolution and higher criticism controversy at BYU results in investigation and dismissal of professors with advanced training "abroad"

1912   Publication of *The Fundamentals*, seen as the origin of twentieth-century Protestant fundamentalism

1915   Nationally publicized academic freedom controversy at the University of Utah

1918   Mormon E. E. Ericksen completes his University of Chicago dissertation, "Psychological and Ethical Aspects of Mormon Group Life," an influential social scientific approach to the history of Mormonism

1921   Franklin S. Harris assumes the presidency of BYU and pursues its accreditation, courting LDS professors with advanced degrees

1922   Berkeley education professor Charles Edward Rugh instructs LDS church school teachers on "Religious Education" and "How to Teach the Bible" at the BYU summer school

1925   Historic Scopes "Monkey" Trial in Dayton, Tennessee; Vasco M. Tanner, with a PhD in entomology from Stanford, begins teaching evolution at BYU without incident

1926   The Brigham Young College closes; church establishes first of several LDS "institutes"—social and academic centers adjacent to a state university—for Mormon college students

1928   BYU accredited by Association of American Universities

1930–33   University of Chicago Divinity School professors lecture annually at summer schools for LDS religious educators

1931   Sidney Sperry becomes the first Mormon to earn a PhD from the University of Chicago's Divinity School; ten other Mormons earn advanced degrees there between 1931 and 1942

1934   LDS geologist Sterling B. Talmage (PhD, Harvard) and Apostle Joseph Fielding Smith argue publicly and bitterly over the appropriate boundaries between religion and science

1938   J. Reuben Clark Jr. delivers "The Charted Course of the Church in Education," outlining the "fundamentals" of Latter-day Saint belief in order to check, and condemn, the influence of secular methodologies in LDS religious education

1940   BYU Board of Trustees approves new academic division of religion, which includes faculty trained at the University of Chicago's Divinity School

American Universities and the
Birth of Modern Mormonism, 1867–1940

Introduction

Mormonism Reframed

· ·

Because nineteenth-century Mormons could never fully realize their separatist dream of building the Kingdom of God in North America, the history of Mormonism has involved highly complex contacts and negotiations with non-Mormons. In their attempts to convert, resist, or appease powerful outsiders, Mormons have engaged in a distinctive dialectic of secrecy and self-disclosure, of esoteric rites and strategic public relations. The result has been an extended process of controlled modernization, the evolution of a dynamic, global faith.

Fundamental questions linger, however, about the history and the process: how did the LDS Church grow from a small, persecuted sect into one of the world's fastest-growing religions? More specifically, how did the nineteenth century's "most despised large group" become so loyal to the United States in the twentieth?[1] In other words, how could nineteenth-century Mormons, after decades of principled, costly resistance to federal authority, suddenly jettison their utopian separatism—their polygamy and their communitarian ethics, economy, schools, and politics—and embrace the institutions and values of their tormentors?

To answer the questions, I dove into massive archives of Mormon history, focusing on the unpublished diaries, correspondence, and church records from the critical transitional period of Mormon history: the late nineteenth and early twentieth centuries. What I unearthed is an extraordinary history of Mormon academic migration to the elite universities of the United States. Right at the height of Mormon-"Gentile" hostilities, the American university offered exiled Mormons a unique, quasi-sacred cultural space of freedom and dignity. At schools like Johns Hopkins, Penn, Cornell, Columbia, Harvard, MIT, Michigan, Chicago, Stanford, and Berkeley, a rising, influential generation of Mormon women and men would undergo a radical transformation of consciousness and identity. They would fall in love with America again. Outsiders became insiders; those on the margins entered the mainstream. Indeed, this book's central thesis is that modern Mormonism was born in the American university, and the Mormon path to citizenship—to a genuine, passionate sense of belonging in America—ran directly through it.

It was hardly what the church's aging pioneers and revolutionaries had in mind. Beginning in the 1860s, led by Brigham Young, they authorized academic migration only insofar as it would maintain Mormon independence. Mormon students were supposed to use their limited time in "Babylon," across enemy lines, to acquire the practical and professional expertise they needed to build the kingdom of God, a civilization that would be the envy of the world. Church leaders knew it was a gamble. As devout Mormons, they understood the benefits, even the necessity, of education, but they feared that prolonged association with non-Mormon professors and peers would corrupt the students' faith. They could not foresee a third possibility, between kingdom-building and apostasy: the possibility that devout Mormon students would understand their exhilarating university experiences as compatible with Mormon ideals of freedom, dignity, intelligence, and growth. For these students, the academic errand became a pilgrimage, an eastward migration that reversed the course, and healed the wounds, of exile.[2]

It was precisely what leading American educators had in mind. Unlike rabidly anti-Mormon politicians and preachers, who aimed to destroy "polygamic theocracy" with punitive legislation and evangelical zeal,[3] university presidents like James Angell of Michigan, Charles Eliot of Harvard, and David Starr Jordan of Stanford opted for persuasion rather than coercion, pursuing their nation-building project by inviting Americans, including Mormons, to flourish in zones of religious and academic freedom. This, too, was a gamble, a risk that American intellectuals assumed in order to promote social cohesion in a post–Civil War America threatened by economic inequality, lingering sectional tensions, and racial and ethnic balkanization. They hoped that university-trained scholar-citizens—experts, professionals—would steer the rapidly changing nation through the tumult into a new era of unity and strength.[4] As a result, universities became unique and essential sites of diplomacy during a sort of Mormon-Gentile cold war. In university settings that were neither sectarian nor secularist, Mormons could rehearse for American citizenship and embrace higher education as a spiritual calling. They felt welcome, challenged, and inspired. They would never be the same.[5]

For Mormon students' cultural conversion to matter in Utah, though, it had to be shared and celebrated. Few nineteenth-century Mormons had the leisure or means to study at a university, but with their star students as proxies, Mormons in Utah could participate vicariously in the students' transformation. Relatives and other church members devoted themselves to the students, who could not have succeeded without steady financial and spiritual support from home. Church periodicals then amplified the students' influence by routinely publishing their correspondence and feature articles about American universities. Finally, in the early 1890s, after the church had officially renounced plural marriage, and Utah was mounting its latest campaign for statehood, returning Mormon students brought leading American educators to Utah for enormously popular teacher training institutes. The gatherings allowed Mormons and non-Mormons to unite in service of shared American educational aims and ambitions. As Mormons lost their independence, educational aspiration gave them a way to imagine entering the mainstream of American life without selling their souls.

Nevertheless, the Mormon romance with higher education has always been tempestuous. The success of Mormon scholars, women and men, has filled the Saints with pride, but it has also often left church leaders anxious to defend their authority. In the twentieth century, fierce, protracted battles ensued over academic freedom, scientific evolution, and the historicity of Mormonism's sacred past. As a result, education became the main battleground in the twentieth-century war to define Mormon identity, the struggle for the soul of modern Mormonism. In the crucible of conflict, Mormons developed competing notions of authenticity—of what makes a "good" Mormon—that even a rigidly structured ecclesiastical hierarchy could not reconcile.

By 1940, these basic structures and parameters for Mormon discourse about authority, ambition, and the Mormon mind were firmly established, and these essential frameworks, tensions, and controversies persist. Only by understanding their astonishingly long history can we begin to see how and why modern Mormonism takes its current, hotly contested form.

Academic Migration and the Evolution of Mormonism

Analyzing this pattern of Mormon academic migration adds essential depth to our understanding of Mormon modernization, accommodation, and Americanization.[6] Established narratives of these processes have focused heavily on LDS president Wilford Woodruff's "Manifesto" of 1890, a momentous declaration that Latter-day Saints must cease to contract plural marriages. The Manifesto put an end to the intense federal persecution of the 1880s, when government agents forced husbands of plural wives to go to prison or underground; confiscated Mormon assets; abolished Utah women's right to vote; and secularized Mormons' local schools. President Woodruff's truce with the federal government brought Mormons peace and, eventually, the most meaningful sign of acceptance in their short history: the granting of statehood to Utah in 1896.

Tremendous, lasting changes in Mormonism accompanied the Manifesto and statehood. New patterns and structures in the Mormon family, education, politics, business, and religious practice emerged.[7] Describing the broad sweep of these changes, some scholars have argued that twentieth-century or "modern" Mormonism bore little resemblance to the Mormonism of Joseph Smith and Brigham Young. Mark Leone and others have described the discontinuity in terms of a transition from a closed, communitarian, and theocratic society to an open, individualistic, and republican one. The former was confrontational in its posture toward the Gentile world, the latter accommodating.[8]

Following Leone's lead, R. Laurence Moore asserted that accommodating Mormons "forgot their history" as a persecuted community of American outsiders.[9] Jan Shipps, in some of her important early work, gave the changes a less negative cast but saw them as no less dramatic. Charting new religious practices among Mormons in the late nineteenth and early twentieth centuries, she noted that "the behavioral boundary that had once separated Mormons from the outside world was being seriously eroded."[10] To preserve a sense of sainthood, Mormons cultivated practices that softened their separatism. They began to pay more attention to regulations concerning diet and appearance. Devotion to genealogy and temple work on behalf of the dead also intensified. No longer distinguished by their communitarianism or theocracy, Mormons found in these new gestures, interests, and callings a way to feel faithful to their principles and their past.

All the scholarly attention to the 1890s, however, has obscured crucial contingencies of Mormonism's historical evolution and important continuities between pre- and post-Manifesto Mormonism. Mormon academic migration began decades before the Manifesto, and the mentalities of the early participants in the migration (as well as their supporters) defy simple categories of resistance, accommodation, and assimilation. In the 1870s and 1880s, Latter-day Saints took advantage of new opportunities available in education and transportation, confident that they could remain "a people set apart" from the worst influences and vices of the wider culture. Neither rejecting American culture nor assimilating to it, Mormons made strategic choices, and engaged in fierce debates, about how to use education to build the kingdom. Their attitudes toward church authority, gender, polygamy, politics, and America itself varied widely. Their stories offer a glimpse of deeper truths: the Mormon path to modernization was neither narrow nor fixed, and external pressure alone could not have produced modern Mormonism.

After the Manifesto brought a certain peace, and Mormons began to think of their Zion as more of a spiritual than physical kingdom, education in America's elite universities remained deeply desirable to Mormons seeking to stimulate the growth of Utah's fledgling universities and broader regional infrastructures of agriculture, law, and medicine. As a result, as early as the 1890s, Mormons started becoming increasingly aware of, and sympathetic to, national trends in education. Building on the gains and contacts made by their university-educated predecessors, Mormons started striking up friendships with elite educators like Charles Eliot, G. Stanley Hall, and John Dewey, all of whom lectured in Utah at the invitation of leaders at Provo's Brigham Young Academy. (The Academy, chartered in 1875, would begin calling itself Brigham Young University in 1903.)

As pragmatist philosophy and evolutionary science began to sway increasing numbers of Mormons studying "abroad" in the early twentieth century, however, Mormon intellectual and theological consensus proved elusive. Influenced directly by the likes of William James and John Dewey, some returned to Utah with a diminished belief in divine providence, a new openness to modern biblical scholarship, and a robust devotion to academic freedom. As a result, Mormons debated the nature of truth, revelation, and authority as never before, spurring the church's president and prophet, Joseph F. Smith, to proclaim: "God has revealed to us a simple and effectual way of serving Him, and we should regret very much to see the simplicity of those revelations involved in all sorts of philosophical speculations. If we encouraged them it would not be long before we should have a *theological scholastic aristocracy* in the Church, and we should therefore not enjoy the brotherhood that now is, or should be common to rich and poor, learned and unlearned among the Saints."[11] Controversies at Brigham Young University in 1911 and the University of Utah in 1915 signified the shift with a wave of heresy trials, firings, and resignations.

Smith's attempt to thwart a "theological scholastic aristocracy" reflected deeply rooted "populist" sensibilities in Mormonism, which had shaped the church from the beginning. Historian Nathan Hatch has argued that religious populism was characteristic of the influential "democratizing" Christian movements of early nineteenth-century America—including Mormon, Methodist, Baptist, "Christian," and African American churches—that permanently altered the American religious landscape. This populist orientation entailed reverence for the wisdom of ordinary folk and a suspicion of learned elites. Hatch writes, "At the very time that British clergy were confounded by their own gentility in trying to influence working-class culture, America exalted religious leaders short on social graces, family connections, and literary education. These religious activists pitched their messages to the unschooled and unsophisticated. Their movements offered the humble a marvelous sense of individual and collective aspiration."[12]

Mormons' populism led them to distrust philosophical speculation, believing that it obscured and even corrupted simple, common-sense truths. The Book of Mormon itself gave its adherents ample reason to distrust the "learned." A passage from 2 Nephi, for example, links learning to unbelief and exploitation of the poor. "And the Gentiles are lifted up in the pride of their eyes," it reads, "and have stumbled, because of the greatness of their stumbling block, that they have built up many churches; nevertheless, they put down the power and miracles of God, and preach up unto themselves their own wisdom and their own learning, that they may get gain and grind upon the face of the poor."[13] Learning was not inherently dangerous, however, according to the same text. As long as the devotees of learning "hearken unto the counsels of God,"[14] the Saints could keep infidelity and class division at bay.

The resulting tension and struggle would preoccupy church leaders throughout the twentieth century and well into the twenty-first, as young Mormons' quest for intellectual cultivation endured. Church leaders continued to give students their (often qualified) sanction for studying in elite American universities, but controversy surfaced repeatedly. In the 1920s and 1930s, for example, Mormons trained at the theologically liberal University of Chicago Divinity School strove to reform religious education in Utah, and conservative church leaders responded forcefully. In 1938, J. Reuben Clark Jr., a high-ranking authority in the church, a Columbia law graduate, and a former official in the U.S. State Department, rebuked the Chicago graduates. He asserted that "On more than one occasion our Church members have gone to other places for special training in particular lines; they have had the training which was supposedly the last word, the most modern view, the ne plus ultra of up-to-dateness; then they have brought it back and dosed it upon us without any thought as to whether we needed it or not."[15] Although Mormons continued to flock to American universities after Clark's speech, the address articulated a deep ambivalence about higher education that remains strong among Mormon leaders today. As long as higher education was "practical" and "faith-promoting," church leaders supported it unequivocally, but maintaining those ideal boundaries proved impossible.

The history of Mormon academic migration has received scant scholarly attention. Histories of higher education in Utah offer a partial view, insofar as they provide biographical information on Mormon faculty trained in universities outside the Intermountain West. Histories of the legal and medical professions offer additional source material. No one, however, has attempted to analyze the migration in its full scope. In his 1965 master's thesis, John Parley Dunford called attention to the phenomenon, but his study had severe limitations: it treated student migration as an exclusively male, post-Manifesto phenomenon, and it discussed only a few of the best-known examples.[16] My research has yielded information on hundreds of students from Utah and southern Idaho who enrolled in universities outside the Intermountain West and left records of their experiences. The vast majority returned to the region, and they assumed a disproportionate role in the building of regional institutions. (The databases in Appendices A–E, which I developed from my research, offer a glimpse of the data informing the story I tell and opportunities for further research.) By examining the full extent and history of Mormon student migration, we can see how badly, and for how long, Mormons have wanted to be as "scientific" and "progressive" as other Americans, even as they have maintained a strong sense of cultural distinctiveness.

Gender, Ethnicity, and Outsiders in American Higher Education

This revised cultural and intellectual history of Mormonism sheds light on the emergence and domestication of nineteenth-century Mormon feminism, the evolution of Mormon ethnicity, the development of Mormon intellectual life and anti-intellectualism, and the history of outsiders in American higher education.[17]

The chronology of Mormon academic migration, in fact, converges in striking ways with the history of other outsiders' forays into the American academy. When the University of Michigan began admitting women in the 1870s, for example, Mormon women were there.[18] In the 1890s, when Harvard president Charles Eliot denied graduates of Jesuit colleges regular admission to the Law School,[19] and when W. E. B. Du Bois became the first African American to earn a PhD from Harvard, Mormons were there. In the early twentieth century, when elite institutions like Harvard and Columbia wrestled with what they perceived as a growing "Jewish problem" and began implementing admissions quotas, Mormons were there.[20]

In other words, at a time when American Protestant elites were anxious to defend their own authority and supremacy in an evolving America, Mormons, like other outsiders, posed a significant threat. Yet as those elites increasingly equated authentic American identity with evolving notions of "whiteness," Mormons stood to benefit in the long run. In comparison with other outsiders, Mormons enjoyed relative freedom in the American university to join the club and play the game—to cover the outward markers of ethnic outsider status and "pass" as white (and even as monogamous, in some remarkable nineteenth-century cases discussed in the first two chapters of this book).[21]

Despite such relative privilege, the Mormon migration to the American university was fraught, because first-generation Mormon university students were still cultural outsiders in profound ways. They carried the hopes, and bore the anxieties, of their elders. New forms of accommodation and mobility became available to this rising intellectual class, threatening to tear at the fabric of the pioneers' prized, communitarian solidarity but promising to bring Mormonism unprecedented influence and respect.

Insider Mormon Language: A Primer

Throughout the book, for the sake of simplicity and brevity, I refer to members of The Church of Jesus Christ of Latter-day Saints as "Mormons," "Latter-day Saints," or "Saints," employing the corresponding adjectives "Mormon" and "LDS." Church members themselves customarily used these designations in their published and unpublished writings during the period that I have examined. In using this shorthand myself, I do not intend to obscure the church's claim to be not only Christian but also the one true "Church of Jesus Christ." Understanding that claim is essential to any analysis of "Mormon" history, especially the history of Mormon thought. The church's inherent Christian exclusivism gives it its comprehensive sense of authority in matters of Christian doctrine and practice, its dark view of the Christian past, and its suspicion of "outside" theology and philosophy. The history of Mormon thought reflects the ways in which Mormons have embraced or modified these basic dispositions.

The unique organization of the church also gives rise to a distinctive institutional language that bears some explanation. The Mormon priesthood, exclusively male yet nonprofessional, forms the base of a pyramid of church authority. (Mormons affirm that church leaders, except at the very highest, full-time levels, should neither be paid a salary nor be required to have formal training the way that clergy in many other denominations are.) Advancement through the ranks of the priesthood, starting at age twelve, carries young men through the offices of deacon, teacher, priest, and elder. At the highest level of ecclesiastical authority stands the president, also designated as the living "Prophet, Seer, and Revelator." With two "counselors" the prophet forms a body called the First Presidency. Like the prophets of the Hebrew Scriptures, the prophet acts as a conduit for divine revelation, embodying the Mormon belief that revelation is an ongoing historical process. Immediately below the First Presidency in the chain of authority are the Twelve Apostles, the senior member of which often fills any vacancy in the First Presidency.

Although women do not hold the priesthood, they do hold the highest offices in church women's organizations like the Relief Society (dedicated to charitable and humanitarian work), the Young Women's Mutual Improvement Association (promoting the spiritual and cultural development of young women), and the Primary Association (for the spiritual and cultural development of children).

On the local level, the basic unit of organization is the "ward," over which a lay bishop presides. A "stake" is the next largest regional unit, which comprises multiple wards and is governed by a stake presidency. Semiannually, as many leaders and members as are able gather for a "general conference" in Salt Lake City.

Mormons customarily address each other as "brother" or "sister," and in earlier times it was not uncommon for them to refer to non-Mormons as "Gentiles." In ordinary usage "Gentile" often simply meant non-Mormon, but in many cases the term was reserved for dogged anti-Mormons. In my writing, I have tried to use "non-Mormon" as much as possible, employing "Gentile" or "outsider" only as a way of evoking the sense of opposition that has pervaded the Mormon past.

Humanizing Mormonism

In a recent meditation on theory in the study of religion, Thomas Tweed describes scholarly accounts of religion as "positioned representations of a changing terrain by an itinerant cartographer."[22] This book is the product of precisely such an intellectual sojourn. I have never been a practicing Mormon—my family's spiritual heritages, influences, and affiliations are exceedingly diverse—but on my father's side of the family, I have a Mormon ancestry that extends to the days of the pioneers. I never took much academic interest in the study of Mormonism, however, until I was in graduate school, specializing in the religious history of the United States after the Civil War. As I prepared for doctoral examinations, the historical evolution of Mormonism increasingly intrigued and puzzled me. My immersions into Davis Bitton's thick *Guide to Mormon Diaries & Autobiographies*, in search of clues to shifts in Mormons' outlook and identity at the turn of the twentieth century, led me to discover the surprising pattern of Mormon academic migration I describe here.[23] As I carried out and reflected on my archival research two thousand miles from home, I relearned old lessons in a startlingly fresh way: that "religions" and "cultures" are irreducibly and irrepressibly diverse, fluid, and contested. Mormonism is no exception, of course, and yet much of the prevailing discourse about the faith—as formulated by insiders and outsiders alike—remains reductive.

It is my hope, then, that this intellectual genealogy, this mosaic of Mormon intellectual and cultural history, will be textured enough to allow us to add essential complexity to the Mormon past, humanizing the Saints by portraying their diversity, conflict, and passion.[24] This history also bears witness to the enduring promise of the American university as—at its best—a radically humanizing, democratic cultural space.[25] Ultimately, and at its heart, this book wrestles with some of our most enduring questions: Can subcultures and minority faiths flourish in modern America? Can a sectarian religious tradition embrace pluralism and survive? And can the religious and scientific mind ever be integrated, or are they destined to be at war?

1 Brigham Young's Romance with American Higher Education, 1867–1877

· ·

In the 1860s, Mormons began knocking at the doors of American colleges and universities. Reversing the course of their westward-bound pioneer ancestors, these academic emigrants sought to retrieve what their fore-runners had left behind, by force or by choice: their access to higher edu-cation. By 1940, hundreds of Mormons had left Utah and Idaho to study "abroad" in the elite universities of the United States. In the earliest cases, church leaders sent the students as missionaries, but not to proselytize. Rather, they tapped these women and men for specialized training in professions ranging from law, medicine, and engineering to education. Mormons saw education in "Gentile" universities as a means to realize a corporate hope: a kingdom of God in the Mountain West. The goal was, in the words of Brigham Young, to gather the world's knowledge to Zion, to help build the perfect society in the "latter days" before God's millen-nial reign.

Religious and secular motives drove the students' migration. Mormons had long believed that education hastened their spiritual progression toward godhood. Before his assassination in 1844, Joseph Smith had taught that "the glory of God is intelligence" and instructed believers to "study and learn, and become acquainted with all good books, and with languages, tongues, and people."[1] The impulse to learn intensified, how-ever, in the 1870s, when the completion of the transcontinental railroad forced Utah Mormons to adopt new strategies for maintaining their cul-tural and economic independence. Higher education was no longer just a means of spiritual progress; it was also a way to survive. In the mind of Brigham Young, sending women and men "abroad" to receive advanced degrees would reduce the church's dependence on outside doctors, lawyers, and teachers, preserving Mormons' dignity and strength.

The first Mormon to venture east for training in the professions ap-pears to have been Elvira Stevens Barney, who left Utah in 1864 to spend nearly two years studying medicine at Illinois's Wheaton College.[2] Mor-mon academic migration would not become a movement, however, until it had the explicit sanction of Young, the church's president and prophet. Earlier in his administration, he had made important practical and theological arguments in support of education. In 1859, for example, he had urged the Saints to go forth and gather the best of the world's knowledge, to build the perfect society. He affirmed that "it is the business of the Elders of this Church . . . to gather up all the truths in the world pertaining to life and salvation, to the Gospel we preach, to mechanism of every kind, to the sciences, and to philosophy, wherever it may be found in every nation, kindred, tongue, and people and bring it to Zion."[3] Later, in 1860, Young proclaimed that "intelligent beings are organized to become Gods, even the Sons of God, to dwell in the presence of the Gods, and become associated with the highest intelligencies [sic] that dwell in eternity. We are now in the school, and must practice upon what we receive."[4] The rewards of education were great, here and in the hereafter.

Young was not especially inclined, however, to promote a large-scale academic migration. In 1866, he told a Mormon correspondent that "going abroad to obtain schooling will be labor spent in vain."[5] Such study would be costly and unnecessary, Young argued, since Utah boasted well-trained teachers in virtually all branches of learning. At best, the claim was debatable; opportunities for higher education in Utah virtually did not exist.[6] The distortion revealed Young's reluctance to endorse education abroad unless it met the urgent needs of the Mormon kingdom.

Authorizing Mormon Study "Abroad"

Pressing concerns about the welfare of the Saints finally prompted Young to approve a limited student migration in 1867. He knew that his developing territory desperately needed trained surgeons, especially in the fledgling settlements north of Salt Lake City. Yet Young hoped that after just one or two students received their eastern degrees, they could train others back home and eliminate the need for additional outside training. Mormon independence was paramount.[7]

Young also harbored suspicions of the medical profession itself. Mormon scripture justified that skepticism, with its abundant testimony to the healing power of faith. Teachings revealed in the *Doctrine and Covenants*, the collection of modern revelations given mainly to Joseph Smith, convinced Mormons that their elders could heal the sick through the laying on of hands. In cases where the patient could not muster the requisite faith, Smith forbade medical care at "the hand of an enemy," prescribing

Brigham Young first authorized Mormon study "abroad" in the 1860s. Used by permission, L. Tom Perry Special Collections, Harold B. Lee Library, Brigham Young University, Provo.

only "herbs and mild food" as treatment.[8] These attitudes toward healing and the medical profession led Brigham Young to allow Mormons to study surgery, but not medicine. He contended that "surgery will be much more useful in our Territory than the practice of medicine, [because] simple remedies such as herbs and mild drinks are in operation in our faith, and it is my opinion that too many of our people run to the doctor if they experience the slightest indisposition, which is decidedly opposed to the revelation which governs us as a people."[9] Young tried to ensure that when he endorsed academic training abroad, he would not lead the faithful to question the sufficiency of revelation or faith. He was walking a tightrope.

With Young's blessing, the first Mormon to train in surgery was Heber John Richards, a twenty-seven-year-old elder living in Salt Lake City. In 1867, Young arranged for Richards to study under Dr. Lewis A. Sayre at the Bellevue Hospital Medical College in New York City. Young had met Sayre the previous year in Salt Lake City, and the Mormon leader recognized in him a wealth of knowledge that "could not perhaps be excelled on this continent."[10] When Sayre offered to train one or two Latter-day Saint students in surgery at Bellevue, Young encouraged Richards to go.[11] In November 1867, Richards left for New York.

Given the financial support and the blessing of the church, Richards understood his academic errand as a mission.[12] Although the prophet did not expect Richards to devote much time to securing converts, he nevertheless wanted Richards to see his studies as a sacred calling. Young instructed him to pursue his course of study diligently, ever mindful that "you hold the priesthood." To help reinforce Richards's religious commitments, the prophet prescribed regular meetings with other Saints in New York; preaching to the inhabitants of the city whenever possible; and, when among non-Mormons at school, association only with "those of steady and virtuous habits." Young offered his admonitions to fortify Richards for his time in "the world."[13]

A more formal, ritualized blessing accompanied the prophet's personal advice. In keeping with Mormon rites established to consecrate a missionary for labors in the world, Elder John Taylor (who would eventually succeed Young as president of the church) "sealed" a blessing upon Richards: "[W]e pray God the Eternal Father to cause His holy spirit to rest down upon you that your mind may be expanded that you may be able to understand correct principles, that the blessings of the Most High God may be with you, that the spirit of inspiration may rest upon you while you are studying those principles to which you have been appointed[.]"[14] Richards left Salt Lake City armed with the blessings of God, God's prophet, and God's holy priesthood. He planned to return with uncorrupted faith and acquired expertise.

Richards's academic and spiritual success mattered to the Saints at home. In their eyes, New York was a dark, lost city of "Babylon," a place of spiritual darkness and omnipresent vice, a proving ground for the righteous. At the same time, paradoxically, many admired New York as a center of culture and refinement. They eagerly awaited news of Richards's exploits. Reports occasionally came in from David M. Stewart, a Mormon in the missionary field. In 1868, Stewart gave the following news: "Br. Heber John Richards writes me . . . occasionally. He says he is . . . preaching the gospel every opportunity that offers. He is hale in body, cheerful in spirit, but says in conclusion, 'there is no place like home.' "[15] In early 1869, Stewart visited Richards and filed another report: "We spent a very interesting day with Bro. Heber John Richards in New York, and we saw sights never to be forgotten in the 'Bellvue [sic] Medical College,' and other places of interest. He is rapidly improving in the study of anatomy, and treasuring up classic lore, which if properly applied will be of great benefit to its possessor."[16] Such accounts reassured and flattered the faithful at home. Richards eventually returned to Salt Lake City with his degree from Bellevue. He had a successful practice in Salt Lake until 1892, when he moved south to Provo and practiced there until his retirement.[17]

By 1869, the importance of sending Mormon students "abroad" became even more apparent in an increasingly diverse, modernizing Utah territory. The transcontinental railroad, which Young famously welcomed because it would hasten the gathering of Mormon converts to Zion,[18] nevertheless introduced unwelcome competition in the realms of business, law, politics, religion, and education. To ensure that he had lawyers to ward off Gentile attacks on his financial holdings, doctors to administer healing to the suffering, and engineers to build the infrastructures of Zion, Young began to consider sending some of his own children east on educational missions. As most contemporary Americans knew, he had dozens from whom to choose.[19]

The first to go east in the 1870s was Willard Young, born in 1852, Brigham's third child by Clarissa Ross Young. Brigham thought his bright, strong son was well suited for an educational mission to a fortress of American patriotism and strength: West Point. (As governor of the Utah territory, it was Brigham's prerogative to choose a representative from the territory to attend the New York military academy.) Brigham knew that Willard would not only receive a first-rate, "practical" education there, but also enjoy a rare opportunity to demonstrate that Mormons were as rational and civilized as other Americans.

To help strengthen Willard for his time in "Babylon," Brigham had him, like Heber John Richards, blessed and "set apart" as a missionary by members of the church's First Presidency. The church's highest-ranking authorities prayed over Willard that he might "go and fulfill this high and holy calling and gain this useful knowledge, and through the light of truth, make it subservient for the building up of the Kingdom of God."[20] Just after Willard arrived in New York, the prophet wrote with additional assurances ("our prayers are constantly exercised in your behalf") and warnings ("the eyes of many are upon you").[21]

By December of his first academic year (1871–72), Willard had good news to report. He felt that the blessings the brethren placed upon him were coming to fulfillment. "I am succeeding quite well in my studies, and I never enjoyed more the spirit of our religion," he avowed. He marveled at the effect he seemed to be having on other cadets, whose anti-Mormon sentiment had waned. Some of his non-Mormon peers, he said, now even went so far as to say that aggressive anti-polygamists were "entirely wrong."[22]

Again, the Saints at home took special notice of how their representative was faring in the eyes of the world. When Willard was interviewed by a curious New York reporter, Salt Lake City's pro-Mormon newspaper, *The Deseret News*, reprinted the exchange in full. With equal insecurity and pride, the Salt Lake editors noted that the interviewer "evidently found the young gentleman, though a resident of these mountains from birth until now, well prepared to answer his questions."[23] Home pride swelled again when Cadet Young graduated in 1875, fourth in his class of forty-three, and was promoted to the Corps of Engineers. *The Deseret Evening News* opined that Willard had vindicated Mormonism and polygamy:

The success of Utah's first West Point cadet further confirms the erroneousness of the idea that the minds of polygamous children are inferior to those of monogamic parentage. The Chicago *Times* of June 28th says—"A son of Brigham Young has graduated from the military academy at West Point, standing third in his class. It has been said that polygamy results in the impairment of the mental faculties of the offspring, but this does not seem to prove the theory."[24]

Willard's success in acquiring "practical" knowledge as an engineer, maintaining his religious commitments, and diminishing anti-Mormon prejudice bolstered Brigham's confidence to send more Saints on academic missions abroad.[25] At the church's semiannual general conference in 1873, Brigham encouraged Mormon men to study law, and he called on both men and women to study medicine.[26] That year, he also privately urged six of his sons to go east to study law or engineering. Three Mormons answered the call in 1873, and others soon followed. Joseph Richards (Heber John's brother) went to the Bellevue Hospital Medical College; LeGrand Young (Brigham's nephew) went to the University of Michigan to study law; and Romania Pratt, the first Mormon woman to accept Brigham's call for more women doctors, left to enroll in the Woman's Medical College of Philadelphia.

Again, however, Young's embrace of higher education was not unrestrained. None of Brigham's sons actually left for an eastern school in 1873 because George A. Smith, Young's counselor and close friend, expressed strong concerns about sending them to non-Mormon schools. Young took Smith's warnings to heart. He required his sons to take two years of preparatory work at Salt Lake City's University of Deseret, and he insisted that they use their education to build up the kingdom of God.[27] Three of Brigham's sons took him up on the offer. Feramorz ("Fera") would leave for the United States Naval Academy in 1874; in 1875, Alfales began a course in law at the University of Michigan, and Don Carlos enrolled at Rensselaer Polytechnic Institute in upstate New York, to pursue a degree in engineering.

The fears of George A. Smith—that Mormons educated abroad might not benefit but corrupt the kingdom of the Saints—received some substantiation in the example of LeGrand Young, Brigham's nephew. From 1873 to 1874, LeGrand worked toward his LLB degree at the University of Michigan. As he approached graduation and surveyed his options for employment in Utah, he made a choice that would aggravate the Mormons. He entered the practice of law in Salt Lake City with Parley Williams, a notorious anti-Mormon, and he became temporarily "inactive" (nonpracticing) as a Mormon. LeGrand's sparse journal reveals no reason for the unpopular decision. Although he later defended Brigham and the church from non-Mormon legal attacks, and even though he later resumed his activity in the church, Mormons would remember LeGrand as an example of the dangers of studying abroad.[28]

There was nothing new in Young's endorsement of the study of medicine and engineering, but giving Mormons his approval to enter the legal profession marked a significant shift. His contempt for lawyers' greed, dishonesty, and corruption was well known.[29] Yet as outside legal pressures on the prophet mounted in the 1870s, the benefits of training Mormon lawyers seemed to outweigh the dangers. In August 1876—the year before Brigham died—he wrote to Alfales in Ann Arbor, "It would be very pleasing to us if at the present time you had finished your course of studies and had been admitted to the bar, for you could materially help me in the numerous vexatious suits that are being brought against me to rob me of my property. The present bench appears to be not only willing but anxious to give my possessions away to anyone who has the effrontery to ask for them."[30] Reeling from legal battles, the prophet hoped to see some of the Saints employ eastern training to thwart the designs of trained, hostile Gentile lawyers and judges.[31]

Gendered Migrations

As he began to encourage Mormon men to study law, Brigham Young made another important shift by calling for Mormon women to study medicine. In 1873, he declared that "the time has come for women to come forth as doctors in these valleys of the mountains."[32] Again, both nation-building and public relations were at play. Brigham thought that having trained female doctors in the church would help Mormon women preserve their modesty, by eliminating the need for medical treatment from outside male doctors. He also hoped that by encouraging higher education for women, he could weaken outsiders' political criticisms of Mormon patriarchy. On both counts, he saw limited success, but Mormon women quickly seized their new opportunity.

Although his doubts about professional medicine lingered, Brigham recognized Mormon settlers' growing needs for medical care. Mormon women, who had seen too many mothers and infants die during childbirth, had pressed the prophet to act. Brigham responded by enlisting the help of LDS women's organizations—the Relief Society and the Young Ladies' Retrenchment Society—to organize classes in medicine, especially nursing and obstetrics.[33] He also encouraged women like Romania Pratt to pursue a medical degree in the East. According to Relief Society president Eliza R. Snow, the prophet's design was to "do away with the necessity of employing male doctors or women [who are] not of our people."[34] The plan was consistent with Mormon women's broader commitment to female modesty and "retrenchment" (reducing Mormon dependence on outsiders' goods and services).

To achieve their desired independence in medical care, a small dose of outside training—something like a vaccine—was necessary. So in December 1873, Romania Pratt, blessed by Brigham Young, left Utah to obtain a medical degree. Early in 1874, she enrolled in the Woman's Medical College of Philadelphia.[35]

The approval that Mormon women physicians received from the highest church officials (all male), the Relief Society, and the Mormon press reflected the church's distinctive and controversial attitudes toward women. Church doctrine excluded women from the Mormon lay priesthood, investing its male elders with spiritual authority over families, congregations, and, for the highest-ranking authorities, the entire church. Politically, however, Utah women enjoyed unusual power in the 1870s. Fifty years before the ratification of the 19th Amendment, they could vote, thanks to a woman suffrage amendment passed by Utah's territorial legislature and approved by Governor Brigham Young in 1870. In that regard, Utah women were almost unique in the United States and its territories.[36]

Of course, non-Mormons in the Utah territory and the United States saw Utah's enfranchisement of women as a shameless Mormon attempt to solidify the church's political power, since political parties in Utah were split largely along Mormon and non-Mormon lines.[37] Young's pragmatism and self-interest naturally played a role. For Young, giving women the right to vote was indeed an attempt to strengthen the church's political clout, in addition to being part of a calculated, even desperate public relations campaign to curb anti-Mormon sentiment in Washington, D.C. Young thought that if he could alter the broad perception that Mormon women were powerless dupes, he could avert a harsh federal crackdown on the Saints.[38]

The strategy helped temporarily stave off federal aggression. Mormon women, for their part, embraced their new political power with impassioned idealism. *The Woman's Exponent* began circulating in 1872, touting itself as an organ dedicated to the rights of women not just in Zion, but in all nations.[39] The semimonthly magazine highlighted Mormon and non-Mormon women's progress in education, politics, medicine, law, and social reform. It supported national and international movements for women's rights, and it asserted "the right of a woman to earn her living in any honorable career for which she has capacity."[40] Even more emphatically, it proclaimed that "woman was designed to be something more than a domestic drudge; and it is not right for her to confine herself exclusively to that monotonous calling, having no thoughts, no interests, hopes or prospects above and beyond so humble a sphere."[41]

The magazine was careful, however, to temper bold ambition with reverence for Brigham Young, the church, and polygamy. "A Mormon Woman's View of Marriage," published in the fall of 1877, was typical:

> It is known to the world far and wide that the Latter-day Saints believe in direct revelation. Through this channel (revelation) they obtained the knowledge of the principles of plural marriage and in no other way would pure and devotional women, who had been educated and traditionated in the ideas of the present age accept it. It is truly the sacred phase of polygamy which gives it prestige. . . . It is grossly absurd to say plural marriage is a sin in the sight of heaven when we have abundant testimony before us, that God has blessed this people in a most wonderful manner ever since its practice. More than this, physicians, men of science, and phrenologists have all failed to discover in the children born in plural marriage any inequalities, or lack of brain, or muscle and fibre that would characterize children born of suitable parentage.[42]

The Woman's Exponent promoted a consciousness among Mormon women as those "who are to build up Zion and redeem the nation" with religious purity and idealism.[43] It allowed Mormon women to make arguments, based on revelation and reason, for women's rights, higher education, professionalization, social reform, and polygamy. It was unlike any magazine in America.

In this unique climate of freedom and hierarchy, distinctive obstacles, frustrations, and networks of support shaped the experiences of Mormon women who pursued the MD. Financial troubles forced Romania Pratt to come back to Salt Lake City early in 1875, before she had earned her degree, but the Relief Society banded together to raise the funds she needed to complete her work.[44] Romania especially needed the help of her sisters in the faith because her husband, Parley, had exacerbated the family's financial woes by taking another wife.[45] In the fall of 1875, Romania returned to the Woman's Medical College of Philadelphia. The financial support, and the high hopes, of her sister Saints accompanied her.[46]

This time, Romania also enjoyed the company of a fellow Mormon, Maggie Curtis Shipp, but Maggie did not last long. After just four weeks at the Woman's Medical College, homesickness overwhelmed her, and by early November she was back in Utah.[47] But Maggie had an ambitious "sister-wife," Ellis Reynolds Shipp, who was happy to take her place. Ellis had been hoping for years to pursue a "useful" calling, something more consistent with her Mormon and Victorian ideals of womanhood and motherhood, something beyond the mind-numbing routine of daily chores. As early as 1872, she had recorded her exasperation in her diary. "I know that I am tired of this life of uselessness and unaccomplished desires," she wrote, "only as far as cooking, washing dishes and doing general housework goes. I believe that woman's life should not consist wholly and solely of these routine duties. I think she should have ample time and opportunity to study and improve her mind, to add polish and grace to her manners, to cultivate those finer tastes and refined and delicate feelings that are so beautiful in women and that are so truly requisite in a mother."[48] Three years later, finally, the opportunity had come for her to study medicine. Ellis marveled, "What a strange fatality!"[49]

Although Brigham Young did not specifically call her to the work, Ellis did seek the prophet's approval, which he granted.[50] When she arrived in Philadelphia, she found additional comfort in the company of Romania Pratt. Boarding with Sister Pratt, Ellis acclimated quickly. In January 1876, on her twenty-ninth birthday, she wrote, "truly no ideal romance could be fraught with more exciting changes."[51]

Ellis approached her studies with the theological and epistemological conviction that her quest for scientific truth would blend harmoniously with her faith. She affirmed, "*All truth*, all knowledge is of God—it has its origin in the Heavens. And with a proper degree of humility and reverence for the 'Author of every good and perfect gift' there is no danger of becoming too wise. I verily believe that He is pleased with those who seek after knowledge, that it is His desire in so much that it becomes a duty, and indeed a responsible duty, to improve and cultivate the talents He has given us."[52] Brigham Young shared her confidence. In the decades to come, Mormons would struggle to uphold the kind of optimism that Shipp and Young displayed in asserting that all truth emanated from one divine source, and that in the humble search for truth "there is no danger of becoming too wise." Some would abandon that optimism altogether.

Ellis did recognize some of the tensions between her faith and her scientific pursuits, but her awe at the "beautifully and wonderfully made" human body—and a little naiveté—helped her sail toward her medical degree with an untarnished, even deepened, faith. When one of her professors pressed her to account for "the lack of coloring matter upon the soles of the feet and the palm of the hands of the Negro," Ellis declared it to be "a design of the great Creator, which like many of his other works is alike wonderful and incomprehensible." Ellis knew the answer would not satisfy her professor, who was "one of the believers in Huxley and Darwin," but Ellis relished the exchange. It seemed to prove her fidelity to God in the face of encroaching irreligion.[53]

Although deeply committed to Mormonism, Ellis never went out of her way to let people know that she was part of a polygamous household.[54] She must have known how shocked they would have been, and in many ways she enjoyed her reprieve from the difficulties of life at home. Ellis's married life had never been easy. From 1869 to 1871, she had endured the trials of loneliness while her husband, Milford, went on a mission. She prayed fervently that he would be comforted while he was away. She got her wish and then some: Milford returned with another wife, Elizabeth Hilstead, whom he had married late in 1871. Ellis knew that it would take "all my power to be kind, considerate, and charitable" in response.[55] Yet despite tempestuous household affairs, Ellis agreed with Milford that joyous exaltation awaited polygamists in the afterlife. Borne patiently, all her frustration and boredom, all the "trials of polygamy," would translate into glory in the life to come.[56]

In Philadelphia, Ellis enjoyed some relief from domestic life, and yet she also drew strength from her unusual web of relations back home. In fact, she depended heavily on her sister-wives for financial and emotional support. Ellis felt closest to Maggie (Milford had four wives in all), who had come to Philadelphia as a student briefly in 1875. Acknowledging "an occasional discord" in her dealings with Maggie, Ellis nevertheless found over time that "a sympathy and love" unique to sister-wives suffused their relationship. For instance, when Ellis battled loneliness and homesickness, Maggie convinced her to stay in Philadelphia. Maggie pleaded, "Recall your feelings when you were here, willing to endure *any thing* [sic] for a while to give your boys great advantages. Now you are just in the right place, for not only your boys will receive an everlasting benefit, but you will be every thing woman could desire."[57] On at least three occasions, sister-wives Maggie and Elizabeth gave Ellis money that allowed her to continue her studies. On New Year's Day in 1877, Ellis had just a dollar left when money unexpectedly arrived from "Lizzie." When Lizzie came through again in April, Ellis rejoiced: "How pure and heavenly is the relationship of sisters in the holy order of Polygamy. Even the kindred ties of blood could not be more pure and sacred, nor more unselfish and enduring. How beautiful to contemplate the picture of a family where each one works for the interest, advancement and well being of all. *Unity is strength*."[58] As Ellis saw them, the complicated ties between sister-wives involved spiritual and economic cooperation, whose benefits helped them endure the strains of sharing a husband.

Ellis's second year at the Woman's Medical College was her most difficult financially and physically, but she performed well academically. In March 1877, she earned high marks in anatomy, physiology, and chemistry, her three main branches of study, winning "the esteem of my Professors for my energy and perseverance." A year away from graduation, she began to feel "prepared for a life of usefulness among the Saints of God."[59] She counted her success as a blessing of God, her Heavenly Father, without whose assistance she could not have won acclaim in the eyes of the world. Ellis graduated in 1878, and by then Maggie Shipp was on her way to securing an MD of her own.[60]

Back in Utah, the Saints applauded Romania Pratt and Ellis Reynolds Shipp, Utah's "woman physicians." In April 1877, *The Woman's Exponent* published a notice of Dr. Pratt's graduation, noting that she was one of just fifteen women (and one of only two from the West) to receive the MD from the Woman's Medical College.[61] When Pratt conducted postgraduate research on the use of healing baths in upstate New York during the summer of 1877, *The Woman's Exponent* devoted nearly a full page to Pratt's correspondence with the magazine's editor. Pratt's account of her life in the East gave the readers at home a sense of her enduring commitment to the church, her emerging scientific expertise, and her aching desire to return to her "mountain home." "I go home heart hungry and soul starved," she wrote, "to feast on the society of my friends. . . . I did not come east to preach the Gospel, but I know I have in many times and in many ways broken down prejudices against my people. It has often been said to me 'I am glad I have met you, for I shall always feel differently now towards your people.'"[62] Sister Pratt's letter made for good press. *The Woman's Exponent* treated her success as a student and a Saint as

At times in the late nineteenth century, the ambitious pursuit of higher education occurred even within the complicated frameworks of Mormon polygamy. Pictured clockwise from bottom right: "sister-wives" Ellis Reynolds Shipp, MD; Margaret Curtis Shipp, MD; Mary Elizabeth Hillstead Shipp, and Mary Catherine [Smith] Shipp. Used by permission, International Society Daughters of Utah Pioneers, Salt Lake City.

exemplary. Academically, she could stand shoulder to shoulder with the best students, and in matters of the spirit she never came unmoored. She looked forward to the day when all might "grow eye to eye in faith and scientific knowledge." Moreover, in keeping with the prophet's educational ideals, she understood her intellectual attainments as gifts to be offered to her fellow Saints, a humble "mite" used to build the kingdom of God.[63]

Authorities' Abiding Ambivalence

While Mormon women offered each other support and a rationale for higher education, Mormon men who studied abroad in the 1870s often enjoyed the personal attention and oversight of Brigham Young. As he had with Willard, Brigham corresponded closely with Fera, Don Carlos, and Alfales. He also made sure that they received *The Deseret News* and other news from Utah, so that they would not feel isolated or tempted to forget their mountain home.

Brigham advised his sons that the best way for them to maintain their Mormon identity and diminish anti-Mormon prejudice would be to live honest, upright lives. He told Fera, who was just sixteen when he entered the Naval Academy, that "wisdom dictates a kind, courteous, forbearing and gentlemanly course under all circumstances, and a careful obedience to all the rules of the academy and the requirements of its officers[.]"[64] He discouraged them from preaching gratuitously, although they should "never be afraid to acknowledge your faith."[65] He recommended that they let their lives and conduct speak; he thought Willard's success at West Point in this regard to be exemplary.[66]

Brigham felt that his sons' good character would help them defuse prejudice and make friends, but he did not want them to blend in too much. Young worried about the temptations his sons would face in schools where students indulged in swearing, smoking, or irreligion. The intellectual environment of the university concerned Brigham as much as the moral.[67] He warned his sons about the corrupting intellectual influences of rationalistic skepticism, scientific naturalism, and poisonous—that is, capitalistic—economic notions. In an 1876 letter, Brigham linked these fears, writing: "We have enough and to spare, at present in these mountains, of schools where young infidels are made because the teachers are so tender-footed that they dare not mention the principles of the gospel to their pupils, but have no hesitancy in introducing into the classroom the theories of Huxley, of Darwin, or of Mill and the false political economy which contends against co-operation and the United Order."[68] The "United Order" was the Mormons' radically cooperative economic experiment, which Brigham had implemented in 1874. Although the Saints would abandon it in the 1880s because of mounting internal and external opposition, the United Order represented Brigham's hope that Mormon civilization could avoid the kind of selfishness, inequality, and discord that seemed to characterize the largest cities of the United States. After the dissolution of the United Order, Mormons would gradually embrace capitalism, becoming more integrated into national markets and muting their separatism as they mounted campaigns for statehood. Once Mormons became good capitalists, those who worried about the corrupting influences of higher education would proceed with Brigham's old attacks on Huxley and Darwin, but they quietly dropped the critique of Mill.

Brigham never foresaw such accommodations, however, and as he worked to ward off capitalism through the United Order, he also tried to prevent the influx of skepticism by laying the foundations for private, Mormon institutions of higher learning. In 1875, just as he was sending some of his sons east to school, Brigham donated land for a "Brigham Young Academy" in Provo, which later became Brigham Young University. In 1877, a separate and shorter-lived "Brigham Young College" opened in Logan, also on land donated by the prophet. It would be decades before either school offered college-level work.

Conclusion

Until his death in the summer of 1877, Brigham Young vigorously pursued his nation- and empire-building project in the Intermountain West. As he neared his end he saw gloom ahead for the United States, whose class conflict, political corruption, and persecution of Mormons seemed to foreshadow "the breakup of our present form of government" and millennial catastrophe. He wrote, "The revolution foreshadowed should be averted by all the effort the people could exert against plague or famine, for it means a common ruin for workingman and capitalist, which will be irretrievable if the people permit it. In fact, it means the fall of Babylon, or as much thereof that spreads over this fair land of Joseph. It can only be prevented by a complete change in the hearts and lives of the people and an obedience to the plan of salvation, revealed by God in this generation. But we fear it is too late, the masses have gone too far, the body politic too corrupt, the tree is too rotten, it is fit only for the burning."[69] Despite this pessimism, and even because of it, Mormons continued to build the kingdom of God in their promised land, gathering converts, expanding settlements, experimenting with radically cooperative economics, and working desperately to ward off the seductions and corruptions of the outside world. Under these circumstances, Brigham Young's original sanction for studying abroad still held. The Saints who survived him believed that trained professionals in medicine, engineering, and law would help strengthen and protect their emerging civilization, which they thought would be the envy of the world. Relief Society women continued their study of medicine at the Woman's Medical College of Philadelphia and the University of Michigan; Mormon men gravitated to Ann Arbor and New York City for the study of law or medicine. And although it was still common for Mormon students to seek the blessing of the church for their educational pursuits, it became just as common for students to be spurred by private ambitions for intellectual and professional advancement.

Unwittingly, Brigham Young had helped set the stage for American universities to become sites of a profound transformation of Mormon consciousness and identity. Mormon ambivalence toward scholarship and the intellect has a long history, and it has much to do with Brigham Young's original, protectionist desire to gather all the world's knowledge to Zion— his blend of intellectual prudishness and promiscuity.

2 The Death of Mormon Separatism in American Universities, 1877–1896

· ·

By all accounts, the last quarter of the nineteenth century was critical for Mormonism's evolution and modernization. During that period, under immense external pressure, Mormons jettisoned their utopian separatism in favor of monogamy, market capitalism, public schools, national political parties, and military service. Nevertheless, the rapidity of the transformation leaves nagging questions. We know that "regime change" is rarely smooth. Brute force can bully an enemy into submission, but it cannot destroy an ideology of resistance or manufacture loyal subjects. Somehow, Mormons must have determined that a pact with America was not a deal with the devil. Otherwise, the fires of resistance would have continued to rage among far more than the handful of "Fundamentalist" Mormons who clung to polygamy and spent the twentieth century huddling in the darkest corners of America. In the late nineteenth century, however, prospects for Mormon-Gentile reconciliation remained bleak. Mutual hostilities raged in their primary realms of encounter: Salt Lake City, missionary fields, and the halls of Congress.

Yet right when Mormon-Gentile animosity was at fever pitch—in the two decades between the death of Brigham Young (1877) and Utah's admission into the Union as the forty-fifth state (1896)—American universities offered a rising, influential generation of Mormons rare, revivifying freedom from Gentile aggression and ecclesiastical oversight. A realm of genuine hospitality, dignity, and freedom, the American university became a liminal, quasi-sacred space where nineteenth-century Mormons could undergo a radical transformation of consciousness and identity. As a result, they developed an enduring devotion to non-Mormons' institutions, deference to non-Mormons' expertise, and respect for non-Mormons' wisdom. These extra-ecclesial loyalties would dismantle the ideological framework of Mormon separatism and pave the way for Mormons' voluntary reimmersion into the mainstream of American life.

For Mormon students and their supporters to help give birth to modern Mormonism—a Mormonism at home in America—a complex history had to unfold. It started in the late 1870s, when hostile Gentile reformers, frustrated by the aborted federal Reconstruction in the South but reemboldened by the death of Brigham Young, took the war on barbarism to a new theater, Mormon Utah.[1] At the same time, Mormon students returned from abroad and began to exert their influence at home.

Dismantling Populism, Rehearsing for Citizenship

The ideological underpinning of Mormon separatism was the church's "populism," an egalitarian, antielitist mentality that characterized much of American Christianity and culture in the nineteenth century.[2] Mormon populism entailed profound reverence for the wisdom of ordinary people like the young, untutored Joseph Smith, whose humble quest for truth and righteousness, uncorrupted by the learning of "the world," had guaranteed his access to pure truth and salvation. Decades of persecution only reinforced Mormons' populist self-reliance.

Yet shortly after the death of Brigham Young, and long before the church's surrender to federal power, Romania Pratt, an eastern-trained Mormon doctor, began publicly criticizing Mormon populism, and she won influential support. Taking enormous pride in the accomplishments of learned professionals like Dr. Pratt, Mormons began to move beyond Young's limited, pragmatic endorsement of medical training. Upon Pratt's return to Salt Lake City, in September 1877, with an MD from the Woman's Medical College of Philadelphia, the city's pro-Mormon newspaper, *The Deseret News*, celebrated Utah's "Lady Professional" and encouraged all its readers to take advantage of her expertise as a physician and surgeon.[3] The following spring, the paper offered the same endorsement to Ellis Reynolds Shipp, a recent graduate of the Woman's Medical College with specialties in obstetrics and women's diseases. The *News* editorialized, "We are pleased to see ladies belonging to the community of Latter-day Saints adopting the medical profession. The thorough course of training they receive in medical colleges abroad, combined with the further advantage of faith in the efficacy of the gospel, should prepare them admirably for that pursuit."[4]

High-ranking church leaders also approved. In August 1878, Apostles John Taylor and George Q. Cannon[5] gave ceremonial blessings of consecration to Romania Pratt, Ellis Reynolds Shipp, Maggie Curtis Shipp, and Martha Hughes Paul "to practice medicine and surgery among the Saints." Romania Pratt and Ellis Shipp had completed their studies, Maggie Shipp was in the midst of hers at the Woman's Medical College of

Philadelphia, and Martha Hughes Paul (later Cannon) was about to begin her medical training at the University of Michigan.[6]

The youngest of the four, "Mattie" Paul was the first of several Mormon women to enroll in the University of Michigan's Medical Department in the late 1870s and 1880s. The University of Michigan had established the first university hospital in 1869, and the school had begun to admit women in 1870.[7] The Woman's Exponent, a Mormon periodical, hailed the school for opening its doors to women. It made sure that its readers, like Mattie, knew about the opportunity to study at a school that was neither as expensive nor as distant as schools of similar quality on the East Coast. In just its second issue, published in June 1872, the magazine reported that sixty-three women were enrolled at the University of Michigan.[8] The University of Michigan also attracted Mormons because it offered a special freedom from religious compulsion and prejudice. Like other growing American universities, the university promoted a broad, nonsectarian Christianity. Chapel services were regular but not mandatory. By the 1880s, leading figures in the university, including John Dewey and the university's president, James B. Angell, were deftly and publicly linking the Christian life with the life of the mind.[9]

In the minds of Mormon authorities, however, questions persisted about whether a doctor's scientific expertise could be reconciled with divine revelations. Romania Pratt knew it, so in 1879, confident that her fellow Saints considered her exemplary, she boldly offered Mormons an anti-populist rationale for professional training in medicine. In the pages of The Woman's Exponent, the church's official magazine for women, Dr. Pratt argued that when it came to the health of the Saints, the church's populism was naïve, obsolete, and even dangerous. She pleaded with her sisters and brothers in the faith to make room for "cultivated skill," "reason," and "progress":

> It is neither safe nor right for any one [sic] with a smattering [of] knowledge picked up promiscuously to undertake the practice of medicine, and go forth to hold the balance of life and death in their unskillful hands, too often unnecessarily resulting in the desolation of hearts and homes. . . .

> Our reason, the greatest gift of God to man[,] was given us for cultivation and our life here on earth presents a series of opportunities of transforming circumstances into eternal knowledge. Progress is the keystone of heavenly thought and plan, and . . .

[t]rue medical knowledge can never corrode the soul or unfit us for usefulness in any way. It is said in Holy Writ that "faith without works is dead," and it is a matter of correct observation that good intelligent common-sense work is very frequently a most excellent subordinate to faith.[10]

Like any effective proponent of reform, Pratt owned the tradition she dared to modify.

Church leaders found Dr. Pratt's arguments unsettling. Dangers lurked, they insisted, in relying too heavily on the authorities and wisdom of "the world." Joseph F. Smith made the hierarchy's concerns explicit in his formal blessing of Dr. Pratt in 1881. Smith, one of two counselors to John Taylor in the church's First Presidency, asked God to grant Dr. Pratt special success in her labors as a doctor, midwife, and teacher among the Saints. Yet he was quick to add a prayer "that faith may not be crowded out of the hearts of the people of God through the science of medicine[.]" President Smith recognized the value of Dr. Pratt's training in "the science of the world," but he insisted that only the Holy Spirit could impart "that knowledge which cannot be false and . . . cometh from the Lord God."[11] Smith wanted to ensure that Pratt's expertise functioned only to deepen and clarify—not challenge or surpass—the divine principles of healing revealed exclusively to the church.[12]

In 1882, the living prophet himself, John Taylor, chose the same theme for his dedicatory address at Salt Lake City's new Deseret Hospital. The institution represented Mormons' initial attempts to integrate the healing powers of the professionally skilled and the divinely anointed. Mormon women rejoiced.[13] President Taylor labored. Commenting on the special training that several Mormon women had acquired in medicine, he issued a statement suffused with ambivalence. "We [are] commanded of the Lord," he said, "to 'seek out of the best books words of wisdom,' and to seek knowledge by learning. Yet we must not forget to call in the aid of faith, but while we acquire all the intelligence possible to be attained, at the same time we must exercise faith that the blessings of the Lord might be upon our efforts."[14] Taylor's strained rhetoric—with the reversals "yet," "but," and "at the same time" all in one sentence—reveals a moment in Mormon history when the arguments of populists and their critics began to have equal force.

President Taylor's misgivings about higher education carried over into his dealings with younger Mormons seeking his blessing to study "abroad."

Romania Pratt, MD, played a crucial role in dismantling Mormon populism after
the death of Brigham Young. Used by permission, Utah State Historical Society,
all rights reserved.

In 1881, Taylor had kept an eager student, Horace Hall Cummings, home out of fear that education abroad would corrupt him spiritually.[15] The next year, James Talmage and James Moyle had better luck securing the church's approval for their university training (in the sciences and law, respectively), but emphatically conditional language continued to permeate the hierarchy's ritual blessings. Praying over James Talmage, Brigham Young Jr., one of the church's twelve apostles, promised: "If you seek inspiration you will perform your mission profitably; and your mind shall expand in the faith of the gospel as well as in letters." Young concluded with a plea that God would "guard your mind from yielding in the least degree to the spirit of infidelity[.]"[16] President Taylor was more ominously evocative in his blessing of Moyle:

> As thou has had in thine heart a desire to go forth to study law
> in order that thou mayest become proficient therein, we say unto
> thee that this is a dangerous profession, one that leads many people
> down to destruction; yet if you wilt with clean hands and a pure
> heart, fearing God and working righteousness, and with a desire
> to maintain the truth and defend the rights of the Church and
> Kingdom of God on the earth;—if thou wilt abstain from arguing
> falsely and on false principles maintaining only the things that can
> be honorably sustained by honorable men, if thou wilt dedicate
> thyself unto God every day and ask for His blessing and guidance,
> the Lord God will bless thee in this calling; and thou shalt be
> blessed with wisdom and intelligence, and with the light of reve-
> lation, and thou shalt be an instrument in the hands of God to
> assist, to protect the rights and liberties of His people. But if thou
> doest not these things thou wilt go down and wither away.[17]

Taylor's fears reflected enduring Mormon suspicion of the legal profession, inherited from Brigham Young. In fact, one of President Taylor's own sons, Bruce, had been among the select group Young had tapped to study law at the University of Michigan in the mid-1870s, but Bruce would never practice law in Utah, nor would he maintain his commitments to the church. Allegedly, he even confessed his own homosexuality to Apostle (and future church president) Joseph F. Smith. In any case, Bruce Taylor spent the rest of his life in Oregon, using neither his brain nor his body to build the Mormon kingdom.[18]

Specters of treason and idolatry thus accompanied any Saint who ventured into "Babylon" on an educational quest. Departing Mormon students often pledged to remain true to the church, but their experiences would change them in unforeseen ways, even when they kept the faith. For example, before leaving for his studies at Lehigh and Johns Hopkins, James Talmage proclaimed that it was the "mission" of devout Mormons like himself to "redeem" the sciences from "infidelity & skepticism."[19] His ideas quickly became more sophisticated. Like Romania Pratt before him, Talmage came to understand that populist self-reliance can lead to simplistic interpretations of complex phenomena. In 1884, less than two years into his studies, Talmage excoriated religious and intellectual naïveté in response to a Baltimore Presbyterian minister's sermon on Darwin. The preacher, Talmage recorded in his journal, "spoke much as an ordinary person would—'Darwin. Ah Yes—says we come from monkeys'—then condemns." Talmage concluded, "I certainly think 'tis the ministers themselves who have bred the disgust with which most scientific people regard them—because they will dabble with matters from which their ignorance should keep them at a safe distance. . . . Darwin wrote for those who can understand him; some of whom will agree with & others oppose him; but he did not write for ministers who never read beyond others' opinions of the man, anymore [sic] than Plato or Socrates wrote for babes and sucklings."[20] In the early twentieth century, as one of the church's twelve apostles, Talmage would watch some of his colleagues in the hierarchy ape the Baltimore preacher. He would have to hold his tongue.[21]

In the meantime, as the young Talmage completed his studies at Johns Hopkins, federal aggression against Mormons escalated to a full-scale raid, ultimately leaving thousands of Mormons either imprisoned or exiled.[22] Under the circumstances, the Saints needed extra assurance that students abroad had not become "intoxicated with the allurements of Babylon."[23] In early 1885, a Mormon student's firsthand account of the rampant "evils" at West Point, published in *The Woman's Exponent*, must have left persecuted Mormons both wary and self-satisfied. The author[24] testified that he had remained pure at a school pervaded by "effeminate" self-indulgence, vanity, idleness, drinking, smoking, and "a brutal contest called foot ball [sic]."[25] Validating Mormon populism, he asserted that "For [every] thoroughly educated man a college turns out there are a dozen numbskulls ground through, and full as many young men unsettled and unfitted for life by lack of discipline, and by the acquisition of vices which, not only corrupt and waste them bodily, but which totally undermine that true and abiding love for moral instincts, without which it is absolutely impossible to lead a correct life."[26] The boy adrift in Babylon concluded that Mormon parents, instead of sending their children to schools abroad, should keep them home, under the ennobling shelter and sway of the church.

It was not long before young Mormon scholars started feeling heat from home. In the spring of 1885, rumors circulated in Utah that James Henry Moyle "was turning infidel" in Ann Arbor.[27] He was furious. He had left Salt Lake City full of desire to remain "true to Israel."[28] Rattled, Moyle turned on the other Mormons at Michigan.[29] Henry Rolapp, he said, "seems anxious not to be known as a Mormon," because in a law school debate he defended Utah's quest for statehood without openly supporting the church.[30] Worse, Rolapp "seems to love the sensual, licentious, and intemperate, so also the vulgar & obscene," while boasting that "he will go on [his church] mission [merely] to keep up appearance."[31] Rolapp and David Evans aggravated Moyle all the more when they worked to defeat him in class elections.[32] Another Mormon law student, Waldemar Van Cott, proudly declared himself to be "an uncompromising enemy of polygamy" because of the "great injustice" it had visited upon himself and his mother.[33]

Moyle's defensiveness obscured the real changes that he and other students had been undergoing in their outlook and attitudes. Even with his strong sense of solidarity with the church, Moyle privately admitted a welcome "broadening" and "liberalizing" of his political and religious views at Michigan.[34] He and Henry Rolapp, despite their differences, had for years welcomed the opportunity to wrangle with non-Mormon classmates over polygamy, the church, and Utah's bid for statehood.[35] They earned the clear, abiding respect of their peers not by proselytizing but by engaging them in rational discourse and debate about law and politics, leaving matters of faith off the table, private. In correspondence published in 1883 for Mormons in rural, southern Idaho, Rolapp wrote, "We have had quite [a] severe time in our class regarding our religion, but after we determinedly let them understand, that while we were not on a preaching mission, we were nevertheless proud of our religion, and could not be converted by ridicule—they let us alone."[36] Non-Mormons did more than leave them alone. They would support Moyle in his bid for the junior class presidency and elect Rolapp to the Law Department's Supreme Court. For the downcast Saints at home, Rolapp exulted, "we have held our own in spite of coming from Utah."[37]

The experiences of Moyle and Rolapp indicated how universities could transform Mormon-Gentile relations, allowing mutual respect to replace entrenched hostility. They offered Mormon students the chance to rehearse for American citizenship, instilling them with confidence that they could be rewarded for their discipline, hard work, and loyalty in an integrated, diverse society. The result was not merely Mormon-Gentile détente, but a genuine mutual esteem that left Mormon students ambivalent at best about Mormon independence.

Evading Oversight, Rejecting the Resistance

Church leaders were quick to recognize universities as institutional rivals in the formation and transformation of Mormon students' identity and character. In the nonsectarian modern university, students were free to retain their faith, but they were also free to privatize, reform, and reject it. This range of options—a hallmark of the modern Mormon American experience—worried President Taylor and Karl G. Maeser, the period's preeminent Mormon educator and the principal of the fledgling Brigham Young Academy in Provo.

To prevent the students' attrition and apostasy, President Taylor and Karl Maeser tried to bring order and discipline to the religious life of the Mormons at Michigan. Even though Taylor was busy trying to avoid federal prosecution, he had to attend to the students abroad. Because of their special training, they were likely to mature into figures of real influence in Utah, with the power to shape the church's destiny. (As it turned out, the aging Taylor, born in 1808, had less than a year to live; he would die in exile in July 1887.) After Maeser wrote to Taylor concerning the "young men of our people now studying at Ann Arbor . . . whose spiritual development for the future causes me some anxiety,"[38] the prophet and the principal devised a plan. Under the watchful eye of Benjamin Cluff Jr., an Academy teacher about to depart for Ann Arbor, the Mormons at Michigan would hold regular religious meetings. In response to this special calling, Cluff vowed "to do everything in his power" to execute the will of his superiors "with the help of the Spirit of God."[39] Cluff seemed to be the perfect choice. He was devout and eager to commence his university-level studies in engineering, in service to the church. A polygamist, he would also enjoy the opportunity to make himself scarce, and useful, during the raid. Officials at the University of Michigan welcomed Cluff in 1886, unaware that their esteemed institution would become part of the Mormon underground.

Because of the diversity and independence of the Mormon students at Michigan, Cluff's dutiful efforts to corral them produced mixed results and unintended consequences. He found that while some of his companions took their religious commitments seriously, others proved "rather backward in [their] duties"[40] and irregular in their attendance of religious meetings. As the delegate of Taylor and Maeser, he had expected more deference to his authority. He did not hide his disapproval. When two students missed a religious meeting in the fall of 1888, he wrote, "Their absence may have been caused by forgetfulness, but I doubt it."[41] After a June 1889 meeting, he lamented that only three of the Saints had come, noting that one of the missing, Garrie van Schoonhoven, "has again taken to smoking."[42] Months later, Cluff snapped when Van Schoonhoven spoke ill of the recently deceased President Taylor. "At dinner today," Cluff wrote privately, "an unpleasantness occurred. Bro. Ericksen[43] commenced to criticise [sic] some of the church authorities, I and others took the opposite side. When in the midst of our conversation Garrie Van Schoonhoeven [sic] burst forth with 'John Taylor was nothing but a coward,' 'Why didn't he stand up and take his medicine'? Van S. is a boy (20 yrs) with the least sense of any person I ever saw. He never has an opinion of his own, but having been brought up with a lot of outsiders in Salt Lake City repeats now the arguments and expressions he heard from them. . . . I shall be glad when we are rid of him."[44]

Just days later, Cluff had a bitter "falling out" with two of the other Mormon students, who defied him and moved out of the Saints' boarding house early in 1890. Cluff fumed, "There is no manhood in Hart[,] and Ericksen naturally opposes everything. He has always something to say against his bishop, his stake president or against the authorities in general."[45] Disputes over the proper attitude toward church authorities and the proper course in the face of persecution rankled Cluff and his brethren. A common heritage and faith, and a common identity as "outsiders" in the halls of the American academy, could not unite the fractious collection of Mormons at Michigan in service of any ecclesiastical agenda.

Even during a hailstorm of new anti-Mormon legislation and persecution, unleashed by the Edmunds–Tucker Act of 1887,[46] Mormon students failed to unite in service of the resistance. Even worse, in the eyes of Karl Maeser and his sympathizers, Mormons were emigrating to American universities in the greatest numbers yet. Particularly striking in this regard is the published correspondence of "Cactus,"[47] a Mormon medical student who felt in no way disloyal to the faith when she told Mormon girls that the University of Michigan was a promised land. As she progressed toward her MD from 1887 to 1889, she came to see the university as the place that "had long been the wished-for goal of our hopes and ambitions."[48] Rigorous in its curriculum and affordable for people of "low estate," the university possessed a redemptive power that lifted her to heights of romantic eloquence. "Here is one place in the world," she enthused, "where money and position are of little avail, unless coupled with ability, and conscientious application to study. . . . So may it ever be, fair Michigan, thou queen of western universities. Be ever as now, the friend and helper of the poor and struggling student, who but for such aid must needs sink beneath his load of poverty, and the frowns of those more fortunate than himself. Thus by thine assistance thousands of earth's noblest sons and daughters will rise from their low estate to positions of honor and trust; and pointing to thee with pride will cry: 'Blessed be our Alma Mater.'"[49]

In the business of exaltation—helping individuals reach their glorious destiny—the church was supposed to enjoy a monopoly. Devout Mormon separatists worked to eliminate the competition. In this spirit, from 1889 to 1890, a Mormon obstetrician named Hannah Sorenson condemned the academic migrations of the Saints in a series of "letters to the young women of Zion," published in *The Young Woman's Journal*, the same church magazine that was publishing the correspondence of "Cactus." Sorenson noted that before converting to the Mormon church in 1883 and emigrating to Utah, she had received high-level medical training in Denmark's Royal Hospital, graduating in 1861. Yet when she joined the despised Mormon sect, she paid dearly; she was promptly dismissed from government service. After arriving in Utah, she used her medical skill to build the Mormon kingdom. She taught health classes to young women, and by 1890, according to her estimate, she had assisted with 4,500 births.

Sorenson was populist to the core. Her experience of conversion and rejection across the Atlantic had left her with an undying loyalty to the church and an understandable contempt for "the world." Although she never repudiated her own medical training, she fought desperately to keep other Mormon women from studying with the doctors of "Babylon." In Mormonism, she found divine principles of knowledge and health, fully accessible to ordinary people, which surpassed anything that Gentile doctors knew or taught. Those doctors, practicing without divine guidance, spewed a Babel of confusing, contradictory, and even deadly advice. Like the young Joseph Smith, who had been bewildered by an array of competing Christianities, the modern patient could only wonder which philosophy of health was true. She wrote: "What a confusion, I say. Consult one doctor; consult ten doctors, consult twenty doctors, and you will not find two of them who would give you the same advise [sic], even for the same sickness. What does all that mean, and which of them is the right one? If you will be satisfied with my answer, I will say: "they are all wrong." . . . I will say as I have said before, medicine never has and never will cure a single person. But it is the proper care and treatment connected with the blessings of God, which will restore a person to health, and not the drugs administered."[50]

Like all truth, Sorenson asserted, truth about healing comes through revelation and prayer, not through misguided pilgrimages to the schools of the East. "We do not need," she said, "to go to Philadelphia, Chicago, or New York, to study these things, they are obtainable for the humblest of God's daughters, if you will plead with Him to tell you how, to inspire you how you shall be a worthy, noble, pure and virtuous mother."[51] Sorenson thought that thoroughgoing observance of the divine laws of health would usher in a "millennium of purity," when women would no longer study in "the most wicked cities and places on the earth," but enjoy such a state of holiness that they would even give birth without pain.[52]

As she reprimanded girls with dreams of studying abroad, Sorenson fought an uphill battle. For more than a decade, ever since Romania Pratt and Ellis Reynolds Shipp returned from Philadelphia with the MD, Mormon periodicals had been offering a pulpit to eastern-trained women doctors and medical students, who were a tremendous source of pride for the Saints at home. By giving more than equal time to Mormon doctors trained abroad, Mormon periodicals robbed Sorenson's arguments of much of their force. In fact, in 1889, just after *The Young Woman's Journal* began publishing Sorenson's letters, the same magazine printed an article by "Cactus," who, from Ann Arbor, unequivocally endorsed education abroad. "Never before in the history of our people," she said, "have the opportunities for obtaining a broad, liberal education . . . been so promising as at present."[53]

Even Benjamin Cluff, the church's appointed overseer in Ann Arbor, was as effusive as "Cactus," leaving Karl Maeser incensed and desperate. By the spring of 1889, Maeser had grown weary as he tried to oversee both the Brigham Young Academy (in Provo) and the church's new General Board of Education, headquartered in Salt Lake City. He was now directly responsible for strengthening the Mormon educational system and keeping it free from Gentile control. It was an enormous task. Maeser needed someone to take the helm in Provo, but he had his reservations about Cluff, who, at just past thirty, was half Maeser's age. Maeser sent Cluff a stern letter. "I have been careful," he said, "not to suggest your recall during this present academic year, surely expecting that you intend returning on your own account this summer. . . . Now Bros. D. John and H. H. Cluff[54] tell me that it is your firm determination to remain yet another year or two East. I do not recognize the necessity nor the wisdom for that course, and I have good reasons for supposing that I am sustained in my position in regard to it by the President and the bretheren [sic] of the General Board."[55] The educational destiny of the church was at stake, and Maeser could not stand the thought of Cluff basking in the rays of an "eastern" education, fiddling while Zion burned, as it were. He told Cluff that he could stay in Ann Arbor long enough to earn his bachelor's degree. Just be sure, Maeser warned, that "your long stay does not imbue you with a preference for eastern methods and notions."[56]

Maeser's suspicions about secular education, nursed in Prussia and brought to maturity in Utah, matched Hannah Sorenson's, and in the late 1880s, Gentiles in Utah did little to disabuse Maeser of the notion that Mormons had few friends outside the faith. Maeser conceded that students educated abroad could help the church reach some of its goals, but he, like Brigham Young, did not want educational missions to become a permanent practice. In May 1889, he reminded Cluff that the church's hierarchy wanted a first-rate, Mormon-run educational system that would "open up chances for satisfying the aspirations of intelligent young people at home, *without going abroad*[.]"[57]

Maeser's stress became even more acute when church leaders ambitiously designated three Mormon schools as "colleges": the BYA in Provo, the Latter-day Saints' College in Salt Lake City, and the Brigham Young College in Logan. The hierarchy looked to Maeser to place one of the best Mormon minds at the head of each.[58] Again Maeser turned to Cluff, but he hardly begged. Before handing the BYA over, he would need to discover "to what extent [Cluff's] spirit and methods have been influenced by his eastern sojourn."[59] As Cluff neared graduation in the spring of 1890, he tried to assure Maeser of his own worthiness. "My studies in this University," Cluff maintained, "have only tended to increase my confidence in your methods of discipline and instruction." Yet he wanted to leave himself room for innovation. Should he become principal of the

BYA, he said, he would "introduc[e] only such changes from time to time as the progress of the times seem [sic] to demand."[60] The comment revealed the extent of Cluff's faith in the American university's modern creed: changing circumstances often render established ideas obsolete, and they demand forward-looking, "progressive" adjustment in response. Cluff, raised in a church with strong, distinctive notions of eternal progression and ongoing revelation, thought he was being perfectly orthodox.

Claiming Authority, (En)Gendering Reform

Even after church leaders bowed to federal pressure and vowed, in 1890, to cease contracting plural marriages, they clung as tightly as ever to the dream of a strong, independent Mormon educational subculture. Mormon scholars, however, continued to stray from the agenda of their superiors. In 1891, Joseph Marion Tanner, the polygamist principal of the Brigham Young College, defied Karl Maeser when he left Logan to enroll in Harvard's law school.[61] He took six promising students and educators with him, including John A. Widtsoe and George Thomas, both destined to become extraordinarily important figures in the development of secular higher education in Utah.[62] Maeser legitimately feared that Tanner's departure would destroy the Brigham Young College, which was locked in a Darwinian struggle with its local rival, the Agricultural College of Utah (later Utah State University). With the Brigham Young Academy in Provo unstable as well, Maeser appealed to LDS president Woodruff:

> I beg leave to call your attention also to the B. Y. College at Logan.
> Bro. J. M. Tanner has announced his intention to go East after the
> close of the schoolyear, and study also for a year or two as Bros.
> Talmage and Cluff have done, in order "to be even with them."
> Now, there is the Agricultural College at Logan with its financial
> advantages gaining in influence and power in ever increasing ratio.
> The B. Y. College must not be suffered to be swamped by that Gentile
> Institution [sic], which it certainly would be if Bro. Tanner, who has
> been working up a fine spirit among the young people there, leaves
> and no suitable man [is available] to continue the work.[63]

Maeser's protests notwithstanding, Tanner was off to Cambridge in the fall.[64]

Tanner's desire to "be even" with the university-educated Talmage and Cluff reveals much about the rising Mormon generation's reverence for

American universities, even among unrepentant polygamists. The private correspondence of one of Tanner's three wives, Jennie, reveals even more. Jennie would not accompany her beloved "Marion" to Cambridge; if he took more than one of his wives, they would attract the sort of scrutiny the church abhorred as it mounted its campaign for statehood. At Harvard, Marion would have to pass as monogamous. Jennie agreed to stay in Akron, New York, with plans to reunite with her husband after two years apart. In a letter to her brother, Daniel Harrington, who was studying law at the University of Michigan, Jennie confessed that she dreaded "another siege of two years of widowhood" in her husband's absence, but she was "willing to put up with most anything to have him take a course in some Eastern Institution[;] his ambition has always been for that, and I want to see him gratified."[65]

In the eyes of the Mormon students, Harvard lived up to its reputation. Reflecting years later on his arrival in Cambridge in 1891, John Widtsoe marveled, "History, tradition, science, books—the dream had come true! My prayers had been heard. Who cared for the past, in full view of a glorious future!"[66] Like the Mormons at Michigan, the Mormons at Harvard were no longer in the trenches of Mormon-Gentile conflict. Virtually beyond ecclesiastical oversight, and freed by Harvard from religious coercion of any sort, Mormons luxuriated in the company of Harvard's renowned student body and faculty. Widtsoe studied philosophy, psychology, and religion with university luminaries William James and Josiah Royce, and in chemistry, his major field of study, he came under the profound influence of Josiah Cooke, the head of the department. For years Cooke had wrestled to harmonize his scientific research with religious faith, and ultimately he affirmed that "to him there was no conflict between science and religion. All of nature was but God's speech."[67] With Professor Cooke's aid, Widtsoe became a new breed of Mormon intellectual, at home in the modern university while retaining and even strengthening his faith.

Harvard's president, Charles Eliot, had intentionally created this sort of environment for his students. He exalted the freedom of students by promoting unfettered inquiry, implementing an elective system that allowed students tremendous power to determine their courses of study, and making chapel attendance voluntary.[68] Widtsoe and his companions revered him. Widtsoe enthused, "In my generation he was easily the foremost citizen of America. Such men as he have the power to shape the world, and always for good."[69] Eliot's influence on George Thomas was even more direct. During his sophomore year, desperate financial trouble threatened to cut Thomas's time at Harvard short. Thomas felt he had no choice but to drop out and go home. Utterly dejected, he came across his adviser, the eminent geographer and geologist William M. Davis. Professor Davis was deeply moved and arranged for Thomas to see President Eliot, who asked Thomas to hand over his bills for the rest of the year. With Thomas looking on, Eliot wrote on each one, "Paid in full—Charles William Eliot."[70] The intervention allowed Thomas to finish the year. It felt redemptive. Thomas eventually graduated with high honors and went on to serve as president of the University of Utah for some twenty years."[71]

Ordinary Americans had no idea that Mormons were enjoying such lavish hospitality at Harvard. They found out in 1892, when the personal connections that Mormons had established with Charles Eliot led him to visit Salt Lake City.[72] Before a crowd of seven thousand Mormons and non-Mormons in the Salt Lake Tabernacle, Eliot delivered a speech on one of his favorite topics, religious liberty. He expressed admiration for the Mormons, who, he said, resembled the early Puritans in their willingness to endure hardship and travel great distances in pursuit of a religious ideal. Apparently, non-Mormons in Salt Lake City and throughout the nation found Eliot's comparison intolerable, even traitorous. Eliot only added to the storm of controversy when he acknowledged that there was a "colony" of Mormon students at Harvard.[73]

The aftermath of Eliot's speech illustrated how badly Mormons wanted to be considered fully American, and how far most of the country still was from seeing them that way. Mormons rejoiced when President Eliot continued to stand up for them in the face of public criticism. "Polygamy is completely abandoned as a doctrine of the Mormon Church," Eliot said, "and has been made a crime by the votes of the Mormons. I think they should now be treated, as regards their property rights and their freedom of thought and worship, precisely like Roman Catholics, Jews, Methodists, or any other religious denomination."[74] The controversy followed Eliot to San Francisco, where he added that Mormons were "sober and industrious, and . . . anxious to give their children the benefits of a higher education."[75] Pressed about the Saints at Harvard, Eliot defended his students. At a time when the notion of a "colony" suggested a menacing enclave of the ethnically unassimilated and un-American, Eliot praised his Mormon students as model citizens of the university. "They live together," Eliot conceded, "but they are not colonists in the sense of propagating Mormon doctrines or endeavoring to secure proselytes. They are

Mormons from Utah and Idaho studying in Boston and Cambridge, 1893. The presence of the Mormon "colony" at Harvard was a subject of public controversy when Harvard's famed president, Charles Eliot, visited Salt Lake City the previous year. Courtesy of Church History Library, Church of Jesus Christ of Latter-day Saints, Salt Lake City.

good students, but do not differ greatly from other young men in their habits and customs."[76] Mormons savored the soul-stirring respect.

Back east, New Englanders made "a great ado" over Eliot's Tabernacle address and the Mormons at Harvard, according to an Associated Press dispatch. A reporter reached one of the Mormon students for comment. "The truth of it is," the student said, "President Eliot said a kind word for the Mormons and the Gentiles misconstrued his meaning." He added, "there are ten of us here studying in Boston and Cambridge. I don't know that we should be called a colony of Mormons. We are of Mormon parents, brought up in Mormon families and hold to that belief. We are all single except one of my brothers, who leaves his wife and family at home and comes here just as a student like any one [*sic*] else."[77] The student, misidentified as "J. L. Tanner," must have been Caleb Tanner, Joseph

Marion's unmarried brother, who was in the Lawrence Scientific School studying to be an engineer. Caleb's description of his brother as "a student like any one else" who left "his wife and family at home" was thoroughly disingenuous; in the 1890s, however, he simply could not have admitted otherwise. What mattered most to Caleb was that Mormons had won the public support of academic royalty. They were gaining ground.

Eliot's visit was just one of a number of appearances by the nation's leading educators in Utah in the 1890s. Early in that decade, the passionately idealistic and ambitious Benjamin Cluff inaugurated a series of summer schools at the Brigham Young Academy, which allowed Cluff to rival his superior, Karl Maeser, as the most influential figure in Mormon education. Cluff had failed in his narrow ecclesiastical mission to unite the Mormon students at Michigan, but he was spectacularly successful in his broader, independent quest to bring the church, and Utah, into close communion with America's foremost educators. The summer schools' guest lecturers included Col. Francis Parker of the Cook County Normal School in Chicago (1892), James Baldwin of the University of Texas (1893), and Burke Hinsdale of the University of Michigan (1894). (G. Stanley Hall of Clark University would follow in 1897, and John Dewey would come from the University of Chicago in 1901.) In a common spirit of aspiration and professionalism, hundreds of Mormon and non-Mormon teachers attended the summer schools to hear lectures on some of the latest methods in education and psychology.[78] John C. Swenson, a member of the BYA faculty who had never set foot outside of Utah, recalled the event as a "remarkable and enthusiastic gathering" that fueled his desire to pursue university training in pedagogy and psychology, which he did at Stanford beginning in 1894."[79]

The interest in the summer schools spread far beyond the teachers. In 1892, *The Deseret News* offered detailed reports of Col. Parker's lectures. Parker, a devotee of Herbert Spencer, troubled Mormons at times; his assertion that "the child is a born savage," for example, struck them as patently false.[80] Yet Parker's eloquence, practical illustrations, and praise won over the assembly. At the Salt Lake Tabernacle, he proclaimed before some seven thousand people, "Let me say right here that we met five hundred of the sharpest thinkers, most earnest and intelligent teachers and students that I have ever seen in the United States and I have held a great many institutes in my day."[81] When Parker left after two weeks, he told a delighted *Deseret News* reporter that he would spread the word "at home and abroad" about the high quality of teaching in the Utah territory."[82]

Subsequent summer sessions at the BYA involved similar explorations of the practical and moral aims of education, which elicited assent from Mormons and non-Mormons alike. Visiting lecturers encouraged teachers to master their profession, to set high personal standards of character, and to direct strategically the will of the child. "Be what you would have your pupils become," James Baldwin of the University of Texas pronounced in the summer of 1893. "The old teachers drove," he went on to say, "the modern teacher must lead."[83] University of Michigan professor Burke Hinsdale echoed the sentiment in the summer of 1894. The duty of the teacher, he contended, "is to take charge of the pupil's mind, to prepare him for the duties of life, to form his character, and give him motives in this direction."[84] The instructors' broad aphorisms allowed Mormons to demonstrate genuine loyalty to an emerging national consensus about the nature and aims of education. As Mormons lost their independence, educational aspiration gave them a way to imagine entering the mainstream of American life without selling their souls.

As he orchestrated the first summer schools, Benjamin Cluff further promoted professionalism in the ranks of Mormon teachers by adding a bachelor's degree in pedagogy to the Brigham Young Academy's offerings. In 1893 eight of Cluff's protégés earned the first BPd degrees that the school conferred. Each of the students had adopted a pseudonym from the canon of Western thought, like "Locke," "Pascal," or "Rousseau," and four of them went on to obtain graduate degrees (at Harvard, Tufts, Columbia, Illinois Wesleyan, and Stanford).[85] Cluff himself was eager to return to Ann Arbor to work toward a master's degree, and he left the Brigham Young Academy for the 1893–94 academic year.[86]

Cluff's admiration for the University of Michigan was nearly boundless. When he arrived, he sighed, "I wish I could spend the next two years of my life in these laboratories."[87] A few months later, he wrote to his students at the Brigham Young Academy, "It is an inspiration . . . to come into the society of those whose knowledge and attainments so far exceeds ones [sic] own that he feels as though he had hardly taken the first step."[88] Cluff studied with George Herbert Mead, the trendsetting social psychologist, whose lectures and experiments made Cluff eager to construct a version of Mead's laboratory at the BYA. Making a permanent break with his populist elders, he began to characterize higher education as a spiritual imperative, populism a sin. He wrote, "there is so much benefit to be

Benjamin Cluff Jr., president of the Brigham Young Academy, possessed an almost boundless faith in higher education. He told bright young Mormons that it would be "a sin to miss the opportunities" that America's finest universities afforded. Used by permission, L. Tom Perry Special Collections, Harold B. Lee Library, Brigham Young University, Provo.

derived from a few courses in this university that I feel it is a sin to miss the opportunities. I have often said that we as teachers don't know enough. Now I am fully convinced, especially in my own case, and I am determined to see that the teachers in the Academy so long as I am principal shall have opportunities for self culture, and if possible original work."[89]

To complete his work toward the master's degree, in the spring of 1894, Cluff embarked on a wide-ranging tour of American schools to gather additional, firsthand information about educational trends in the United States and Canada. The visits expanded the already impressive list of contacts Cluff had made with prominent educators.[90] To each destination, he carried a letter of introduction from President Angell of the University of Michigan, which "opens all doors to me, and enables me to get any information I desire."[91] Highlights included meeting with the esteemed Clark University psychologist G. Stanley Hall, whose services Cluff would later secure for the 1897 summer school at the BYA; visiting the Mormon colony at Harvard and dining and discussing Mormonism with William James;[92] and observing the work at leading normal schools, like the Oswego State Normal School in New York and the Cook County Normal School in Illinois.

When he returned to Utah, Cluff resumed the summer schools at the BYA and continued training the next generation of Mormon scholars. Cluff's successes at the BYA stood in stark contrast to the church hierarchy's failure to launch a "church university." National economic panic sealed the school's fate before it could open its doors. A capitulating, but ideologically unwavering, Karl Maeser instructed church schools to now "consider themselves feeders to the State University," the University of Utah. "The reason for this is obvious," he claimed. "It is better to have our young people pursue their university course at our home institution, instead of going abroad for that purpose away from our control and influence."[93] Maeser clung to his hope that "Gentile" institutions of higher education would offer Mormon youth a world-class, but narrowly practical, education that would leave the church's patriarchal authority intact.

Church periodicals, however, continued to offer Mormons an alternative to Maeser's siege mentality, showcasing, and openly celebrating, the accomplishments of Mormons studying abroad. In the early 1890s, *The Young Woman's Journal* and *The Woman's Exponent* published correspondence from LDS students at the University of Michigan, as they had through the storm of federal persecution. In 1894 and 1895, the church's magazines for young men, *The Juvenile Instructor* and *The Contributor*, featured correspondence and feature articles by Mormon students at Harvard, MIT, Cornell, Michigan, the U.S. Naval Academy, and the art schools of Paris.[94] Most of the articles appeared in the *Instructor*, edited by George Q. Cannon, the church's most prominent national political figure and a strong advocate of Utah's statehood.

Each student dispatch introduced a distant, prestigious school to Mormon youth. The articles contained large photographs and ample descriptions of each school's distinctive strengths, religious milieu, entrance requirements, daily routine, social life, and insider language like "quiz" and "flunk."[95] At the invitation of their supportive elders, the students thus assumed authority as culturally bilingual diplomats who allowed the Saints at home to experience, vicariously, the thrill of being welcome in America.

Richard Lyman, writing from Ann Arbor, bore perhaps the most ebullient testimony. He described the University of Michigan campus and the surrounding town as "a perfect little garden of Eden," evoking the university's power to resacralize the American landscape for Mormons.[96] At first, he had entered such space with fear and trembling, because all Mormons "go out into the world feeling that in some degree, at least, we shall be curiosities to people[.]"[97] Anxiety nearly overcame Lyman when he had to introduce himself to James B. Angell. The university's president carefully looked over the documents testifying to Lyman's educational qualifications and said, "I am very glad to see you. We have had a great many students from your state, and among them we have found only good workers." Lyman's relief was inexpressible.[98]

Lyman and his peers emphasized that the modern university, unmoored from sectarian religious constraints, held vast opportunities for hard-working men and women of all backgrounds. They assured the Utah Saints that Mormons could flourish at such places, which felt neither viciously anti-Mormon nor awash in godlessness. "The best preachers of the various Christian denominations" could be heard at Cornell; the Students' Christian Association at the University of Michigan could be counted on for boundless hospitality and assistance in getting oriented to campus; and Harvard's chapel services, though optional, were well-attended and graced by a "perfectly trained" boys' choir.[99] The authors exalted their freedom from bigotry and their seemingly limitless educational opportunity. Lewis T. Cannon reported that MIT boasted "the most modern apparatus for all kinds of research."[100] Lyman remarked that he was "always busy" at the University of Michigan, but at a school "second to no institution in our land" he could hardly complain.[101]

In her articles for *The Woman's Exponent*, Ellis Reynolds Shipp exhibited a faith in higher education that was undimmed by changing circumstance and passing time. Shipp, nearly fifteen years after earning her MD at the Woman's Medical College of Philadelphia, had traveled to Ann Arbor in 1892 to take an additional year's worth of graduate courses in medicine. At the University of Michigan, she averred, "woman is every where [sic] received with the greatest consideration and respect, and in all the numerous avenues of learning, stands on an equal footing with her brother man."[102] She reported that women made up a full two-thirds of the literary department and one-third of the medical department. President Angell had lauded them as "an army of earnest workers."[103] Shipp, now 45, joined "Cactus" and other university-trained Mormon women to ensure that Hannah Sorenson's populism would not possess the daughters of Zion.

Conclusion

The student correspondence published in *The Juvenile Instructor* during the 1890s presented a positive account of Mormon life in the American university. Obscured or excluded in such narratives were many of the real struggles and complexities of life in and out of the classroom, information revealed only in Mormon students' private journals. There, we find evidence of simmering internal disputes, even before statehood, that would reach a boiling point in the early twentieth century and threaten to tear the church apart.

The experiences of Josiah Hickman, a student of physics and pedagogy at Michigan from 1892 to 1895, were representative. For him, university life was a disorderly mix of success and secrecy. Early in his studies, Hickman had won the confidence of the church's First Presidency, who appointed him to preside over the meetings of Mormon students at the university.[104] He was also a skilled public speaker. At Michigan, he relished the opportunity to defend the honor of his home state and the Mormon church. In his senior year, he took third place in a highly competitive university oratorical contest at Michigan, in which he portrayed the Mormons as patriotic and long-suffering.[105]

Yet as a polygamist who lived with both of his wives (at different times) in Ann Arbor, he struck fear into the hearts of the First Presidency. When they ordered him to send his wife Martha home, Hickman was "plunged in great grief," but he conceded that the scandal could cause the church "great trouble."[106] Hickman's vigorous public testimony and private turmoil were products of a peculiar historical moment for the church, the brief interlude between the Manifesto (1890) and statehood (1896). During that period, Mormons had to muster every argument in defense of their patriotism and morality, and they had to shield from public view any embarrassing, lingering reminders of their all-too-recent past.

Hickman's strong performance in the university's oratorical contest was not the only instance of public success for the Mormon "colony" at Michigan. The class of 1895 elected Richard Lyman as its president,[107] and in early 1895, James Talmage visited Ann Arbor and delivered a lecture on "the story of Mormonism." Josiah Hickman called it "sublime" and delighted in the warm response Talmage received.[108] The recognition that Hickman, Lyman, and Talmage gained seemed to fulfill the church's hope that the true gospel would eventually reach the social classes of "the rich and learned."[109]

Despite considerable achievement in the public realm, unity continued to elude the Mormon colony at Michigan. For Josiah Hickman, as for Benjamin Cluff, presiding over the religious affairs of the community proved to be a curse as well as a blessing. In part, Hickman was troubled by the skeptical leanings of professors and even of fellow Saints, who cast doubt on the church's millennial prophecies about the imminent vindication of the righteous and the destruction of the wicked. Hickman complained, "It is hard for me to keep the spirit of God while surrounded with such skeptical teachings. It takes constant prayer and reading of scriptures to keep me from becoming doubtful at certain hours. I find several of the young people here growing indifferent and skeptical. It grieves me to see it. Some begin to think the prophecies of the wicked too strong and that our people wrongly interpret the scriptures and that the destructions will not come in our days."[110]

Hickman's companions did not always welcome his brotherly concern for their spiritual condition. At one fast meeting, Hickman chose to address biological evolution. Moved by the spirit of God, he "felt to predict" that it would require the Saints' utmost vigilance to avoid being "polluted with these theories of men." The weak, he said, would reject the gospel for "the learning of the world." Not all the Saints, however, shared Hickman's intense fear. Jed Woolley, speaking after Hickman, openly disagreed with him. He thought Hickman's wariness excessive. Hickman responded by charging that Woolley's words lacked the spirit of God.[111]

Other Mormons at Michigan, who committed themselves to the work of the church as strongly as Hickman, did not see the university as an

In her remarkable educational, professional, and political career, Martha Hughes Cannon, MD, embodied the powerful and wide-ranging aspirations of the children of Mormon pioneers. Courtesy of Church History Library, Church of Jesus Christ of Latter-day Saints, Salt Lake City.

agent of spiritual corruption. Richard Lyman thought that his college years had been the best of his life. James L. Brown mourned his impending departure before he graduated in 1897. He wrote to Benjamin Cluff that he and his wife "feel quite at home here and will, no doubt, take leave of our dear friends and surroundings with some feeling of sadness."[112] Hickman portrayed the university as noxious; Brown saw it as ennobling. The church school system would employ them both, and subsequent decades would see a growing tension between their representative points of view.

Nonetheless, at the dawn of statehood, university-trained Mormon students demonstrated just how much Mormonism had evolved since the death of Brigham Young. They possessed a new status and authority perhaps best exemplified in the career of Martha Hughes Cannon, MD. In 1896, Cannon became the first American woman to serve in a state senate; she even defeated her polygamist husband, Angus, in the process.[113] She held three degrees from institutions outside Utah, all earned in the early 1880s: an MD from the University of Michigan, a bachelor's degree in medicine from the University of Pennsylvania, and another bachelor's degree from Philadelphia's National School of Elocution and Oratory. During the raid, she had gone into exile in Europe, pregnant, to help Angus avoid arrest.[114] There, she visited training schools for nurses, whose methods inspired her as she opened her own training school in Salt Lake City in 1889, before pondering a new life in politics.[115] Such resilience and success made the mid-1890s heady times for the young scholars of the church. From Stanford, John C. Swenson wrote to Benjamin Cluff that with statehood secured, there was no telling "what we can not do."[116]

Celebration of the students' success would forestall a resurgent Mormon anti-intellectualism until the early twentieth century, when conservative members of the church's hierarchy, even some highly educated ones, began to fear that Mormons' respect for "the theories of men" had gone too far and a "theological scholastic aristocracy" might destroy the Saints' culture of brotherhood and lay religious authority.[117] Mormon populists then began to cast the students' enthusiasm as arrogance, their diplomacy as treason. As education turned into the main battleground in the twentieth-century war to define Mormon identity, patriarchal scrutiny would often make Mormon scholars rebel or cower. In the tumultuous late nineteenth century, however, Utah's Mormons needed their intellectuals—and American universities—to show them that becoming American would be neither humiliating nor irrational.

3 Evolution and Its Discontents, 1896–1920

. . . .

After Utah attained its statehood, Mormons inhabited altered landscapes of anxiety and aspiration. Despite experiencing meaningful new forms of acceptance and freedom, they still felt the sting of external hostility, while fresh internal disputes—about evolution, biblical authority, and academic freedom—emerged as the LDS Church's defining controversies of the age. These new circumstances produced new, enduring Mormon mentalities.

One of the most striking developments at the turn of the century was the domestication of Mormon feminism. The change accompanied an important shift in Mormon women's educational aims. After two decades of almost exclusive devotion to medicine, Mormon women interested in education abroad shifted their focus to increasingly popular fields for women: teacher training and "domestic science." Mormon women studying at the Harvard summer school had started the trend in 1892 and 1893. By 1895, Mormon women from Utah had begun enrolling more permanently at schools like the Pratt Institute in Brooklyn and the Oswego State Normal School in upstate New York.

Mormon women studying abroad in the 1890s had many of the same broad aspirations as their predecessors. They hoped to "do good in Zion."[1] The Mormon women who had studied medicine in the 1870s and 1880s had sought to offer the best medical care to the people of God; in the 1890s, women set out to learn the latest scientific methods in teaching and home-making in order to strengthen Mormon civilization. Leah Dunford, a student at the Pratt Institute, articulated the connection between traditional hopes and new academic disciplines. She wrote in 1897 that she hoped to teach "household ethics" in one of the church colleges. "I am ambitious to see the homes of Utah [become] the best and happiest in the land," she said, "and I am desirous that every daughter in Zion will sense the dignity and responsibility of her position as a home-maker."[2] Aretta Young had similar hopes for her work in the teaching profession at Oswego. Having won the accolades of her professors, Young recognized the power that outside experts' testimony could carry in Utah's increasingly competitive educational profession. It carried a weight even Gentiles had to respect. Young wrote to Benjamin Cluff, "Should my work come from the Oswego Normal with the approval of professionals with high reputation it might do a wider good."[3]

Along with the change in disciplines, however, came a rather sudden depoliticization of Mormon women's ambitions. It was an ironic result of cultural success. After the triumph of statehood, the Saints could celebrate, but they had lost some of the powerful, driving opposition that had prompted them to marshal every resource for the struggle. The Mormon women who studied abroad in the 1870s and 1880s had played a major role in the battle with Gentiles. The subjects of well-crafted publicity, they stood strong on the front lines, defying outsiders' stereotypes. As they earned higher degrees and joined national and international suffrage organizations, they had overseen a crucial aspect of Mormonism's public relations campaign. When the need for such an aggressive campaign waned, the political and intellectual force of Mormon women dissipated.[4] In the twentieth century, the public struggle to define Mormon identity would be a man's game, with women on the sidelines.[5]

Making a New Mormon Scholar

At the same time, right as the United States absorbed Utah, the bitter conflicts of the wider Christian world began to absorb the young LDS Church. In the last decade of the nineteenth century and the first decade of the twentieth, nationally publicized clergy heresy trials revealed growing fissures in American Protestantism. In the crucible of the debates about Darwin, biblical authority, and the future of American civilization, new, vibrant, and enduring Christian movements emerged, permanently altering the American religious and cultural landscape: a "social gospel" emphasizing economic justice and the coming kingdom of God, and a "fundamentalism" defending what it saw as the essentials of the pure Christian faith. American Catholics wrangled with similarly pressing concerns. In their ranks, liberal ideas about scientific evolution, biblical scholarship, democratic politics, and the separation of church and state were growing so strong that a defensive Pope Pius X felt the need to condemn this dangerous new Catholic "modernism."[6]

Mormons studying abroad found themselves in the path of the storm. When they and their fellow Saints at home felt its full force, it would threaten to tear Mormons, like Protestants and Catholics, apart. For them, the definition—and the fate—of true Christianity were at stake.

The arguments between Josiah Hickman and his Mormon peers at Michigan, discussed in the previous chapter, were typical. As they wrestled with the implications of new ideas about evolution and the Bible, their fellow Mormons at Stanford were beginning to navigate the same thrilling and forbidding terrain.[7] Stanford's reputation had skyrocketed in the 1890s, and Mormon students, especially those interested in psychology and pedagogy, had begun to see Stanford as ideal. John C. Swenson, one of the first to earn Brigham Young Academy's new bachelor's degree in pedagogy, was among the first, accompanied by two other Saints from Utah, Clinton Ray and Newell Bullock. Before they left, Swenson sought and received the blessing of President Joseph F. Smith, counselor to President Woodruff, for his special educational mission to Stanford. The missionary's certificate Swenson received authorized him to preach the gospel in his California environs, but Swenson elected to take a more indirect approach to evangelization. Careful not to alienate his new colleagues, Swenson "preached by my general attitude and conduct to a group at Stanford that the regular missionaries could not easily reach."[8] His hard work, intelligence, and cordiality, he thought, would serve the church far better than his proselytizing.

At Stanford, the Saints found an academic and religious environment much like that at Harvard, Cornell, and Michigan: academically rigorous and religiously nonsectarian. President Jordan valorized scientific inquiry, and the institution's promotion of Christianity, though sincere and beautifully manifest in its prominent chapel, was subsumed into a broader pursuit of truth and morality. In some ways, Swenson welcomed the change. "The life at Stanford," he reflected, "was strangely different from the life at the Brigham Young Academy. It was free and unconventional— no outward evidence of any religious life; but after I had been there two years, I came to feel that underneath it was deeply and genuinely spiritual."[9] Swenson also enjoyed Stanford's curricular freedom, evidence of President Jordan's conviction "that the average student was mature enough and intelligent enough to know what he wanted."[10]

It took time, however, for Swenson to appreciate fully his new surroundings. From Provo, Swenson brought not only Benjamin Cluff's enthusiasm for education abroad, but also Karl Maeser's wariness of evolutionary theory. When Swenson took a course on "Factors in Organic Evolution," taught by President Jordan and other faculty, the effect "was at once enlightening and disturbing. I had been taught the theory of evolution was wrong, but the evidences presented in this course were so clear and convincing that I could not doubt them. So began the painful struggle of adjustment between traditional ideas of creation and the demonstrated ideas of modern science."[11] In letters to Benjamin Cluff, Swenson shared his developing ideas about religion, science, and ultimate truth. He articulated how intellectual life at Stanford blended values deeply appealing to Latter-day Saints—the quest for truth, the importance of clean and moral living—with ideals broader than those Latter-day Saints ordinarily embraced. He recognized that some critics saw Stanford as a threat to traditional conceptions of religion, but he remained confident that an open, sincere search for truth would yield a conviction of the harmony between religion and science. Late in 1895, he wrote to Cluff, "Many people of California regard Stanford as a dangerous school in some respects. It is thought that unless a student is very strong[ly] orthodox he will come out an evolutionist. I am not prepared to say how much truth there may be in this, I only know that among the professors at least, there is a high moral tone. A clean personal life is regarded above the forms and ceremonies of religion. The question as to whether a thing is orthodox or not is never given a thought; the only question is, is it true. And in following this rule it is surprising how nearly science and true religion harmonize. So long as one is true to his best ideals, his orthodox[y] will take care of itself."[12]

It had never been customary for the Saints to let their orthodoxy "take care of itself." Nevertheless, Swenson pressed ahead, trying fervently to balance his love for Stanford with his commitment to the church and its unique claims. He wanted to assure Benjamin Cluff that despite the genuine reverence he had for his Stanford professors, his intellect would develop only within the framework of Latter-day Saint belief. "If one has the inspiration of God to guide him constantly," he wrote, "there is little danger of his being led astray. In my private devotions I seek to know God's will concerning my course of action. But there is no use denying the fact that some of the professors here have a great influence over me. They are men of high ideals, and, so far as I am able to judge, of spotless characters. And yet I am sure they are not wholly right in their philosophy of life. It is my aim to receive what truth they have to give that does not conflict with the principles of our Faith [*sic*] as I understand them. I have yet to see the religion or the philosophy that can compare with the religion of the Latter Day Saints [*sic*] in its fundamental conceptions of human life."[13] To ensure that he would remain anchored in the faith, Swenson worshiped with other Stanford Saints twice a semester in San

Francisco, the location of the nearest LDS mission headquarters. George Q. Cannon had encouraged Swenson, Newell Bullock, and Clinton Ray to hold regular meetings together in Palo Alto, but the students felt that the group was too small to keep the meetings going. Meetings in San Francisco offered them a chance to partake of the sacrament and renew old patterns of devotion.[14]

Swenson's searching analysis of his spiritual and intellectual life would be replicated by subsequent Mormons at Stanford. They, however, did not always share Swenson's esteem for both Provo and Palo Alto. For example, P. J. Jensen, studying physiology at Stanford in the fall of 1900, raged against the university's embrace of evolution. He wrote to George Brimhall, acting president of the Brigham Young Academy, "I have not yet learned to control myself emotionally when I hear so many evolutionary principles advanced daily. My being boils, as it were, in defense of truth."[15] Engaging in spiritual warfare, Jensen claimed that he had received visions and revelations confirming his sense of righteousness. In one vision, he glimpsed the future greatness of the BYA; two months later, the Lord assured him that "the *truth* is the broad way, and you need not fear the theories of men, if you keep the commandments of the Lord. For he will make known the truth."[16]

Jensen was severe and uncompromising toward fellow Saints who seemed to have strayed. He informed Brimhall that Newell Bullock, now a graduate student, had become the favorite student of an evolutionist professor[17] and had missed all of the Saints' meetings with the nearby San Jose branch. "I am very anxious to see him return to our dear Utah and get warmed up by the spirit of the Gospel," Jensen wrote. In the meantime, Jensen offered to track down records of Bullock's tithing and ward activity for Brimhall. It would be a simple matter of "righteously inquiring after his welfare," he said.[18] Jensen's sanctified contempt for Stanford and his peers drained any passion he might have had to excel academically. As he prepared to graduate in 1903, he could boast of nothing more than "a fair record," but he felt that he had triumphed spiritually.[19]

Despite culture shock, and some formidable challenges to the faith, Mormons' enthusiasm for studying in leading American universities endured. Such enthusiasm, for some, replaced religious passion. Yet Mormon students at the end of the nineteenth century could still often balance the two in ways that felt natural. As he left for Harvard in 1898, for example, Levi Edgar Young wrote, "At last my dream has been realized," but he was incredulous when he failed to convince a Harvard friend, a non-Mormon, of the veracity of the Book of Mormon. Exasperated, Young said, "He couldn't see it my way. How strange!"[20]

Even Benjamin Cluff, utterly enchanted by the University of Michigan, retained a faith of bold simplicity. In 1900, after a decade of overseeing the development of the Brigham Young Academy, Cluff organized a quixotic, ill-fated expedition to Central and South America, whose goal was to find incontrovertible proof of the Book of Mormon's historical and geographical accuracy.[21] He wrote, "It is not a little remarkable that for fifty years we as a people have taught the Book of Mormon in hundreds of Sabbath schools and in many Church Schools and have speculated much about the land in which the recorded events were acted out, and yet not one of all these teachers has ever come over the country and seen for themselves this wonderful land. It is left for the Academy to open up a work which I am confident will be carried on for years to come until the Latter Day Saints of all people will be the most familiar with Central and South America, with their peoples and their ruins."[22] For Cluff, the quest was entirely consistent with his love for modern, scientific investigation. He thought that the expedition, which received coverage in newspapers as far away as New York, would give the BYA a reputation as a leader in "original research," the hallmark of respectability in higher education.

The expedition fell far short of Cluff's expectations, dogged from the start by internal wrangling and wavering church support. Companions attacked Cluff, accusing him of erratic behavior, even of taking a third wife. Revolution in Colombia finally forced the travelers to turn back. The taint of the expedition and polygamy forced Cluff out of the BYA in 1903, just as it began to call itself Brigham Young University.

Cluff would live for decades more in professional obscurity—he would prove difficult to enshrine—but his vision for Mormon education endured. In an 1898 address to BYA students, he powerfully articulated the connection between educational and spiritual advancement. Cluff asserted that both forms of progress required the same concerted "self-effort."[23] In fact, he argued, Mormons' pursuit of education was intimately tied to their pursuit of godhood. "Education," he said, "has for its chief aim the proper evolution of man from his mortal, selfish, ignorant state to an immortal, exalted, and intelligent state."[24] Pursued fervently by the people of God, education held the power to eliminate sin and create a blessed community of righteousness:

When the young men and women of Zion . . . understand that the wisdom which a man gains in this life follows him in the world to come; when they see the harmony and beauty of the Gospel plan, and sense the fact that they are God's children, capable of becoming as He is, all-wise and all-intelligent; when these facts dawn upon their minds and possess them as a boundless faith, then indeed will they arise and put forth every needed effort; then will they strive for knowledge, for grace, for moral perfection and for intellectual advancement in harmony with the mind and will of God. Then the idler, the loafer, the profaner, the drunkard, the smoker, the scoffer, and the infidel among us will be no more; and from the children of Zion, from among the sons and daughters of the Latter-day saints [sic] there will be found learned philosophers, great scholars, great statesmen, great men in every vocation and avocation in life, and especially will there be found men and women great in keeping the commandments and the laws of God.[25]

In Benjamin Cluff, the utopianism of Brigham Young and the progressivism of John Dewey fluidly merged, but the church's pressing need to purge potentially embarrassing figures like him would diminish his legacy. In 1903, the election of Reed Smoot, a Mormon apostle, to the United States Senate provoked a political firestorm in Washington. At the center of the controversy were serious allegations that Mormons had continued to contract plural marriages after the Manifesto. That led to protracted, publicized hearings that, in effect, put the church on trial. Once more, church leaders were on the ropes, forced to mount a defensive campaign to prove that Mormons were Christian and law-abiding, not the priest-ridden pawns of a debased authoritarian regime.[26]

The public scrutiny resulting from the hearings forced the church's president, Joseph F. Smith, to issue a "Second Manifesto" in 1904. Smith admitted that some Mormons, even the apostles John W. Taylor and Matthias F. Cowley, had indeed contracted plural marriages after the Woodruff Manifesto, without official church sanction. From now on, he declared, any Mormon entering into plural marriage would face excommunication. Taylor and Cowley were eventual casualties of the Second Manifesto, forced to resign in 1906.

The crackdown cut short the academic career not only of Benjamin Cluff, who resigned from his post as principal of the Brigham Young Academy in 1903, but also Church School Superintendent Joseph Marion Tanner, who would leave his position in 1906.[27] Both Cluff and Tanner had contracted plural marriages after the Manifesto. In the 1890s, however, they had done as much as anyone to encourage the Saints to study abroad in American universities. Oddly, the purge of unrepentant polygamists slowed the progress of Mormon intellectual history.[28]

Cluff and Tanner did manage to have a lasting influence, despite seeing their academic careers end prematurely. Tanner had failed to complete his Harvard law degree, apparently because of strain on his health,[29] but when he came home, he found real success as president of the Utah Agricultural College. Like Benjamin Cluff at the Brigham Young Academy, he had recruited brilliant, promising young teachers, offering them furloughs to study in universities outside the Intermountain West. In 1900, however, his tenure had abruptly come to an end, when a state appropriations committee began to worry that Tanner's wide-ranging marital ties would threaten the school's federal funding.[30] Tanner ultimately resigned, but in 1901, the death of Karl Maeser left a vacancy at the helm of the church's General Board of Education. Tanner was glad to fill it, even though he had defied Maeser a decade earlier by leading the first Mormon migration to Harvard.

During Tanner's brief tenure as superintendent, the General Board of Education established a new education fund, which would be his most significant legacy. It would help shape the next generation of Mormon scholarship by providing low-interest loans to students and church school teachers who wanted to pursue higher education "at home or abroad." Tanner recommended that church school teachers contribute one-half of one percent of their salary to the fund, and he wanted the church to provide an initial appropriation of one thousand dollars to give the fund stability. Tanner hoped that the loans would solidify recipients' loyalty to the church school system and improve its overall quality.[31] Approved by LDS president Joseph F. Smith, the fund was instituted in the spring of 1903.[32]

At first, applicants were numerous. So were detractors. Some teachers did not want to contribute to a fund from which they might never benefit. In 1907, as teaching began to occupy a more secure place among the professions nationally, and as pensions became an increasingly common method for securing retired workers' financial well-being, some Mormon teachers understandably began to ask whether pensions might better serve the interests of all the church school teachers. As a result, board secretary Arthur Winter reported in early 1907 that teachers' contributions to the educational fund were slow in coming. The shortfall seemed to threaten the fund's existence, but the board voted to continue it, holding fast to hopes for "the good that can be accomplished by it."[33]

On the recommendation of Willard Young, the General Board decided to issue a circular letter to the church school teachers explaining the purpose of the fund. The circular, signed by President Smith, reflected an enduring Mormon vision—now forty years old—of promoting study abroad in order to build and maintain Mormons' cultural independence and strength. It declared: "Since the Church schools must depend for teachers upon persons of our own faith, we cannot import them, and must therefore educate them. It often happens that persons having teaching ability do not have the means to qualify themselves for teaching in our schools without some such assistance as this Fund affords, and the number of applications for loans constantly on file in the Superintendent's office testify to the value and need of such a fund. The General Board trusts, therefore, that the teachers will cheerfully do their part in giving the small amount asked to aid the general cause of education."[34] The prophet's endorsement of the education fund ensured its continuance, but lingering bitterness from teachers over mandatory contributions and the lack of a pension system shadowed the fund's history. President Smith had perhaps been more assertive than convincing when he said of the fund, "There is no question [that] it is productive of good."[35] It would not be long before he himself had his doubts.

A notorious case of a loan gone bad could not have helped the reputation of the fund. One of the earliest recipients, Nathaniel Baldwin, had used his funding to study physics and engineering for a year at Stanford. Baldwin started out well enough, accepting a teaching position at the head of BYU's physical sciences department in 1905, but his persistent, brash advocacy of polygamy quickly got him fired. Baldwin spent the rest of his life not as an employee of the church school system, but as a Salt Lake City inventor who supported the emergent, offshoot Mormon "fundamentalist" movement, whose adherents continued to affirm the sanctity and, more important, the practice of plural marriage. After enjoying some notable success as an inventor, he died poor in Salt Lake City in 1961.[36]

Despite such exceptions, use of the fund usually comported with Tanner's original designs. The board issued loans, generally in amounts of two hundred to four hundred dollars, to members of the church school system at 6 percent interest. By 1907, the fund had accumulated over four thousand dollars from teacher contributions, matching church appropriations, and interest. Almost all of that money, President Smith noted, was out on loan. Loan recipients used the money to enroll—sometimes just for a summer, other times for a year or more—at leading American universities. Most recipients sought training in education at emerging centers like the University of Chicago and Columbia University's Teachers College. John Dewey's visit to the BYA in 1901 had inspired many of them, as had the First Presidency's encouragement of the Saints to train for the teaching profession in order to meet the needs of the growing public school system in Utah.[37]

This new wave of academic migration, under new circumstances, produced a new Mormon intellectual culture. In the first decade of the twentieth century, returning Mormon students tried, as never before, to harmonize the teachings of Mormonism with the findings of academic scholarship in the natural sciences, the social sciences, and biblical criticism. In the pages of *The Improvement Era*, the official magazine of the LDS Young Men's Mutual Improvement Association,[38] eastern-trained Mormons like John and Osborne Widtsoe, Milton Bennion, and Frank West tried to demonstrate that Mormons could be scholars and scientists of the highest order without abandoning the faith. All the writers possessed eastern degrees, and all were teaching in the colleges and universities of Utah. Their articles sought explicitly—and quite optimistically—to reconcile Mormon life with the life of the mind. *The Improvement Era* thus became a showcase for some of the leading Mormon minds of the early twentieth century.

The most ambitious work in the early issues of *The Improvement Era* was a series of articles called "Joseph Smith as Scientist" by John Widtsoe, the PhD chemist who had earned his higher degrees at Harvard and Goettingen. From 1903 to 1904, Widtsoe, the director of the agricultural experiment station at the Agricultural College of Utah, contributed the articles that tried "to show that not only do 'Mormonism' and science harmonize; but that 'Mormonism' is abreast of the most modern of the established views of science, and that it has held them many years—in some cases before science adopted them."[39] Attempting to reconcile the new science with traditional Mormon populism, Widtsoe wanted to demonstrate that modern science was merely catching up to what Joseph Smith, "the humble, unlearned boy prophet," had declared decades earlier.[40] Published as a full-length volume in 1908, under the auspices of the General Board of Education and the Young Men's Mutual

John A. Widtsoe, PhD, represented a new brand and breed of Mormon scholar. As president of the University of Utah and an apostle in the LDS Church, he would spend decades trying to reconcile divine truths and the revelations of modern science. Used by permission, Utah State Historical Society, all rights reserved.

Improvement Association, *Joseph Smith as Scientist* was Widtsoe's first work of apologetics.[41]

The aim of *Joseph Smith as Scientist*, ironically, was not to show that Smith had been a scientist in any ordinary sense of the word. At the outset, Widtsoe made it clear that Smith "did not know the science of his day,"[42] nor was Smith preoccupied with science in his own writings. According to Widtsoe, the prophet Joseph could be seen as a scientist because, despite limited education and vocabulary, he had managed to articulate broad principles that, in Widtsoe's view, harmonized with the independent findings of the world's leading scientists. Widtsoe thought that Smith's ignorance made his teachings all the more remarkable, all the more evident of divine inspiration.

Widtsoe gave examples: whereas Smith affirmed the materiality and persistence of all things earthly and heavenly, physicists now asserted the indestructibility of matter and energy; Smith's description of "worlds without number" seemed to foreshadow astronomers' discovery of multiple solar systems; the Mormon doctrine of eternal progression, applied even to the Heavenly Father himself, seemed compatible with scientific theories of evolution, which posited that all things undergo "ceaseless change"; and Smith had sensed the poisonous effects of tobacco, alcohol, and "hot drinks," which scientists of his time were only beginning to demonstrate. Only divine revelation, Widtsoe concluded, could have made the prophet Joseph such a good "scientist."

Widtsoe addressed himself directly to Mormon youth interested in higher education, trying to steel them for the difficult journey ahead. His preface began: "In the life of every person, who receives a higher education, in or out of schools, there is a time when there seems to be opposition between science and religion; between man-made and God-made knowledge. The struggle for reconciliation between the contending forces is not an easy one. It cuts deep into the soul and usually leaves scars that ache while life endures. There are thousands of young people in the Church to-day [sic], and hundreds of thousands throughout the world, who are struggling to set themselves right with the God above and the world about them. It is for these young people, primarily, that the following chapters have been written."[43] Widtsoe wanted to reaffirm the church's long-standing belief that Mormonism embraced all truth, regardless of its source. He was exceedingly optimistic about Mormonism's ability to withstand upheavals in the broader intellectual and religious life of the western world. "Because of its comprehensive philosophy," Widtsoe maintained, "'Mormonism' will survive all religious disturbances and become the system of religious faith which all men may accept without yielding the least part of the knowledge of nature as discovered in the laboratories or in the fields."[44] Widtsoe felt sure that the ongoing accumulation of empirical, scientific knowledge would never threaten, but only confirm, the teachings of the prophet Joseph Smith.[45]

Other *Improvement Era* articles on higher education treated its destructive as well as ennobling effects. Representative of these articles was "The Mormon Boy at College" by Osborne Widtsoe, John's younger brother. Osborne wrote the article in 1905, after he had returned from Harvard with a master's degree in English. Now teaching at the Latter-day Saints' University in Salt Lake City, he undertook to explain why some Mormon students, exposed to higher education, might fall away from the faith.

University life, Widtsoe explained, entailed a series of trials and temptations for a good Latter-day Saint. At social events, students and faculty routinely smoked and drank. Inside the classroom, the dangers were more subtle but no less real. When professors dealt with religion, for example, they often introduced troubling methods for dealing with religious texts and claims. The professors' approach, borrowing from the influential German biblical scholarship of the nineteenth century, treated religious texts as contingent products of a particular social, cultural, and historical environment, whose constraints the original authors could not have transcended. These assumptions led professors and their students to examine texts in all their literary, linguistic, and historical complexity. Some found the new methods invigorating; others found them unnerving. Osborne felt pulled in both directions. Of this approach to biblical study, he said, "It is extreme, of course; yet it is of great value, since it separates the true and authentic from the mythical. Now, as the critical acumen of the young 'Mormon' develops, he comes to know that, as yet, we have had but few real scholars among us. Further, he becomes convinced that some good men have made serious mistakes. In the light of his acquired scholarship, he questions some matters of interpretation. His faith begins to falter."[46]

Pushing past his brother John's more comforting reassurances about the precocious wisdom of Joseph Smith, Osborne Widtsoe more boldly argued that an awareness of the intellectual limitations of Mormon pioneers need not undermine Mormons' confidence in the truth of the church's claims. Perhaps working out of an understanding of the church's belief in ongoing revelation, or perhaps trusting, along with many of his non-Mormon contemporaries, that this was an exciting age of progressive intellectual development, he told Mormon youth not to worry. He wrote, "Doubts that arise when the searchlight of modern criticism is turned upon our religion, are perhaps pardonable; but they need never be of long duration. In the course of our scriptural and religious interpretations, we have no doubt made mistakes; but they have arisen from the conditions of the people. Poor, oppressed, and untrained, they could do no better than they did; and they erred much less often than even learned men who work without divine assistance. A broad-minded scholar always makes allowance for the opportunities and the environments of the people he is studying."[47] Like John Widtsoe, Osborne wanted to convince a rising generation of Mormon scholars that they could balance piety and scholarship. Yet his "broad-minded" view of his "poor" ancestors represented a major intellectual and theological concession for a Mormon, whose populist tradition sanctified the unlearned.

Osborne Widtsoe concluded that Mormon students could adopt "the critical attitude" of a scholar and still possess a strong testimony of the truth of the restored gospel. "If he has struggled and overcome [doubts]," he claimed, "his testimony may be built more firmly on a sure foundation than that of his friends."[48] The temptations of university life, moreover, "should not deter any parent from sending his son to a good school."[49] He believed that neither higher education, nor any narrowness in Mormonism, was to blame for apostasy among the educated. Rather, only the weak character of apostates themselves would cause them to fall away from the church. As long as parents developed in their children "honest, manly strength to resist temptation," the university posed no threat to the souls of Mormon youth.

Similar assurances came from Frank L. West, a Mormon physics professor at the Agricultural College of Utah, who wrote in 1908 that "our religion is natural and rational."[50] West made his claim in an *Improvement Era* article called "How Knowledge Comes," which reflected his experience in university laboratories. West was on his way to earning a PhD from the University of Chicago, and the magazine's editors hailed him as "one of the best physicists in the state," whose "study of science does not seem to have interfered with his religious faith at all." Best of all, according to the editors, West had made his analysis of science and religion "faith-strengthening" for Mormon youth.[51]

West recognized that believing in phenomena beyond empirical verification made Mormons vulnerable to the criticism of skeptics. "Because we believe in that which we have not seen and heard," he conceded, "we are sometimes looked upon as simple-minded, credulous, superstitious, and anything else that stands for a low order of intellect."[52] He reminded his readers, however, that scientists routinely investigate invisible realities, charting the activity of molecules, atoms, and electrons that "no one ever saw."[53] West speculated that scientists might be able to describe operations of the spirit much in the same way that they discussed the transference of light, sound, and electricity. "In all three [cases]," West explained, "we have a disturbance, a connecting medium, and a receiving apparatus. . . . Transference of intelligence from God to man need be no more mysterious than light propagation."[54] West noted that at a recent World's Fair, scientists had used "singing mice" to demonstrate the different auditory capacities of human beings. Some audience members could hear the high-frequency sound waves emitted by the mice, while others heard nothing. West wondered if the capacity to perceive the communications of the divine might vary similarly from person to person. That would explain, he said, why "in religious gatherings and temples, some have seen heavenly visitors, and others present have seen nothing extraordinary."[55] West's argument was cleverly crafted to assure scientifically minded Mormons that they could trust their religious experience, even if non-Mormon scientists might never corroborate it.

The Mormon student's struggle with doubt and skepticism was the central theme of another typical *Improvement Era* article from the first decade of the twentieth century, Milton Bennion's "The Modern Skeptic." Bennion, a professor of philosophy at the University of Utah, had studied briefly at the University of Chicago before earning his master's degree from Columbia in 1901. Bennion's article displayed a deference to modern psychology that, he trusted, would only strengthen his argument that educated Mormon youth need not succumb to skepticism. Bennion argued that a period of profound doubt "commonly occurs in the life of the individual somewhere between the beginning of the teens and maturity. It is characterized by a tendency to renounce previously accepted opinions, to repel external authority, and to become a law unto themselves. . . . It comes very frequently as a reaction to a childish mythology, or illogical faith, or as a rebellion against an arbitrary and oppressive authority. In case of both individual and race development this condition is normally outgrown and is followed by a more rational faith and a deeper insight into the necessity of institutions and lawful authority."[56] Intellectual maturity, Bennion asserted, involved moving beyond skepticism to an awareness "that the most real thing in the universe is God."[57] Scientific claims about "natural laws" and the evolutionary process did not alter

Bennion's belief that behind natural processes stood a purposive, ordering God.

Questions remained, however, about the nature of religious knowledge and experience. Modern psychology, Bennion said, leads students to believe that a revelation or vision, if "not observed by everyone," is an hallucination.[58] It was a familiar question, the central point of discussion between William James and Benjamin Cluff a decade earlier.[59] Bennion found a solution in reducing knowledge to the subjective. He wrote, "Indeed, psychology has shown that all knowing, as such, is private. . . . Science and scientific methods have great value and are perfectly legitimate in their place, but they do not cover all human experience. The most vital questions pertaining to man, his spiritual powers and obligations, lie outside the domain of positive science. Religious knowledge and experience are as private and individual as the knowledge and experience of love, pain, or desire. How, then, can this knowledge be attained? Only by individual experience. . . . The feelings and the will are more fundamental in life than is knowledge."[60] Bennion's "The Modern Skeptic" was a bold flirtation with subjectivist epistemology. It skirted Joseph Smith's desperate efforts to prove, through corroborating external testimony, that his experiences had been more than a private affair.

Bennion's conclusions contrasted sharply with those of Frank West, the physicist who was unwilling to reduce religious experience to the subjective as he groped for a Mormon epistemology. The fact that "The Modern Skeptic" and "How Knowledge Comes" appeared in the same *issue* of an official LDS periodical revealed the eclectic, experimental quality of Mormon theology and philosophy at the beginning of the twentieth century. For a time, at least, what mattered most was that Mormons were becoming real scholars, even if their conclusions were contradictory. It would not be long before this intellectual heterogeneity would draw the attention of influential and fierce Mormon critics.[61]

Struggling for the Soul of Modern Mormonism

Twentieth-century Mormon intellectual life saw its first real crisis in the so-called modernist controversy at Brigham Young University in early 1911. Mormon opponents and defenders of a "modernist" theology were not terribly precise in defining modernism, but it was clear to all sides that it connoted a certain comfort with scientific theories of evolution and

German biblical criticism. The lack of conceptual clarity added fuel to an already heated debate.

Imprecision characterized the Mormon debate over "modernism" partly because the term was not original to Mormonism but borrowed from the transatlantic world of Protestant and Roman Catholic theology. For liberal Protestants, modernism was a byword and a state of mind. It signified an intentional, ongoing adjustment of religious ideas to their changing contexts, a profound sense of the immanence of God in human affairs, and a passionate desire to make this world approximate the kingdom of God.[62] Clashes between "modernists" and "fundamentalists" would not engulf Protestantism until the 1920s, but by the late nineteenth century, modernism had already established itself as an influential and controversial theological mode.

In the world of Roman Catholicism, modernism carried its own meaning. It was an almost exclusively European phenomenon, but Pope Pius X's condemnation of it in 1907 rattled American Catholics. Pius X associated modernism with a range of theological errors and political threats; he condemned no fewer than sixty-five allegedly modernist theses. Some of his main concerns included: subjectivism, which denied the objective reality of revelation and the lawful authority of the pope; political liberalism, which sought to transfer political power to the people and sever ties between church and state; scientific theories of evolution, which seemed to remove God from the natural order; and post-Enlightenment views of scripture and Christ, which treated the Bible as a time-bound cultural production and Jesus as little more than a great moral teacher. Although such "modernist" propositions had gained little traction among Catholics in the United States, the papal condemnation had a pervasive chilling effect on American Catholic intellectual life until the 1940s.[63]

The Mormon debate over modernism resembled the Protestant and Catholic debates in its focus on scriptural and ecclesiastical authority. Yet concerns distinctive and central to Mormonism—the credibility of Joseph Smith, the historicity of the Book of Mormon, and the importance of instilling a missionary's faith in the young—added a fierceness to the storm of controversy that would last for decades.

The trouble at BYU in 1911 had its origin in changes that had affected the church educational system and BYU years earlier. In 1906, Horace Hall Cummings took Joseph Marion Tanner's place as church school superintendent, and by all accounts, Cummings was no intellectual heavyweight. As a young man in the early 1880s, Cummings had harbored aspirations for going east to study, but President John Taylor denied Cummings his consent. Disappointed, Cummings over time came to see his lack of eastern training as a badge of honor.[64] His opponents saw him a small-minded but dogged foe.

Cummings did not dogmatically oppose study in non-Mormon schools. Through the General Board's education fund, he strongly supported church school teachers who wanted to pursue teacher training at leading schools like Columbia University's Teachers College.[65] Sending Mormon teachers to Columbia, Cummings thought, made more financial sense than using scarce church resources to conduct teacher training at three different Mormon schools: the Brigham Young College in Logan, the Latter-day Saints' College in Salt Lake City, and BYU.[66]

By the time the church decided to consolidate its teacher training work and make BYU its flagship normal school in 1909, Columbia had become well-established as a destination for Mormon teachers-in-training (see Appendix D). Many of the teachers in the new education department at BYU—Ida Smoot Dusenberry, Aretta Young, and Ella Larson Brown—had trained at Columbia. Imitating Columbia, BYU officials customarily referred to their new program as their "teachers college," and to make sure that the college work got off the ground, BYU president George Brimhall even hired a non-Mormon graduate of Columbia's Teachers College, Alma Binzel, whom Ella Larson Brown had met in New York. Binzel would only last a few years at BYU, because Brimhall and Superintendent Cummings did not want to make hiring "outsiders" a habit, but the hiring demonstrated a continuing openness, even in Cummings, to certain kinds of "eastern" training and methods.

Despite disappointment in parts of the state, many Mormon educators entertained high hopes for BYU's normal and other college work.[67] In 1907, BYU president Brimhall wrote to Ellis R. Shipp (a daughter of Ellis Reynolds Shipp) at Columbia, "We expect to make our training school one of the greatest in the West."[68] The desire to have a church normal school of the first rank, while continuing to conduct wider college-level work, prompted BYU's president, George Brimhall, to recruit Mormon faculty of high scholarly attainments. His efforts bore immediate fruit. The academic credentials of the faculty soared between 1908 and 1910, when Brimhall secured the services of Ralph Chamberlin, a PhD biologist from Cornell; Joseph Peterson, a PhD psychologist from the University of Chicago; Henry Peterson, who held a master's degree in psychology from Harvard; and William H. Chamberlin, who had a master's degree in philosophy from the University of California at Berkeley and had logged an additional year of graduate work in philosophy at Harvard. The new faculty represented the new generation of Mormon scholarship; all had earned their advanced degrees in the twentieth century.

The Petersons and Chamberlins proved idealistic and provocative. In the democratic spirit of John Dewey, they held their students in high esteem, treating them as adults capable of wrestling with the great intellectual questions of the age. They desperately wanted BYU to shed its image as a backward "farm school" with little interest in "genuine scholarship."[69] To help the Provo school conform to their vision of educational advancement, Ralph Chamberlin introduced students to scientific theories of evolution; Henry Peterson and William H. Chamberlin encouraged their theology students to move beyond a narrowly literal interpretation of the Bible; and Joseph Peterson approached religion from the methodological point of view of the social sciences. New courses like "Ecclesiastical Sociology" and "The Psychology of Religion" marked the shift in curriculum and emphasis.[70]

The new approach quickly produced devotees and critics. For Latter-day Saints who wanted the church to be respectable intellectually—a hope cherished for decades by the promoters of Mormon study "abroad"—the arrival of the Petersons and Chamberlins at BYU promised to hasten the coming of that long-awaited day. For other Saints, the new teachers' influence signaled decadence, not progress. For them, the Petersons' and Chamberlins' immersion in the natural and social sciences betrayed too much dependence on "outside" teachings that could undermine faith in the authority of the church, its teachings, and its leaders.

Strong concerns about the use of non-Mormon texts in the church schools quickly surfaced. In 1908, the General Board of Education forbade "the use of any text book on the New or Old Testament written by a non-member of our church."[71] When the modernist controversy came to a head in early 1911, Superintendent Cummings, after conducting an investigation at BYU, noted with disdain that "several of the teachers . . . use Dr. Lyman Abbot's [sic] writings as authority."[72] The charge was damning, pitting the authorities of the church against the authorities of "the world."

The author in question, Lyman Abbott, was a towering figure in American religious life, a New England minister-turned-journalist whom American religious historian William Hutchison has called the "champion popularizer" of higher biblical criticism.[73] In *The Evolution of Christian-*

ity (1892), Abbott had attempted "to maintain faith by expressing it in terms which are more intelligible and credible" than ancient formulations.[74] He claimed that "all scientific men to-day are evolutionists," and he wanted to construct a theology that avoided literalism on the one hand and skepticism on the other.

The Evolution of Christianity appealed to Mormons like Henry Peterson because it offered a path through the thickets of modern thought. More than that, Abbott's work lent itself well to Mormon appropriation. Abbott's treatment of evolution as "continuous progression" echoed Mormon ideas of eternal progression, and he looked forward to the culmination of the evolutionary process in the realization of the kingdom of God.[75] Abbott wanted "not to destroy, but to reconstruct" Christian theology, not only to make it more intellectually consistent, but also to promote the spread of human righteousness.[76] To some Mormons, these broad intellectual and social aims seemed unobjectionable.

Soon, however, it was clear that the embrace of evolution at BYU would be anything but unobjectionable. After the General Board issued its 1908 ban on books authored by non-Mormons, the First Presidency issued a statement in 1909 entitled "The Origin of Man," which would be enormously influential in shaping the intellectual and theological landscape of modern Mormonism. It declared: "It is held by some that Adam was not the first man upon this earth, and that the original human being was a development from lower orders of the animal creation. These, however, are the theories of men. The word of the Lord declares that Adam was 'the first man of all men' (Moses 1:34), and we are therefore in duty bound to regard him as the primal parent of our race."[77] In 1910, two Mormon apostles, Francis M. Lyman and Charles W. Penrose, followed with stern addresses against evolution at a quarterly conference of the Utah Stake (the regional church entity to which BYU belonged). According to newspaper accounts, the majority of BYU students heard the apostles' addresses, which characterized evolution as "antagonistic to the teachings of the church."[78]

The addresses of Apostles Lyman and Penrose prompted the General Church Board of Education to send Superintendent Cummings to BYU in late November 1910 to conduct a nine-day investigation "concerning the nature and effect of certain theological instructions given, mostly by the College Professors [*sic*] in that school."[79] Cummings reported that he talked with as many teachers, students, and "leading citizens of

Provo" as he could about conditions at BYU, although he never claimed to have met with the Petersons and Chamberlins themselves. Henry Peterson scoffed at Cummings's claim that he had "conscientiously" investigated the situation. He alleged that Cummings "did not visit the classes of the three of us who were accused, and, so far as I could learn, he didn't talk with my students; and probably not with the students of the other accused professors. He didn't want the truth as they would tell it. He wanted gossip and the rumors that were afloat. He conversed with teachers but said not a word to any of the three accused. We hardly saw him during the nine days. I doubt that patrons [of BYU] complained. In the two years that I taught there I never heard a complaint from a parent about my teaching."[80]

The Cummings report to the General Board of Education was detailed and forceful. Like a syllabus of errors, it presented ten major causes for offense, including: treating the Bible "as a collection of myths, folklore, dramas, literary productions, and some inspiration"; considering "the theory of evolution . . . a demonstrated law"; asserting that "all truths change as we change" and "nothing is fixed or reliable"; and challenging "the objective reality of the presence of the Father and the Son, in Joseph Smith's first vision." The superintendent placed blame squarely on "the skillfully formed theories of learned men"—higher criticism, evolution, Deweyan pragmatism, and modern psychology—which had been imported from "eastern colleges" by Mormon scholars like the Petersons and Chamberlins. Cummings wrote, "The responsibility for this state of affairs seems to rest upon no more than four or five of the teachers, all of whom I regard as clean, earnest men, conscientious in what they do and teach; but, being so long in college with so little to help them resist the skillfully formed theories of learned men, they have accepted many which are erroneous; and being zealous teachers, are vigorously laboring to convince others of their views. Such attitudes of mind, from the beginning, have been a common experience with our students in eastern colleges; but fortunately they often get rid of these errors when they again plunge into church work at home."[81] Cummings thought that the professors' intemperate passion for "the theories of men" threatened "the soundness of doctrine, the sweetness of spirit, and the general faithfulness" he was accustomed to seeing in graduates of BYU. He acknowledged that "practically all the College students whom I met . . . were most zealous in defending and propagating the new views." Yet he could not ignore the students who had told him that learning to divest the Bible of its supernatural and miraculous qualities resembled the childhood experience of being "told there is no Santa Claus."[82]

The General Board of Education responded to Cummings's report by appointing a committee of eight men to conduct further investigation of conditions at BYU. The committee called Joseph Peterson, Henry Peterson, and Ralph Chamberlin to Salt Lake City on February 11, 1911, to assess the accuracy of Cummings's allegations. (William H. Chamberlin, hired the previous fall, was not summoned, perhaps because the investigation had begun so early in his tenure at BYU.) The accused felt that the deck was stacked against them. Among their eight interlocutors were the anti-evolution apostles Lyman and Penrose, as well as Superintendent Cummings himself.[83] It came as little surprise, then, that at the end of a day of questioning, the committee judged Cummings's charges to be "substantially correct." Rendering their decision to President Joseph F. Smith and the rest of the BYU Board of Trustees, they recommended "that the services of those three teachers . . . be dispensed with unless they change their teachings to conform to the decisions and instructions of the Board of Trustees of the Brigham Young University and the General Church Board of Education."[84] On February 20, the BYU Board of Trustees adopted the committee's recommendation unanimously.[85]

Utah's leading newspapers gave sustained, full-throated publicity to the case. Predictably, the pro-Mormon *Deseret News* sided with Cummings and the inquiring committee, while the anti-Mormon *Salt Lake Tribune* took up the cause of the professors. Anonymous editorials in *The Deseret News*—with titles like "The Book of Jonah," "Thoughts on Evolution," "Higher Criticism," "True Philosophy," and "Another Monkey Theory"— began attacking higher criticism and evolution as early as February 8.

The arguments in the editorials of *The Deseret News* tended to resemble those put forth by early Protestant "fundamentalists," whose seminal work, *The Fundamentals*, came out in twelve volumes between 1910 and 1915.[86] Authored by British and American biblical scholars grounded in inductive, Scottish Common Sense philosophy, the volumes on the Bible rejected German biblical criticism as hopelessly speculative and "unscientific." These early fundamentalists also sought to uphold the authority of the Bible by preserving belief in the miraculous and supernatural qualities of God's activity.[87]

The *Deseret News* editorials took these positions as their own, even though the Protestant fundamentalists were no friends of the Mormons. (One of the twelve volumes of *The Fundamentals* was devoted exclusively to attacking Mormonism.) The first *Deseret News* piece, "The Book of Jonah," made the connection to early Protestant fundamentalism clear. Allegorical and demythologizing interpretations of the Book of Jonah, the author argued, did not "appeal to anyone but those who are anxious to get rid of miracles and the direct intervention of God in human affairs." A more satisfying reckoning with the biblical account, the author said, came from Reuben A. Torrey, superintendent of Chicago's Moody Bible Institute, a bastion of the new Protestant conservatism. Torrey thought that Jonah may have died inside the fish and then experienced resurrection, "which makes Jonah a still more remarkable type of Christ."[88] The early Protestant fundamentalists and Mormon editorialists were strange bedfellows. Their alliance shows how the opponents of the BYU professors, facing important new questions about biblical authority, were forced to adopt Gentile biblical hermeneutics while castigating the professors for doing the same.

Mormon editorialists did not rely wholly on outsiders' arguments to make their case. Analysis of the Book of Mormon in light of the claims of higher criticism raised questions that never would have occurred to Protestants. The author of the editorial "True Philosophy," for instance, pointed to the chronology in the Book of Mormon in order to dispute the conclusions of higher critics. One target was Julius Wellhausen's influential theory that the Pentateuch was not a unitary work authored by Moses, but a compilation of four distinct sources gathered and edited over several centuries, from the time of David and Solomon all the way to the fifth century BCE.[89] The Mormon critic of Wellhausen, citing Book of Mormon descriptions of the "Law of Moses" in 1 Nephi, said that the four-source theory simply cannot be true. "The Book of Mormon," he argued, "confirms the Ancient Scriptures against the modern school of destructive criticism, for it shows us that the Law of Moses was engraved on plates and in circulation among the people at the time Lehi left Jerusalem, 600 BC, and also the sacred writings of the early prophets. But, according to some 'higher critics' the Law was not given in its present form until some time between 525 and 425 BC. The Book of Mormon refutes this theory and therefore becomes 'a new witness for God' in our age, when such witness is so much needed."[90] An argument based on evidence from the Book of Mormon, of course, never would have convinced Wellhausen, but that was not the point. The point was that Mormons, in evaluating the claims of higher criticism, relied not only on the traditional Christian canon, but also on the inflexible truths of their own unique revelations.

A similar assault on higher criticism from a Mormon point of view came from B. H. Roberts, in an April 1911 Logan tabernacle lecture called "Higher Criticism and the Book of Mormon." Before an audience of two thousand, Roberts took up the issue of the authorship of the Book of Isaiah. Higher critics had identified a clear break between chapters 39 and 40, where the historical context of the book suddenly shifted from the upheavals of the eighth century BCE to the conditions of exile and return during the sixth century BCE. Roberts said that the shift did not necessarily mean that Isaiah had multiple authors. He defended the transcendent character of prophecy:

> The prime reason why we are asked to believe that this second
> part of the Book of Isaiah could not have been written by the one
> who wrote the first part is that if we suppose the first Isaiah to
> have written the latter part of the book, then we must believe
> in the possibility of a man being wrenched from the environment
> in which he stands, so to speak, and be projected forward in time,
> and become so immersed in a different environment as to speak
> by the spirit of prophecy in a new style and spirit, and from the
> midst of future events, as if they were present. Higher critics,
> as a rule, insist that the miraculous does not happen, that
> wherever the miraculous appears, there you must halt, and
> dismiss the miraculous parts of narratives, since they suggest
> fraud on the one hand and credulity on the other.[91]

Roberts challenged the higher critics' bedrock assumption—an assumption shared by Mormons like Osborne Widtsoe in his 1905 article, "The Mormon Boy at College"—that the authors of biblical texts could not have risen above the limitations of their historical and cultural environments. Refusing to concede that point, Roberts felt impervious to the destructive assertions of arrogant brethren who had gone east. He wrote, "In conversation with one of our young men who recently returned from an eastern college, where he had come in contact with higher criticism, he remarked to me, 'Yes, higher criticism shoots to pieces the Book of Mormon.' 'Pardon me, my brother,' I answered, 'you have misstated the matter; you mean that the Book of Mormon shoots holes into higher criticism!'"[92] Just a decade later, Roberts would embark upon a rigorous investigation of the authenticity of the Book of Mormon, which left him far less self-assured.[93] Yet in 1911, Roberts thought the Book of Mormon was unassailable, and he assured his audience that they had nothing to fear from arrogant Mormons returning from esteemed "eastern colleges."

The *Salt Lake Tribune* responded to such apologetics with characteristic disdain. Soon after the BYU Board of Trustees had rendered its decision against the professors, the *Tribune* scoffed, "A school that is presided over by a polygamist [George Brimhall], and in which the divinity of polygamy is allowed to be taught, can hardly commend itself to intelligent opinion by opposition to evolution and the higher criticism."[94] When the editorial "On Evolution" appeared in *The Deseret News* in March, the *Tribune* called it "appalling in its stupidity and ignorance"[95] for arguing that:

> if it is true that man has evolved from lower forms of life by a gradual process, history would give us some incontestible [*sic*] proofs of this process. But it does not. We do not find a lower man in the 17th, or 16th, or first century, than now. In the 17th century we have a Galileo and a Newton. The sixteenth gave us Luther and Shakespeare. The first century gave us Paul, whose influence is felt throughout the world today. Four centuries before Christ we find a Socrates and a Plato. A thousand years before Christ, David composed his matchless poems and Solomon penned his inimitable proverbs. The Laws of Moses are unsurpassed. The Chinese had their Confucius 2,400 years ago. And back in the dim antiquity we meet a Lycurgus among the Greeks, and a Homer. Still further back there was an Egyptian civilization which is still the admiration of the world. No matter how far back we go, history gives no encouragement to the theory that man evolved slowly from a lower kingdom. These facts the evolutionists ignore, but by doing so they renounce all claims to the honor of true philosophers. There should be a theory equally consistent with the facts of history and biology.[96]

The accused professors—Henry Peterson, Joseph Peterson, and Ralph Chamberlin—did get a chance to have their say in the newspapers. Just days after what he called an "inquisition" in Salt Lake City, Henry Peterson wanted to make his position on evolution clear. He said, "Evolution, as I view it, does not mean that man sprang from the monkey. Neither does it mean that the universe came by chance. Those are the views of people ignorant of evolution. Man is the son of God, and the universe His great creation. Evolution is the process by which God creates. It means in the language of some people, 'eternal progress.' Viewed as the creative process of God, evolution is faith promoting, not faith destroying."[97] In defense of his colleagues, W. H. Chamberlin put forth a similar view of evolution that emphasized its compatibility with Mormonism. Responding to the *Deseret News* editorial "Another Monkey Theory," he tried to convince readers that scientific investigation did not entail a "godless" view of the universe. Chamberlin wrote that "even when the way in which organic forms have come into existence has been fully worked out by scientists, what it is that is developing or evolving or what cause is back of the process will remain untouched by true science."[98] What constituted "true science," of course, stood at the heart of the debate.

The professors' attempts to make evolution palatable failed to convince Superintendent Cummings, BYU president Brimhall, and the rest of the BYU Board of Trustees that the school would not be better off without them. Early in March, Joseph Peterson resigned. On March 16, the presidency of BYU (Brimhall and his counselors, J. B. Keeler and Edwin Hinckley) informed Henry Peterson that "under existing conditions, we can not see our way clear to recommend you to the Board of Trustees as a member of the faculty of the Brigham Young University for the academic year 1911–1912."[99] Ralph Chamberlin, for his part, was sufficiently repentant to avoid being fired. The BYU Presidency granted him a one-year leave of absence to study at the University of Pennsylvania, but he would never teach at BYU again, an outcome doubtless agreeable to both sides.

Once it became clear that the professors would not return to BYU in the fall, their allies offered impassioned but futile support. Ninety-five of the one hundred fourteen students doing college work at BYU sent a lengthy petition to the *Deseret News* and the *Salt Lake Tribune*, declaring that firing the professors and ruling out discussion of evolution would be "a death-blow to our college work."[100] The students worried that the firings would hamper the school's ability to recruit professors of high scholarship and hurt the students' chances for success in institutions of higher learning abroad. Evolutionary theory was unavoidable in those schools, they said, and the best preparation for them would be to learn the theory from committed, faithful Mormon scholars. "Every man or woman who goes east or west to colleges of high rank must face the questions," they wrote. The petition concluded with a plea for the church to embrace a vital, progressive intellectual life, rich in theological reflection and outreach to a suffering world. "We have great faith in the church," the students affirmed, "and can hardly imagine that any policy contrary to its best needs will be adopted, but we ask you to consider what the proposed restriction would mean for us educationally, and what it would mean to our critics, and what it would mean to our standing in the educational world. Some of our fondest hopes have been for the future of the 'dear old B.Y.U.'—that it would continue to adapt itself to the growing needs of humanity and demonstrate to the world, as only that can demonstrate, that Mormonism is a real, vitalized, divine institution."[101] The *Salt Lake Tribune* immediately published the petition, relishing the students' rebellion. When the *Deseret News* failed to publish the petition, the *Tribune* took the alleged suppression as additional confirmation that the *News* was a staunch enemy of fairness and truth.

Defining Academic Freedom: "The School Follows the Church"

The *Tribune*, not unlike the professors themselves, liked to cast the debate in terms of "academic freedom," the byword of educators across the country interested in protecting themselves from powerful, antagonistic trustees and legislators. In the heat of the controversy, Henry Peterson had written, "Where [academic freedom] is hampered or circumscribed by authoritative limitations, higher study cannot be carried on. Fear of honest truth-seeking investigation is inconsistent with college work. It is certainly inconsistent with the views of those who hold that the gospel embraces all truth."[102] Milton Bennion, the University of Utah professor who had written "The Modern Skeptic" for the *Improvement Era* three years earlier, issued a vigorous defense of the professors in the March 1911 edition of the *Utah Educational Review*, the professional magazine of the Utah Education Association. Calling the controversy "the most significant happening in recent Utah educational history," Bennion wondered, "Is it not probable that any serious attempt on the part of church officials to dictate the methods and results of science in the church schools would mean the death of higher education in these schools?"[103] It was a bold gesture for which the Petersons and Ralph Chamberlin would long be grateful. Coming from a Mormon at the University of Utah, the criticism in Bennion's editorial carried a particular sting for BYU.

For BYU president George Brimhall, the protest from various quarters became especially infuriating. For months, he had held out the hope that some gradual resolution would emerge. In December 1910, Brimhall had said of the professors, "I believe I understand them. While I believe they are from their point of view perfectly right, still I think they are a little over zealous in their desires to bring people to their point of view. As they look at it their teachings are in perfect harmony with the principles of the Gospel, but there are certainly many who cannot perceive that harmony, and, therefore it seems to me that a little waiting with their working will be in keeping with greater wisdom on their part."[104] By the middle of March 1911, however, Brimhall had had enough. In a March 16 devotional address at BYU, he chastised his professors and students for their presumption, reminding them that "You are the guests of the Church, and you are also the guests of the board. I hope none of you will assume to be host or hostess. I hope you will have sufficient confidence in those who have been providing this progressive educational feast; I hope you will have sufficient confidence in the institution known as the Church, and in those whom the Lord has called to direct in that Church, to feel that it is amply able to take care of its children."[105] It was a powerful reassertion of hierarchy in contentious times.

Brimhall's remarks exemplified the paradox of his administration. Enamored by the famously democratic John Dewey—as the Brigham Young Academy's acting president, Brimhall had brought him to Provo in 1901—he also had a penchant for autocracy. The circumstances of early 1911 forced him to embrace the latter as never before. That year, he reduced the complexities of Mormon education to a slogan: "the school follows the Church."[106] In April, the General Board of Education turned the slogan into official policy for all church schools when it issued the following decree:

On account of some teachers indulging in the teaching of erroneous doctrine to the pupils of the church schools the General Board of Education passed the following resolution at a recent meeting, and principals in engaging their teachers for next year will please read it to them:

"Moved that it be the sense of this Board that any church school teacher who holds and persists in the expression of ideas contrary to the teachings of the Presidency and Apostles of the church be not re-engaged to teach in the church schools, and that at the time of the engagement of teachers for church school service, it be definitely understood that the teaching of doctrine opposed to the preaching of the Presidency and Apostles shall be sufficient cause for dismissal without recourse." The resolution was adopted unanimously.[107]

Despite and even because of the new restrictions, President Brimhall remained optimistic about the future of BYU. He thought that keeping the school closely in line with the teachings of church authorities would help shore up church appropriations for the school, which had endured financial difficulties from the start. By the spring of 1912, when enrollment and faculty recruitment seemed still to be healthy, Brimhall proudly told a student's parent that "the spirit of the school is such today that a visit from an apostle or any of the general authorities will elicit as much applause as that of an eastern educator—and as a rule more because we have never been deceived by our brethren—they always 'deliver the goods', but we have been badly fooled by the men from abroad sometimes."[108] Brimhall's feeling of being "badly fooled" evoked the disillusionment of spoiled romance, a romance that had emboldened him to court Dewey, the Petersons, and the Chamberlins. The spring of 1911 left him with the feeling that all along he had only been courting disaster.

Response to the controversy from the prophet himself, Joseph F. Smith (a nephew of Mormonism's founder), followed the stern, definitive statements of Brimhall and the General Board. In April editorials for *The Juvenile Instructor* and *The Improvement Era* called "Philosophy and the Church Schools" and "Theory and Divine Revelation," President Smith argued that teaching evolution and higher criticism was not only theologically suspect, but also pedagogically misguided. It would only confuse the majority of Mormon youth, he said. "The ordinary student," Smith pronounced, "cannot delve into these subjects deep enough to make them of any practical use to him, and a smattering of knowledge in this line only tends to upset his simple faith in the gospel, which is of more value to him in life than all the learning of the world without it."[109] Smith went on to say that "philosophical discussions," over which the learned disagree, are at odds with the mission of church schools. "In the first place," he said, "it is the mission of our institutions of learning to qualify our young people for the practical duties of life. It is much to be preferred that they emphasize the industrial and practical side of education. Students are very apt to draw the conclusion that whichever side of a controversial question they adopt is the truth, the whole truth, and nothing but the truth; and it is very doubtful, therefore, whether the great mass of our students have sufficient discriminating judgment to understand very much about some of the advanced theories of philosophy or science."[110] What one might call Smith's pedagogical anthropology—his estimation of the intellectual capacity of Mormon students—was at odds with that of a professor like Henry Peterson. Peterson thought that Mormon students needed to wrestle with evolution and higher criticism under the compassionate care of Mormon professors in order to avoid intellectual crisis and ridicule when confronted with those issues outside the church. Reacting directly to the *Juvenile Instructor* editorial, Peterson told President Smith, "Evolution is no longer a mere theory. I have laboured under the impression that our young people, *who cannot avoid hearing it and reading of it*, had better hear and read it in our church schools . . . that are pervaded by the spirit of God and where they are taught the doctrines of the church right along with it."[111] In the 1920s, after the Brimhall administration had ended, Peterson's point of view would be welcome at BYU, but by then he would be long gone, finishing his career at the publicly funded Agricultural College of Utah.

The difference between Henry Peterson and President Smith over the capacity of Mormon students was part of a broader conversation about education and social mobility in a rapidly industrializing America.[112] In the Mormon context, President Smith worried that "philosophical discussions" would not only distract and confuse Mormon youth, but also promote a catastrophic stratification in Mormonism between the learned and those who lacked formal education. Such division Smith could not countenance. Warnings from the Book of Mormon about the misuse of learning by the powerful, and the destructive results of division within the church, were too strong. Smith sought to restore the "simplicity" of church authority and prevent the rise of a rival hierarchy of the learned. He wrote, "God has revealed to us a simple and effectual way of serving Him, and we should regret very much to see the simplicity of those revelations involved in all sorts of philosophical speculations. If we encouraged them it would not be long before we should have a theological scholastic aristocracy in the Church, and we should therefore not enjoy the brotherhood that now is, or should be common to rich and poor, learned and unlearned among the Saints."[113] Smith's pronouncements reasserted the old Mormon populism, which distrusted the "authorities" of the world in religion, law, medicine, and education. Blending this traditional suspicion with a modern appreciation for conservative biblical interpretation and narrowly "practical" education, Smith launched a wide-ranging attack on a rising generation of Mormon scholars who wanted to see the church shed the intellectual limitations of the past.

Other repercussions from the BYU controversy soon followed. In September 1911, the General Board of Education issued a "Circular of Instructions" to the church schools, the first such declaration since April 1892. The circular announced the narrowing of all LDS college work to training high school teachers. It also stated that "all teachers are expected to be loyal to the school, the church, and the authorities thereof, and especially to refrain from unwise criticism."[114]

Then, in December, after the death of Apostle John Henry Smith, President Smith called on James Talmage to fill the vacancy in the ranks of the apostles. Talmage, whose nonresident work had earned him a doctoral degree from Wesleyan University in 1896, was the first PhD to hold such a high rank in the church. Author of the influential doctrinal work *The Articles of Faith*, first published in 1899, he also enjoyed renown in academic circles as a fellow of the Royal Society of Edinburgh, the Royal Microscopical Society, and the Royal Geological Society.[115] Since his days as a student at Lehigh and Johns Hopkins in the early 1880s, he had wrestled with questions of science and religion, and he had become, like John Widtsoe, one of the ablest expositors of church doctrine in an age of science. Talmage had advised the First Presidency as it prepared its statement on "The Origin of Man" in 1909, and his ascent to the apostleship lent a new intellectual credibility to the leadership of the church.[116]

Talmage could have been a natural ally to Mormons like the Petersons and Chamberlins. As early as 1884, Talmage had condemned "ignorant" Protestant preachers who inflamed prejudice against science by reducing evolution to the belief that "we come from monkeys."[117] Yet in 1911, nearly thirty years after Talmage dismissed that view as hopelessly simple-minded, Mormon newspaper editorials like "Another Monkey Theory" appeared with the implicit sanction of church leaders.[118] To some of his academic peers, it seemed that Talmage had compromised his intellectual integrity by assuming his new role in a conservative ecclesiastical hierarchy, but he had little choice but to defend the church and its pronouncements. Privately, he would indulge in subtler and more controversial opinions until his death in 1933, but publicly he became an extraordinarily influential apologist for the church.

Back in Provo, George Brimhall rejoiced that "those who prophesied the downfall of the school were among the prophets of Baal."[119] Naturally, in order to justify the stand he had taken against the Petersons and Chamberlins in 1911, Brimhall overstated the school's continuing appeal to the best Mormon teachers and scholars. Brimhall pointed to his recruitment of Harvey Fletcher, a PhD physicist from the University of Chicago, as proof of the school's ability to keep drawing teachers of high scholarship and firm commitment to the church. In fact, Dr. Fletcher had wanted desperately to stay in Chicago, where his adviser, the renowned physicist Robert Millikan, had offered him a permanent, lucrative faculty position at the University of Chicago. Fletcher tried to convince Brimhall that a Mormon in such a prominent position could actually do much good for BYU. He thought that he could bolster the reputation of BYU in the eyes of scholars, for example, and help BYU students get their academic credits honored at the University of Chicago. Brimhall was unconvinced and unashamedly manipulative in his response. Brimhall told Fletcher that rejecting the "allurement of wealth" and coming to Provo would be the Christ-like thing to do. Fletcher came, but after five years he was gone again, destined for a long career in New York City as a researcher for Bell Laboratories and professor at Columbia.[120]

Only after the end of the Brimhall administration, and the end of Horace Cummings's tenure as superintendent of church schools, would scholars with PhDs come to BYU again in significant numbers. Although Brimhall and Cummings blamed "eastern" ideas in part for the trouble at BYU, they continued to promote the Education Fund, even as many teachers continued to resist contributing to it.[121] Brimhall especially supported funding students, like his own son Dean, who wanted to pursue graduate work in educational administration, a field of clear practical value for the church schools.[122] Brimhall wrote to Cummings late in 1912, "Why do none of our young men who go East for preparation not take up education, the very thing we most need. We are not the geologists nor the biologists nor the sociologists of the world—more than anything else we are the teachers of the world."[123]

While BYU narrowed its focus, Mormon scholars with bright futures looked elsewhere for employment. Kimball Young, a descendant of Brigham Young who would have a long, prolific career as a sociologist outside of Utah, refused an offer from Brimhall to teach at BYU after earning his PhD at Stanford. Likewise, A. T. Rasmussen, after receiving his PhD in biology from Cornell in 1916, refused an offer from Brimhall to head up the BYU biology department, preferring to stay in his position as head of the anatomy department at the University of Minnesota.

Others, like Arthur Beeley, a PhD in social psychology from the University of Chicago, preferred positions at the University of Utah. It was hard for BYU to shake its reputation for hostility to genuine scholarship.

One of the most penetrating young thinkers to slip through the hands of the church school system was E. E. Ericksen. A product of the Brigham Young College in Logan, Ericksen was just one of dozens of Mormons who had gone to the University of Chicago in the early twentieth century. Much closer than Columbia, the Rockefeller-endowed University of Chicago drew Mormons eager to prepare for careers in law, medicine, and education. Its summer school also became a popular destination for Mormons. Ericksen recalled that by 1908,

> there was a large number of graduate students from Utah at Chicago, although I was the only one majoring in philosophy. Many were in law, others were in medicine or education, a few in the physical and biological sciences. We all attended the popular lectures and were stimulated by the broadminded and creative spirit of the university. Even the Sunday sermons in Mendall Hall stimulated thought and caused much discussion among Utah students. While some of the more critical students attended services at the university, the more orthodox went to [LDS] church [meetings] on Polina Street.
>
> On Sunday afternoons small groups met in the married students' apartments, where we had vigorous and sometimes heated discussions. The conservative wing, dominated by law students and those in the behavioral sciences, seemed not to have been greatly affected by evolutionary ideas. The liberals were in the biological sciences, psychology, history, philosophy, and literature. Many became teachers, spreading the liberalizing effect of these discussions throughout the entire church.[124]

Ericksen identified himself as one of the "liberals," partly because he had come under the profound influence of professors like James Hayden Tufts, a close colleague of John Dewey both at the University of Michigan and the University of Chicago. Tufts, a professor of philosophy, had co-authored *Ethics* with Dewey in 1908. Under the tutelage of Tufts, Ericksen made philosophy and ethics major areas of study. Tufts encouraged Ericksen to "develop a broad foundation in human relations," and that advice led Ericksen to delve into economics, sociology, and psychology as well. By the time he finished at Chicago, his studies had included courses like the "Evolution of Morality," "Socialism," "Research in Labor Problems," "Genetic Psychology," and "Psychology of Religion."[125] He held his professors in the highest esteem. "My teachers," he said, "were not only men of intellectual capacity but men of character who were as anxious as I, my parents, and the leaders of my church to find out what is true, worthy, and noble."[126] Ericksen relished his time at the university; years later, in his autobiography, he would refer to it ironically as his "sojourn in Babylon."

In the summer of 1911, depleted finances forced Ericksen and his family to return to Utah. Ericksen planned to continue working toward the PhD at Chicago by conducting research on the economic dimension of Mormonism. In the meantime, his best hope for employment was as a teacher in the church school system. Ericksen's advisers at Chicago had serious questions about the move. Chicago psychology professor James R. Angell (not to be confused with University of Michigan president James B. Angell), who had advised Joseph Peterson during his doctoral work, wanted to be sure that Ericksen had no plans to teach at BYU. Joseph Peterson, Angell told Ericksen, "is a well-trained psychologist and a splendid gentleman, and yet he was fired from that school. It is not the school that I thought it was, and if you are going to take his place, you are not the man I thought you were."[127]

Superintendent Cummings and President Brimhall, for their part, had their own doubts about Ericksen coming home to teach. Cummings wanted assurance that Ericksen had "full faith in the divinity of our religion,"[128] even though Chicago LDS mission president German Ellsworth had told Cummings that Ericksen was "a good spirited student and attends the mission services quite regularly."[129] Brimhall wanted to know for himself where Ericksen stood on matters of vital importance to BYU. Brimhall declared to Ericksen that every BYU teacher must embrace the motto, "Everything for and nothing against (a) the Church, (b) the school."[130] The motto did not have much of a ring to it, but the point was clear. Ericksen replied that he would "acquiesce without hesitation" to such a policy.[131]

After extended correspondence between Brimhall and Ericksen about a possible position at BYU, it turned out that Brimhall had no position to offer. He did not make his reasons clear.[132] Ericksen ended up taking the principal's position at the LDS Murdock Academy in Beaver, Utah, a remote settlement two hundred miles south of Salt Lake City. Ericksen would replace Josiah Hickman, the University of Michigan orator, who had since earned a master's degree in psychology from Columbia in 1907. Hickman's credentials ordinarily would have qualified him for a position of prominence in church education, but, like Benjamin Cluff and Joseph Marion Tanner, Hickman continued to practice and openly espouse polygamy (as it were). His actions embarrassed the church, and when conflict between Hickman and the stake board of education over finances added to the unpleasantness, Hickman tendered his resignation.[133]

After three years at the Murdock Academy, Ericksen wanted to resume his graduate studies. In 1914, he returned to Chicago for a summer of coursework. There, he became close with Joseph Peterson, now a professor at the University of Utah, who was teaching psychology in a summer session at the University of Chicago. When Peterson returned to Salt Lake City, he was in a position to recommend Ericksen to Milton Bennion, who had become dean of the School of Education at the University of Utah in 1913.

A position opened for Ericksen at the University of Utah in 1915, after a sudden wave of resignations there. The immediate cause for the upheaval was a conflict between faculty and administration over the dismissal of four professors. University president Joseph Kingsbury justified two of the dismissals with vague charges against the professors that they had "worked against the administration of the University" or had "spoken in a depreciatory way about the University."[134] Perhaps hardest to take for the aggrieved faculty, Mormon and non-Mormon alike, was the dismissal of George M. Marshall, who had been teaching at the university since 1892 and had organized its department of English. Faculty protest erupted when news reached them that Osborne Widtsoe would replace Marshall, a non-Mormon. Widtsoe, a Mormon whose professional career had been restricted to teaching and administration at the Latter-day Saints' University in Salt Lake City, seemed unfit to replace the venerated Marshall, even though both men held the same degree: a master's degree from Harvard. To protesting faculty, the hiring of Widtsoe smacked of "church influence," even though most of their ire was directed at the non-Mormon Kingsbury.

The dismissals sparked a cluster of resignations, including that of Joseph Peterson, who would leave for the University of Minnesota. An investigation by the American Association of University Professors ensued, since the controversy involved matters of tenure and academic freedom.[135] The investigating committee, chaired by E. R. A. Seligman of Columbia, found no evidence of undue church influence but did conclude that Kingsbury's grounds for dismissing the professors were insufficient. The turmoil led to Kingsbury's resignation in January 1916.

Charges of church influence resurfaced when Regent Waldemar Van Cott, a Mormon graduate of the University of Michigan law school, spearheaded a hasty but contested hiring of John Widtsoe as Kingsbury's successor. The action did little to appease faculty and students concerned about the school's reputation as being under church control. The previous year, the junior class yearbook had featured a picture of the administration building with a statue of Moroni—which stands at the top of the Salt Lake City temple—superimposed at the top of a university edifice. The caption read, "As Others See Us."[136] The student antics drew a sharp response from Richard W. Young, the Mormon West Point and Columbia Law graduate, whose graduate thesis had dealt with the suppression of unruly elements in society. Young forcefully denied that academic freedom had been curtailed at the university. Young asked the students "to believe that the regents are just as vitally interested in the university as you yourself, and possibly quite as much as certain peripatetic teachers who are seeking to stigmatize the reputation of the school and to discredit the true value of your institution and your diploma."[137] Young doubtless thought of Joseph Peterson as one of the "peripatetic teachers," who seemed unable to hold his tongue and keep a job in any of the schools of Utah.

Conclusion

With some hesitation, E. E. Ericksen accepted a job at the University of Utah in 1915, even after his friend Joseph Peterson had resigned. Ericksen liked Milton Bennion, who offered him the job, and moving to Salt Lake City appealed to Ericksen's wife, Edna. Once established there, Ericksen worked to complete his University of Chicago dissertation. Completed in 1918 and later published as *The Psychological and Ethical Aspects of Mormon Group Life*, Ericksen's dissertation represented an unprecedentedly thorough application of modern psychology and sociology to the history of Mormonism. Ericksen's groundbreaking work was highly provocative. In his introduction, he wrote that "[l]ike every other social system Mormonism has been forced to adjust itself to varying circumstances. This has been true notwithstanding the tendency within the church to regard the system as universal and eternal and entirely beyond human control. And notwithstanding the appropriation of many of the ideals and institutions of ancient Israel the group has absorbed sentiments and ideas from its social environment."[138] Using the tools of functional psychology, Ericksen identified three major "maladjustments" or conflicts that had shaped Mormon history: the early clashes between Mormons and Gentiles, the pioneers' struggle to overcome nature in the West, and the more recent encounter with modern science and democracy.

Ericksen thought that over the course of this brief, tumultuous history, four distinct generations of Mormons had formed. The first generation, amidst great "strife and stress," had enjoyed an outpouring of "strong emotions and spiritual manifestations"; the second was doggedly loyal to the first, largely "unreflective" and living in "a world of sentiment." Intellectual progress began to emerge in the third generation, "a generation of philosophers or theologians who take an intellectual attitude toward Mormonism but whose group sentiments are still strong enough to determine their thinking. They have a feeling that Mormonism must be right and they set themselves the task to prove it." The fourth generation, finally, moved beyond the intellectual parochialism of the third. This generation was "a generation of critics and scientists who seem to sense very little feeling of obligation toward the group but are placing the institutions of their fathers on the dissecting table for analysis. This class is making a demand for greater freedom of thought and discussion and it is this demand which is bringing about a third Mormon crisis. Nearly all of the Mormons of the first generation have passed away but the second and third generations are still strong and it is these two classes on the one hand and the critics on the other that are bringing about the present-day conflict."[139] Of course, Ericksen's analysis placed himself and kindred "critics and scientists" at the top of the pyramid of Mormon intellectual progress. Questions of progress aside, Ericksen had accurately mapped the landscape of Mormon intellectual and cultural conflict in the early twentieth century. Members of Ericksen's second, third, and fourth generations jockeyed simultaneously for power: Joseph F. Smith perhaps best represented the second generation in his fierce loyalty to the past; James Talmage and John Widtsoe represented the generation of theologian apologists; the Petersons, Chamberlins, and Ericksen himself represented the generation of critics.

After statehood, modern Mormonism's intramural battles cast a long shadow and exacted a heavy toll. As a new generation of scholars matured, the intellectual gains of previous generations dissipated. Mormon feminism receded, accomplished mentors Benjamin Cluff and Joseph

Marion Tanner faded into total obscurity, and Mormonism's intellectual center of gravity began to shift toward Provo, where academic freedoms narrowed quickly and considerably. The optimism, fluidity, and diversity of emerging Mormon thought, so evident in church periodicals in the first decade of the twentieth century, would provoke a sharp response, forcing it underground or abroad. The tensions would ease significantly when Superintendent Cummings and President Brimhall left their posts in 1920, but they would remain fundamentally unresolved.

4 Anti-intellectualism Rejected and Reborn, 1920–1940

· ·

Mormon intellectual life suffered acutely after the turmoil at BYU in 1911, but less than a decade later, major changes in church leadership and educational policy would help stimulate renewal. At the same time, Mormons studying abroad began gravitating to new disciplines like history, sociology, and the academic study of religion. A number of these students would become scholarly authorities on the Mormon community and the Mormon past (see Appendix E). The students' epistemology, which placed supreme value on documentary and statistical evidence, was bound eventually to clash with that of theologically conservative church authorities, who exalted the private tutorings of the spirit. Again, Mormons' internal disputes would echo broader American ones, especially the battle between Protestant modernism and fundamentalism, which culminated in the historic Scopes "Monkey" Trial of 1925.

For much of the 1920s and 1930s, however, Mormon scholars and church leaders got along surprisingly well. It helped that some Mormons with advanced degrees had joined the ranks of church leadership. University of Utah engineering professor Richard Lyman (Michigan BS 1895, Cornell PhD 1905) was ordained an apostle in 1918. He served as assistant commissioner of LDS Church Schools from 1919 to 1924. University of Utah president and chemist John Widtsoe (Harvard BS 1894, Goettingen PhD 1900) became an apostle in 1921 and served as the church's commissioner of education from 1921 to 1924 and 1933 to 1936. In fact, all the commissioners and superintendents of church education in the 1920s and 1930s—Adam S. Bennion, Joseph F. Merrill, John A. Widtsoe, and Franklin L. West—had earned the PhD. None shared former superintendent Horace Hall Cummings's raw suspicion of "the skillfully formed theories of learned men"; rather, they encouraged Mormon students and teachers to keep abreast of broader scholarly developments in the fields of pedagogy, psychology, sociology, biblical studies, and the history of Christianity. The ecclesiastical authority of Mormons educated outside Utah was unprecedented.[1]

Other administrative changes after World War I boded well for Mormon higher education. The church's new president, Heber J. Grant, lent critical financial support. A businessman, Grant had never been terribly interested in the life of the mind, but supporting higher education seemed to make good business sense. To Grant, many of the old stake academies seemed unnecessary, since they had curricula similar to those of taxpayer-funded public schools. He thought it best for the church to close many of its academies and focus on seminary and teacher-training work.[2] For the most part, Grant also let church educational administrators direct the affairs of the church school system and determine its policy.[3]

Redeeming the Mormon Scholar

The new openness to scholarship in a range of fields was most clearly evident at BYU. The academic climate there changed considerably when Franklin S. Harris became the school's president. Harris, a 1907 graduate of BYU, had a PhD in chemistry from Cornell. He was the first BYU president to hold the PhD; he was also the first to have never practiced polygamy. A former president of the American Society of Agronomy and a fellow of the Utah Academy of Sciences, he was widely known among Utah's Mormon and non-Mormon scientists.[4]

Harris was eager "to put the BYU on the map educationally"[5] by hiring more faculty with doctoral degrees and trying to raise faculty salaries to match "the very best in the land."[6] Harris was an optimist—in 1920, BYU had just one faculty member with a PhD, while in 1921 the University of Utah had twenty-three—but by 1928, after years of work expanding the library, reorganizing the curriculum, recruiting faculty, and promoting sabbatical leaves for existing faculty to earn higher degrees, Harris would bring BYU to the promised land of accreditation by the Association of American Universities.[7]

Early in Harris's administration, President Grant—ex officio president of the BYU Board of Trustees—made it clear that he would not stand in Harris's way. Supremely proud of BYU, Grant hated to think that it needed any sort of improvement, but he conceded that the time had come for BYU to share in the "educational progress" of the day. At an April 1921 meeting of the BYU Board of Trustees, Grant confessed: "It has been one of the saddest tasks of the General Board's life so to speak, at least since I became a member, to feel that in this day of educational progress there was the least necessity to make a change in the Brigham Young University.

The presidency of Franklin S. Harris, PhD, represented a new era at BYU. He courted the finest university-trained Mormon scholars and ushered the university into the promised land of accreditation. Used by permission, L. Tom Perry Special Collections, Harold B. Lee Library, Brigham Young University, Provo.

So far as I am concerned, having practically no education at all, I am not as capable of understanding these necessities as some other men who have had opportunities in an educational way. But we want this school to be all that it is possible to be, to be worthy of its founder, and to be worthy of the Church."[8] President Grant's unusual deference to others with better academic credentials meant remarkable freedom for Harris at BYU.[9]

With fellow PhD scientist John A. Widtsoe as his sympathetic, supervising LDS commissioner of education, Harris took it upon himself to make the school "all that it is possible to be," in the words of President Grant. Harris set out to recruit a cadre of Mormon scholars with recent PhDs who could help increase the school's prestige. Early on, he secured the services of fellow Cornell PhD Thomas L. Martin to oversee the agriculture department. By the 1922–23 academic year, the BYU faculty boasted seven PhDs, including that of President Harris.[10]

There were notable exceptions, however, to Harris's success in recruiting high-powered Mormon scholars. Dr. Kimball Young, a Chicago- and Stanford-trained sociologist, turned down Harris's offer to teach at BYU in 1921 because of lingering concerns about academic freedom there. Harris tried to assure Young, who had been a student at BYU during the modernist controversy of 1911, that Young would be required only to "teach the truth as near as it can be discovered."[11] Unconvinced, Young took a position at the University of Oregon.

Another frustrated recruiting effort targeted Henry Fletcher, the Chicago-trained physicist who had left BYU back in 1916 for a research position with Bell Laboratories in New York City. Harris's "interest in fundamental scientific studies" appealed to Fletcher, but coming to Provo would have meant a severe pay cut. Fletcher was making $6,000 per year and expected that figure to leap to $8,000 soon, while Harris was having difficulty guaranteeing that he could offer Fletcher a mere $4,000.[12] Fletcher stayed in New York.

In perhaps his boldest move, Harris even tried to court the exiled Ralph Chamberlin. Richard Lyman, the apostle and PhD engineer, seems to have suggested the plan. Lyman thought that the time was right to bring Chamberlin back. Lyman told President Harris, "I am of the opinion that if Dr. Ralph V. Chamberlin can render valuable service in your institution, you can get him to accept a position with you for comparatively small salary. He is extremely anxious to come to Utah where he can be in close touch with his kindred, etc. In fact, I think he will marry an L.D.S. girl if he will but come to Utah and be a real Latter-day Saint."[13] Lyman did not specify what it took to be "a real Latter-day Saint," but he felt confident that Utah would exercise an ennobling influence on the wayward scholar.

Chamberlin, however, had his doubts about coming home. Writing from Harvard, where he was conducting his research, he said he could imagine doing innovative work at BYU, like developing a museum and offering instruction in zoology, entomology, genetics, and even the increasingly popular scientific field of eugenics. Chamberlin told Harris that "It is always a privilege to teach such earnest and capable young people as Utah produces. . . . Probably, however, the difficulty is rather in convincing the Utah executives that I am personally needed rather than in convincing them that there is work of importance that I would do well."[14] Chamberlin never returned to BYU. He found the University of Utah more amenable and accepted a position there in 1926. There, he would teach courses on evolution and the natural sciences until 1948.

Although he had given serious thought to returning to Provo, Ralph Chamberlin's feelings about the modernist controversy of 1911 were still raw. When his brother and former BYU colleague, W. H. Chamberlin, died in 1921, Ralph began conceiving a full-length biography that would vindicate him for posterity. His *Life and Philosophy of W. H. Chamberlin* appeared in 1925, the year of the Scopes Trial. Reflecting on the controversy surrounding the Chamberlins and Petersons at BYU, he characterized men like President Brimhall and Superintendent Cummings as primitive and prescientific in their religious mentality:

The savage mind finds mysterious and arbitrary spiritual powers everywhere, in rivers and springs, inherent in the wind and rain, and presiding over the crops; but, with advance in civilization and the development of ordered knowledge, an ever wider compass is established for the reign of natural laws. Those who base their faith in God on the ever-receding miraculous phenomena, on the tacit assumption that human limitations prove the validity of religious interpretations, are ever pointing out some weak spot in the scientific web of cause and effect and saying, "Here science is baffled, and you must admit the need of God." But science keeps extending her domain; and so the history of the thought of these men is the history of a continuous retreat. Their position is fundamentally a bad one because it makes God a personified symbol of our residuum of ignorance[.][15]

To free W. H. Chamberlin from any lingering disrepute, Ralph included a long series of testimonies from his students and colleagues, which read like hagiography. Alma Ericksen, E. E.'s brother, effused, "I regard Professor Chamberlin as having more nearly approached the life and thought of Jesus Christ than any other person I have known."[16] M. Wilford Poulson, a former student of W. H. Chamberlin now at the head of the BYU psychology department, remembered that "in his presence we could freely express our perplexities and feel assured that on his part there would be forthcoming something better than suspicion, pity, rhetoric, scripture-juggling, mere rationalization, heated argument, or condemnation."[17] Joseph Peterson recalled that for Chamberlin, "religion was a consistent, expanding life, toward the furtherance of which formalities were but means; and he was very charitable toward persons with whom he differed on any of these means. He recognized that many individuals, because of the lack of opportunities which he had enjoyed, could not 'walk without crutches.' "[18] For Mormon professors and students who had looked up to W. H. Chamberlin, these eulogistic appraisals took the form of a ritualistic catharsis, a corporate exorcism. Out from the shadows of the previous decade's condemnations, Mormon scholars emerged in the 1920s with a swagger.

For his part, BYU's President Harris forged ahead, undeterred by his failure to get Ralph Chamberlin back. In 1925, he successfully recruited another unapologetic Mormon evolutionist, Vasco Tanner, a specialist in zoology and entomology. A 1916 BYU graduate, Tanner had just earned his PhD in entomology from Stanford, where former university president David Starr Jordan—himself a zoologist—had influenced Tanner profoundly. Tanner even named one of his own sons "Jordan" after his Stanford mentor, and when he began teaching at BYU, he established a David Starr Jordan Club for students particularly interested in biology.[19] Tanner taught evolution unashamedly at BYU. His confidence offered additional evidence that academic life at BYU had changed drastically under the administration of Franklin Harris.[20]

Embracing the Academic Study of Religion

Outside of Provo, the most significant intellectual development under the new LDS commissioners of education was the Mormon interest in the academic study of religion. Writing decades later, seminary teacher Russel Swensen recalled that in the 1920s, Superintendent Adam S. Bennion was "aware of the limited background of the seminary teachers in biblical studies. To help alleviate this problem he placed scholarly books dealing with historical and literary analysis of the Bible in all seminary libraries."[21] Bennion also invited Charles Edward Rugh, a non-Mormon education professor at Berkeley, to teach "Religious Education" and "How to Teach the Bible" at the BYU summer school in 1922.[22]

Later in the decade, Joseph F. Merrill, Bennion's successor at the head of the church school system, would echo Bennion's call for Mormons to pursue the academic study of religion in greater depth. He wanted BYU to develop a master's program in religious education, whose faculty would be specialists in "Biblical history and interpretation; comparative religion; psychology, including the psychology and philosophy of religion; sociology; science; etc." The program would be designed to produce "well-informed teachers of religion" for the seminaries and institutes.[23]

During this period, the construction of LDS "institutes"—Mormon educational and cultural centers located near state universities—also provided a stimulus for the academic study of religion. Like the seminaries, which provided religious education for Mormons attending public high schools, the institutes were designed to offer religious education—as well as a sense of Mormon community—to Mormons at public universities. Typically, institute directors could offer courses in world religions, the history of Christianity, and the Old and New Testaments for undergraduate credit; they also taught courses on the Book of Mormon, Mormon history, and Mormon doctrine for the students' edification, but not for academic credit. The first LDS institute opened in 1926 at the University of Idaho, and more opened in the 1920s and 1930s at schools like the Idaho Southern Branch College in Pocatello, the University of Utah, the Utah State Agricultural College, the University of Wyoming, the University of Arizona, and the University of Southern California. For the Mormons earning advanced degrees in the field of religion, a subsequent position at an institute or BYU was ideal, since those positions offered the best opportunities to use their expertise in the classroom.

The University of Chicago's Divinity School was the most common, albeit unlikely, destination for Mormons in religious studies. A bastion of liberal Protestantism, the divinity school boasted an all-star cast of faculty in biblical studies and the history of Christianity, including the school's dean, Shailer Mathews, a staunch proponent of theological modernism and the social gospel; Edgar Goodspeed, a renowned New Testament scholar; Shirley Jackson Case, a specialist in the early history of

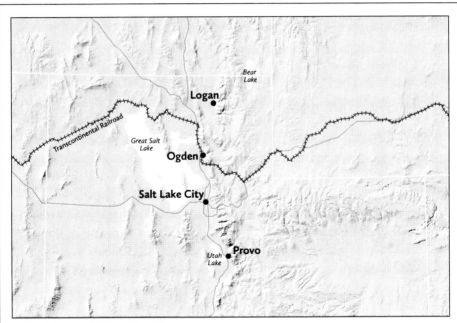

Utah's Colleges and Universities, 1867–1940

Logan
Brigham Young College (1877–1926)

Agricultural College of Utah (1888–1929) / Utah State Agricultural College (1929–1957) / Utah State University (1957–present)

Salt Lake City
University of Deseret (1850–1894) / University of Utah (1894–present)

Latter-day Saints' College (1890–1901, 1927–1931) / Latter-day Saints' University (1901–1927) / LDS Business College (1931–present)

Provo
Brigham Young Academy (1875–1903) / Brigham Young University (1903–present)

LDS/Utah institutions of higher education in the late nineteenth and early twentieth centuries. Map created by Think Spatial, Brigham Young University, Provo.

Christianity; and William Warren Sweet, a towering figure in American religious history. It was nothing new for Mormons to study with some of the most prominent faculty in a particular field. What was surprising about this migration to Chicago, however, was that a cadre of Mormon educational administrators, teachers, and emerging scholars began to acknowledge that expertise—not simply in medicine, law, engineering, or the natural and social sciences, but in *religion*—lay outside their own community.[24] The migration to Chicago thus represented a thorough rejection of the church's traditional theological insularity and populism, an unprecedented display of deference to "outside" authorities on questions of religious significance.[25]

Likewise, the divinity school professors had little reason to expect an influx of Mormon students. The biblical scholars would have lent no credence to the Book of Mormon as "another testament of Jesus Christ." The church historians would have rejected Mormon conceptions of a "great apostasy," after which the gospel, the true church, and priesthood authority finally enjoyed their restoration through the prophetic work of Joseph Smith. A cordial exchange of ideas between the professors and their Mormon students was thus improbable. Yet there were fertile similarities between Mormon theology and the "modernist" theology espoused by many of the Chicago professors. Both theologies evaded traditional conceptions of original sin, embraced optimistic conceptions of human nature and destiny, and urged followers of Christ to hasten the advent of a just social and economic order, a clear sign of the coming Kingdom of God.

An exchange between the Mormons and the divinity school professors, moreover, became possible in the 1920s and 1930s because neither the Mormon students at Chicago nor their divinity school professors were terribly interested in perpetuating traditional theological polemics. The students wanted to help the LDS Church increase its respectability among "learned" non-Mormons, and they were genuinely interested in deepening their understanding of the scriptures and the history of Christianity. The Chicago professors, for their part, had adopted a professional, "scientific" ideal in their analysis of religion, which subordinated apologetics to disinterested inquiry. Decades before ecumenical and interfaith dialogues became common, something of a theological disarmament on both sides allowed eleven Mormons to earn advanced degrees from the divinity school from 1926 to 1942. All but two earned the PhD.[26]

Mormons in Utah soon felt the effects of the new academic migration. At the annual summer gathering of LDS seminary teachers in 1929, Sidney Sperry, who was working toward his PhD at the University of Chicago, offered specialized instruction in the Old Testament that reflected his new expertise. (Heber C. Snell, who had studied the Old Testament at the Pacific School of Religion in Berkeley from 1927 to 1928, also taught at the summer school, which was sponsored by BYU and Commissioner Merrill.) Enthusiastic responses to Sperry's teaching prompted Commissioner Merrill to help send three more seminary teachers—Russel

Swensen, Daryl Chase, and George Tanner—to the University of Chicago, offering them half pay for the year 1930–31. Merrill was especially interested in preparing directors for the new LDS Institutes and, according to Swensen, Merrill tried to ensure a return on his investment by telling the departing teachers that "re-employment in the Church school system would depend upon our faith and continued loyalty to the Church."[27] The deal Merrill struck with Swensen, Chase, and Tanner indicated his concern about the effect that the divinity school might have upon their commitment to the church, but optimism trumped his fear.

The migration went both ways. Because of the strong connections that Mormons made with the divinity school professors at the University of Chicago, it became customary in the early 1930s for one of the professors to offer summer instruction to the LDS seminary teachers in Utah. From 1930 to 1933, visiting University of Chicago professors included: Edgar J. Goodspeed (New Testament), William C. Graham (Old Testament), John T. McNeill (church history), and William C. Bower (religious education). The lectures won the admiration of Commissioner Merrill. In 1930, he wrote that "Dr. Goodspeed is highly praised by our men [at BYU and in the seminaries] for the work he is doing in Provo. They are greatly pleased with what he is giving them. They are learning that the Bible furnishes a subject for the ripest scholarship and for the most interesting lectures."[28] The following year, Merrill reported that "Dr. Graham has measured up most satisfactorily to the standards set by Dr. Goodspeed, and has established himself firmly in the hearts of his students."[29]

The Chicago professors reciprocated. Goodspeed told Sidney Sperry that he would "always remember the summer [in Provo] with great pleasure. My classes were much larger than I anticipated, and everywhere [I] met cordiality and friendliness."[30] Personal contacts with these scholars inspired seven more Mormons to follow Sperry, Swensen, Chase, and Tanner to Chicago.

The bonds with professors had, of course, taken some time to form. When Russel Swensen, Daryl Chase, and George Tanner started school at Chicago in 1930, they were, in Tanner's words, "the objects of a good deal of interest,"[31] but they were received hospitably. Swensen wrote to his father that Dr. Goodspeed "is very interested in our church and assured me that the Divinity School is very pleased to have us come here."[32] Tanner found "not the slightest bigotry" in Shirley Jackson Case, a "real scholar" who quickly became Tanner's favorite professor.[33]

William Warren Sweet, the American religious historian, was perhaps the hardest professor to win over. The same year that Swensen, Chase, and Tanner came to the divinity school, Sweet published an influential work, *The Story of Religion in America*, which described Mormonism as one of many early nineteenth-century "fads and extravagances" that cropped up in New England, including anti-Masonic sentiment, "the Millerite craze," and the spiritualistic sensation surrounding the fraudulent Fox sisters.[34] According to Tanner, Sweet "had his doubts about us Mormon boys" at first, but after getting to know the Mormon students, the professor softened his rigid stance. Reflecting on his treatment of the Mormons in his book, Sweet reportedly declared, "If I could redo that book now, I'd do it quite differently."[35] Russel Swensen, after taking Sweet's American Church History course in the fall, confirmed that a change had taken place in Sweet's thinking about the Mormons. Swensen wrote to George Tanner that Sweet "was not so bad on the mormons [sic] as I expected him to be judging from his text. Evidently you and Daryl have had some effect upon the professor."[36]

Although Tanner boasted that the Mormon students had taught professors like Sweet a lesson in "tolerance and understanding," he and his companions recognized that they themselves had much to learn.[37] Tanner acknowledged that in four quarters at Chicago, he "learned more about the bible [sic] . . . than I had learned in all my previous life." After a year at Chicago, Russel Swensen also offered a glowing review: "One thing is certain, you get real lectures here, well prepared and systematically arranged. When I look back on some classes I had at [BYU] I readily perceive why there was quite a tendency to fall asleep in class. There is certainly a stimulus to study when sitting at the feet of brilliant professors not only from their lectures but the enthusiasm for their work which radiates from them. I think the past year will be a bright spot in my life, especially as I look back on the intellectual stimulus and discipline which is so outstanding here."[38] Commissioner Merrill shared the students' enthusiasm. In his regular "L.D.S. Department of Education" column for *The Deseret News*, Merrill treated Swensen, Chase, and Tanner as exemplary. In their studies, Merrill said, the three offered proof that "as a group the seminary teachers are both progressive and ambitious, educationally and scholastically."[39]

The similarities perhaps ended there. Like their ancestors who had studied abroad, this first group of Mormons at the University of Chicago Divinity School—Sidney Sperry, Russel Swensen, Daryl Chase,

George Tanner, T. Edgar Lyon, and Carl J. Furr—was diverse in theological orientation, and their academic experiences did not exert a uniform influence upon them. Some found the theologically liberal environment stimulating and liberating; others found it disturbing.

Russel Swensen exemplified the former position. He revered his professors, describing them to his concerned father in Utah as men of learning and "genuine humility."[40] Swensen's father was difficult to persuade. He represented something of the old Mormon populism. He suspected that the learned teachers of Russel were arrogant, and he was convinced that they were ill-informed about religious truth—otherwise they would be Latter-day Saints.[41] Russel vigorously defended them. "I believe before you condemn the scholars and thinkers," Russel said, "it would pay to investigate their way of thinking. They have no diabolical scheme to undermine the truth, but the reverse, to discover it."[42] Russel especially admired Shailer Mathews. Russel called him "a courageous defender as well as an expounder of the faith," one who could represent religion as intellectually credible before the university's many "sceptical, agnostic professors"—a skill Russel knew Mormons would need if they were to hold their own in a diverse, modern marketplace of ideas.[43]

The intergenerational debate between Russel and his father could have been a case study in E. E. Ericksen's dissertation on generational conflicts in Mormon history and culture. It continued for years. In 1933, an exasperated Russel mounted his most impassioned defense of his non-Mormon professors:

I want you to realise [sic] . . . that most of these men here in the Divinity School are far from being proud in their knowledge. In fact the greater the scholar the more genuine humility one finds. They realise [sic] so much more keenly the great important things which are still beyond human understanding. In fact Dr. Case, my Church History professor[,] said that the real student is the one with the insight to discover the problems and unsolved difficulties in his field, rather than one who is merely memorizing what someone else has written or says. I think that this frame of mind quite fits in with the great ideal of the Latter-day Saints, "the glory of God is intelligence," and "eternal progression." Its [sic] when we are completely satisfied and complacent that retrogression and stagnation occurs. By praising the fine men here don't think I do it to make an invidious comparison with the Church leaders we have back home. Such is not my intention. The achievements of our people both in the past and present speak for a high and wise type of leadership. But it does not mean that we are to disregard the thirteenth Article of Faith: by seeking all good things and beauty no matter what the source.[44]

Russel tried to convince his father that the academic study of religion, even under Protestant instructors, was compatible with older Mormon affirmations about cultivating intelligence and seeking truth. It was a hard sell.

Honest differences with his father notwithstanding, Russel reveled in his academic surroundings. He regularly attended the university's chapel services, which featured addresses by leading American preachers like Reinhold Niebuhr and Rabbi Stephen Wise. He admired Niebuhr's articulation of a Christian brand of socialism and Wise's eloquent, idealistic defense of religion against pessimism and cynicism.[45] Russel unashamedly reported to his father that "every Sunday we have some such eminent person speak in the University Chapel. Although it means missing our own L.D.S. Sunday School to take these in I feel it is worth the time taken off."[46] Russel's church activity slackened, although it hardly ceased. He took special pride in accepting invitations from fellow divinity students to speak about Mormonism in their churches. On these occasions, Russel felt that he had performed something like missionary work in correcting widespread misconceptions about the church.[47]

Far less sanguine than Russel Swensen about the divinity school experience was T. Edgar Lyon, who would become a revered Mormon teacher and historian in his own right.[48] Whereas Swensen admired his professors for increasing the respectability of religion by bringing it in line with modern thought, Lyon criticized those same teachers for stripping religion of its supernaturalism, turning God into a mere abstraction, and subjecting religious experience to the unrelenting, reductive analysis of the social sciences. Soon after he enrolled, Lyon expressed his frustrations to his father:

I fail to see how a young man can come here to school, and then go out after graduation as a minister of a church, and still preach what we call Christianity. Of course, the U. of Chicago is noted as being the most liberal (and that means Modernism) school in America. All religion is taught as a product of social growth and development, and anything supernatural is looked upon as merely a betrayal of ones [sic] own ignorance and primitive mind. They make no attempt to harmonize Science and the Bible—they merely through [sic] the Bible away, and teach scientific "truths" as the only thing to follow. . . . I have been trying to figure out what kind of God the Christian world accepts, but I can not understand it, and I doubt if any of these professors can, yet they even open classes with prayer at times, and talk about going to God with our troubles. Of course, they merely feel sorry for us, when they hear that we are so ignorant and primitive that we still believe in a personal God. Their God, here at this University, is "the cosmic force of the Universe," "the personality-producing force of the cosmos," the "in all and all" and a few more phrases just as unintelligible and meaningless. I readily see why the modern preachers talk about psychology, sociology, astronomy, prison reform, etc, in their churches on Sunday—that is all there is left to talk about after they have finished robbing Jesus of His Divinity, and miracles and resurrection. . . . I think that they are just as narrow-minded in their interpretations as they claim that we are in ours.[49]

Lyon did his best not to let these aggravations derail his academic progress. By focusing on church history rather than theology or biblical studies, Lyon managed to create a comfortable distance between himself and the professors who infuriated him.

Dealing with fellow Mormons who sympathized with the professors was another matter. Lyon condemned his companions' alleged departure from Mormon orthodoxy. He wrote, "We have several [Mormon students] here on the campus who think that they are outgrowing our little narrow-mindedness about our doctrines, and try to go with the world by attempting to take all of the supernatural elements out of our religion. I talked to one the other day for more than an hour and he was trying to explain to me about Joseph Smith's visions, on the basis that they were merely psychological manifestations to his own mind, hallucinations, etc., etc. The strange thing to me is that they even try to claim that they still believe in Mormonism. They explain away the Book of Mormon, the Doctrine and Covenants and the Pearl of Great Price until they have no more actual value than a story that David [Lyon's three-year-old son] could write, and they say that they still believe in the church and someday we will all come to their way of thinking."[50]

The "liberalizing" tendency of some Mormon students, in Lyon's point of view, threatened bedrock church teachings. He worried about the influence that latter-day Mormon liberals might have in the church and at BYU. Their teachings, he thought, were "far more radical" even than those the notorious Petersons and Chamberlins had disseminated two decades earlier.[51]

Mormon scholars' internal struggles and intramural debates were so intense partly because the divinity school's atmosphere of rigorous investigation led some of them to conclusions that they had not ever expected, or wanted, to reach. George Tanner, whose master's thesis dealt with the origins of Mormonism, became unsettled when his findings did not square with what church leaders had taught him. For example, revelations given to Joseph Smith about the negative effects of liquor and tobacco did not, as Tanner had thought, contradict prevailing early nineteenth-century opinion about those substances. He reflected:

> I'd always been taught that . . . the section of the Doctrine
> and Covenants on the Word of Wisdom [*Doctrine and Covenants*
> 89:1–21] was just like lightning out of a clear sky. I got there and
> started digging in and found the genesis of that thing and the
> roots. I found all over the country there at the time the Word of
> Wisdom revelation was given that there were societies against
> liquor and societies against tobacco. There was no question at all
> that there was as much opposition then against the use of tobacco
> and liquor as there is today. Everywhere we turned we found
> that type of thing—that Joseph Smith instead of getting revela-
> tions which were just brand new was simply giving his own
> sanction to things that were pretty generally known. He was on
> the right side of them, of course; he was on the right side of the
> tobacco issue and on the right side of the liquor issue, but they
> weren't new issues by any manner of means. This is mentioned a
> number of places in my master's thesis.[52]

Tanner concluded that Mormons had overestimated Joseph Smith's originality in urging his followers to abstain from liquor and tobacco, and he
worried that if Mormons persisted in making such overblown claims, they
would invite refutation and ridicule.

T. Edgar Lyon, like Tanner a student of American religious history,
made similarly unsettling discoveries. Although he did not share the
liberal theological orientation of some of his professors and Mormon

peers, he did embrace their methodology in his historical research. For his master's thesis, he conducted original research on Orson Pratt, a close associate of Joseph Smith and one of the church's most influential early apologists. Mormons had long exalted Pratt as a theologian and scientist who had outwitted the "learned" thinkers of the day. Lyon's quest for the historical Orson Pratt, however, led to a different conclusion. In a 1932 letter, Lyon warned his parents that his thesis would not conform to traditional estimations of Pratt: "You will perhaps be surprised [sic] when you read the chapter on [Orson Pratt's] scientific work to see how greatly we have overestimated Orson Pratt as a scientist. But I think that it is far better to make a bold admission of facts and truth, and do it now, than wait until it is forced down our throats at a later date when it will be more embarrassing to us. I am convinced that we must face the future with a little broader view than we have done in the past (I mean certain people in the Church), or we are going to lose our young people and have no power to hold them."[53] Lyon hoped that an honest reckoning with the historical record—and the intellectual limitations of the Mormon pioneers—would help Mormons withstand the encroaching march of historical investigation by Mormons and non-Mormons alike.

The Chicago divinity students were not alone in identifying exaggerated Mormon claims about the church's past. In Utah, a few Mormon scholars had begun following in the footsteps of E. E. Ericksen, narrating the history of the church in a way that shed a tone of defensiveness, played down the role of providence, and paid closer attention to original historical sources. B. H. Roberts's six-volume *Comprehensive History of the Church of Jesus Christ of Latter-day Saints* (1930) exemplified the trend. Roberts, who had come to the church's vigorous defense in 1911 with his address on higher criticism and the Book of Mormon, had become more intellectually independent in the intervening decades. Although he was not himself the beneficiary of formal academic training, his work had a profound, immediate impact on younger Mormon scholars. T. Edgar Lyon wrote in 1932: "I have been rather astonished in reading B. H. Roberts['s] new *Comprehensive History of the Church*, in six volumes, to find that he was allowed to publish some of the things which he has. I imagine he must have had a struggle to get some of it in print. For example, his exposé of the poor judgment used by the Saints in Missouri which caused their persecutions; his criticism of the tendency to become autocratic which displayed itself in Joseph Smith at times; and his criticism of the Nauvoo City Council for destroying the *Nauvoo Expositor*, which he says was absolutely illegal and they should have known better."[54] Roberts's new way of writing Mormon history gave Mormons like T. Edgar Lyon a certain permission to embrace the methodology of professional history in which they were being trained at the University of Chicago.[55]

Mormon students were also paying close attention to the work of BYU psychology professor M. Wilford Poulson. Like George Tanner, Poulson had investigated nineteenth-century attitudes toward liquor and tobacco, in order to assess the originality of the Word of Wisdom. Poulson, a disciple of W. H. Chamberlin and a student at the University of Chicago for seven quarters from 1916 to 1925, came to the conclusion that many in the church had overstated the originality of the church's prohibitions on liquor and tobacco. Poulson denounced Provo doctor Lewis Weston Oaks, whose *Medical Aspects of the Latter-day Saint Word of Wisdom* (1929) asserted that "in strict opposition to the most advanced knowledge of his time, and in face of great uncertainty in the scientific world Joseph Smith, in February 1833, proclaimed as coming direct from God, what is now known as the Mormon Word of Wisdom."[56] Poulson called Oaks's claims "grossly exaggerated."[57] He lamented to Russel Swensen in 1930, "you know of the weakness of our assuming a position which later we will be forced to abandon."[58]

As tensions mounted between divergent narratives of the Mormon past—between sacred and academic Mormon history—M. Wilford Poulson and George Tanner wanted their discoveries about the Word of Wisdom to reach a wide Mormon audience, to prepare them for informed conversations, within and outside the church, about the complexity of Mormon history. It helped that both had the ear of Commissioner Merrill. In the fall of 1931, Merrill published a detailed summary of Tanner's thesis in the "L.D.S. Department of Education" column of *The Deseret News*, followed by Tanner's own frank estimation of the historical record. Tanner tried his best to soften the blow. He declared, "The Word of Wisdom which was given in 1833 cannot be thought of as an addition of much new material. Numerous books and pamphlets published before that date give ample testimony to the fact that both physicians and ministers were keenly alive to the harmfulness of both liquor and tobacco, and of tea, coffee and meats to a lesser degree. . . . [I]t seems to matter little whether this revelation be considered as one giving forth new truth or as the Divine Sanction [*sic*] of truths at least partially known. The results obtained through observance of the Word of Wisdom show it to be worthy of God's revelation to Latter-day Saints whether it be new truth or the sanction of that already known."[59] Tanner may have been disingenuous—he was at least quite optimistic—in claiming that the difference between traditional and revisionist interpretations of Mormon history "seems to matter little."

As Poulson and Tanner begged fellow Mormons to make less exaggerated claims about their past, T. Edgar Lyon argued in a similar fashion that the church needed far more sophisticated appraisals of other Christian traditions. Despite his theological disagreements with many of his professors and fellow students, Lyon concluded that traditional Mormon attacks on other churches simply no longer held. Studying with informed, articulate Protestant ministers and scholars, Lyon began to worry that the LDS Church was training its missionaries to shadow-box with caricatures of Christianity. Lyon wrote to his father, "My experience has taught me that in teaching the younger people of the Church, some radically different approach must be made from what has heretofore been the custom. And our missionaries need more training before coming into the field. It is pitiful to hear some of them get up and try to tell the Protestants about the fallacies of Protestant doctrines. They go over all the hell-fire and brimstone, infant damnation, etc, while the Protestants sit back and laugh. Such doctrines have long since been discarded and re[j]ected by the Protestants, even though they have not taken them out of their prayer-books. I have not met a preacher here this summer, and I have met several hundred, who believed such doctrines. They merely refer to them as outworn dogmas of primitive minds."[60] In Lyon's eyes, missionaries with outmoded tools for debate, just like immoderate amateur historians, threatened to subject the church to ridicule.

As committed as Lyon was to genuine scholarship and softening old Mormon polemics against outsiders, ambivalence about pursuing truth wherever it might lead crept in to his academic work. For example, Lyon was willing to portray Orson Pratt in all his flawed humanity, but he could not bring himself to publish findings that reflected poorly on Joseph Smith. Lyon told his parents that he could not avoid the conclusion that "the Prophet [Joseph Smith] sometimes used poor judgment in 'testing the faith' of his followers." Lyon cited a story from 1841, when Smith tried to convince the church's apostles that it was God's will that Joseph be given their wives. Lyon found the story unpalatable, and he refused to publish it. He hated to think of the pleasure it would give "Mormon-eaters."[61] With the church just a century old, entrenched animosities between Mormons and Gentiles were still strong enough to shape the writing of Mormon history.

Yet because of their unique experiences and qualifications, Mormon students returning from the University of Chicago were poised to revolutionize Mormon religious education. Some would receive a warmer welcome than others. The students generally had support from influential leaders in Mormon educational circles, like Commissioner Merrill, BYU president Franklin Harris, and Apostle Richard Lyman, each of whom held a doctoral degree. Referring to the Chicago students, Lyman said, "When we have more men who can associate with great scholars and can speak and understand the language of great scholars, the work of the Church will go forward much faster."[62] Moreover, the Chicago students and their supporters thought that the returning students were best suited for college work or seminary work in more heavily populated areas. Richard Lyman told Russel Swensen, "You must realize yourself that the only place in which you can fit perfectly here is as a teacher in the Brigham Young University."[63] Swensen ended up joining the faculty of BYU, spending a long career teaching New Testament and history courses there. George Tanner landed a position as the director of the LDS Institute at the University of Idaho. Tanner reported to Swensen: "I am really enjoying my work here and am well pleased with the response of the students. I have forty-four enrolled this semester and they are a fine set. I really enjoy this so much more than the work in the high school that I can hardly understand how I liked that work so much. Last semester I taught the history of the American Churches to a bunch of senior college students and it was very fascinating. This semester I am teaching the History and Religion of the New Testament to a [b]unch of seniors and juniors and it is equally interesting. I also have other courses but these are the ones I have enjoyed the most."[64]

Other returning students were not so fortunate. T. Edgar Lyon told Commissioner Merrill that he wanted a position that would offer "more opportunity for self-improvement" than his old seminary job in remote Midway, Utah, ideally something near Salt Lake City "or some other urban center in Utah."[65] Merrill came up with something far short of the ideal, a position teaching political science at Ricks College, an LDS junior college in Rexburg, Idaho, a school that cash-strapped church leaders hoped to turn over to the state. Lyon was left to wonder why he had spent so much time and money obtaining a master's degree in religion.[66]

Daryl Chase probably would have traded a limb for Lyon's job. Working in a rural Kaysville, Utah, seminary for the year 1933–34 left him thoroughly embittered. Chase complained to Russel Swensen about the onset of mental atrophy. "[M]y students are doing good work," he noted, "but I pray to all the gods that be that I never spend another winter in the country. It is next to impossible to keep from slipping backwards intellectually in such an environment. I was not in love with my position last year, but the situation this year is far less desirable. It is not that I am over-worked, but the monotony is killing—Six classes of O[ld] T[estament] daily to little children who have to be told the meaning of half the words in their text. God of my fathers why am I so cursed!"[67] Chase's career would eventually bring wider opportunities. In 1935, he became the director of the LDS Institute in Pocatello, Idaho, and in 1936, he took the same position at the University of Wyoming in Laramie. In the 1950s and 1960s, he would serve as president of Utah State University.

Like Chase, Carl Furr got off to a rough start, although he generally seemed to enjoy his teaching at the North Cache seminary in the far reaches of northern Utah. The local LDS stake board of education battled Furr, initiating what he called "a heresy trial." The board summoned one of Commissioner Merrill's assistants in the Department of Education, E. Ernest Bramwell, to address the situation. Furr told his side of the story to Russel Swensen: "Our good brother Bramwell was supposed to have made an investigation, but all he did was converse with the stake board of education and then call me in after school and proceed to tell me that there were lots of complaints coming in about my work, that I lacked spirituality and did not have a testimony of the gospel, and that I never paid enough to hold my job (tithing). All in all it was a very disgusting affair."[68] Furr concluded that his "goose was cooked" by a spineless, "jelly-fished chicken raiser" of a stake president.[69] His command of colorful language intact, Furr gathered himself after the unpleasant affair and pressed on, earning his PhD from the University of Chicago in 1937.

Carl Furr's difficulties in the spring of 1934 were not unique among Latter-day Saints with advanced degrees. In fact, they were emblematic and ominous. Enthusiasm for the learning of "the world," though endorsed by eminent men like Joseph Merrill and Franklin Harris, drew sharp criticism from some of the church's highest authorities in the early 1930s. In 1933, J. Reuben Clark Jr. had delivered a forbidding rebuke to an audience of church school teachers, who had just been treated to their fourth consecutive summer school with a University of Chicago Divinity School professor. Clark had seen enough, and as the first counselor to Heber J. Grant in the First Presidency, a Columbia law school graduate, and a former U.S. Ambassador to Mexico, he carried a commanding authority.[70]

Clark's words were not as easy to dismiss as the anti-intellectual harangues of a George Brimhall or Horace Hall Cummings, who lacked the ecclesiastical authority, academic credentials, and rhetorical dexterity of J. Reuben Clark.

In his remarks to the church school teachers, Clark blasted teachers who employed the theories and methods of secular disciplines. Like President Joseph F. Smith in his response to BYU professors in 1911, Clark denounced "wild theories"—pedagogical, metaphysical, or economic—that threatened to corrupt the simplicity of the gospel and the faith of the young. Clark told the gathered teachers:

> I should like to suggest to the seminary teachers that their primary function is to build spirituality, and that the primary qualification for the duties imposed upon them is the same spirituality. I should like to suggest to them that they do not need to use fine spun theories of theoretical pedagogy. They are not supposed to give learned lectures, to indulge in learned psycho-analysis, etc. As I understand it, they are to teach the simple principles of the gospel. . . .
>
> I see no place in the seminary for a discussion of metaphysics. I see no place in the seminary for instruction upon things which are purely sociological and economic. I admit that those problems face us, but they are so vast that personally I have not yet met the man who has the solution. And I seriously object, as a parent and a grandparent, to people who do not themselves understand those things trying to instruct my children and grandchildren on those matters.[71]

Clark's threats bore ultimate, eschatological weight. Excessively "theoretical" or insufficiently "spiritual" teaching, Clark warned, warranted not only dismissal from the church school system, but also "condemnation" in the afterlife for leading a young soul astray.

A year later the prophet himself, Heber J. Grant, denounced secular learning at the same summer gathering of church school teachers. Abandoning the deference to scholars that he had displayed back in 1921, Grant now staked out an ultra-populist position, a radical denial of the existence of truth beyond the borders of the LDS Church. "I want you all to understand," he said, "that you are teachers and that you are in exactly the same position as missionaries who go out into the world to preach the gospel. They go out to teach and preach, and not to learn of the ideas and views of other people. If we have the truth, and everyone in this body ought to have a testimony that we do have the truth, *we do not care what other people believe or what their teachings are.* The main thing that counts with the Latter-day Saint teacher is an individual testimony and knowledge of the divinity of the work in which you and I are engaged."[72] Grant's neo-populism went beyond even the populism of Joseph Smith and Brigham Young, who had instructed the faithful to be wide-ranging in their pursuit of truth. During the 1930s, however, an increasingly contentious theological and political climate—both in the church and in the nation as a whole—made key church leaders desperate to circle the wagons.

The attitudes of Clark and Grant changed the intellectual climate at BYU. Under the new commissioner of Education John A. Widtsoe, it became customary for Widtsoe, BYU president Harris, and one of the church's other twelve apostles to conduct interviews with BYU professors. Lowry Nelson, a BYU sociology professor with a recent PhD from the University of Wisconsin, recalled that "questions about the individual's faith— whether he prayed, paid tithing, attended [ward] meetings, held office in organizations, and so on—were the mainstays of the interviews."[73] Nelson, who felt that Widtsoe and Harris had "complete confidence" in him, got through the interview unscathed. Yet a subsequent slip in private conversation with a fellow Mormon—in which Nelson admitted that he was quite literally "agnostic" (i.e., uncertain) about immortality—made him the subject of scrutiny at the highest levels of church authority. Summoned to meet with the prophet, Nelson worried that he would become the subject of a formal investigation by the First Presidency.

In the end, Nelson eluded such an investigation. He was tremendously relieved. President Harris offered Nelson his continuing support, but Nelson could not escape the conclusion that that BYU professors had been living in a "fool's paradise" of academic freedom in the 1920s and early 1930s. The increasing pressure that Nelson felt at BYU led him to leave and take an advisory position in "rural rehabilitation" with the federal government. In 1937, Nelson accepted a faculty appointment in rural sociology at the University of Minnesota, where he would have his most productive years of scholarship. What Nelson called the church's "benign neglect" of BYU was over.[74]

The church's hierarchy was not, however, uniformly antagonistic to this rising generation of Mormon scholars. While some key church authorities hounded them in the 1930s, others lent them valuable support. David O. McKay, a member of the First Presidency along with J. Reuben

Clark, was widely known as a friend of educators and scholars. Institute directors especially appreciated his sympathy. A former church commissioner of education, McKay gave institute directors the freedom to conduct their work as they saw fit. His attitude was virtually antithetical to Clark's. When the LDS Institute at the University of Utah opened in 1935, for example, McKay told its director, Lowell Bennion, "I don't care what you do or what you draw upon, but be true to yourself and loyal to the cause."[75]

What it meant to be "loyal to the cause," of course, was up for debate; in fact, it was the ultimate question of twentieth-century Mormon identity. Yet Bennion appreciated McKay's vote of confidence, and he set out in his work with enthusiasm. With a recently minted PhD in sociology from the University of Strasbourg—his thesis was "The Methodology of Max Weber," among the earliest American scholarly treatments of Weber— Bennion was eager to help LDS college students relate the study of religion to their own lives and the "problems of modern life." He taught courses like "Comparative Religions," "The Position of Mormonism in the Religious Thought of Western Civilization," and "Religion and the Rise of Our Modern Economic Order."[76]

At the LDS Institute in Pocatello, Idaho (adjacent to the Idaho Southern Branch College), Heber C. Snell was similarly ambitious and optimistic. In 1937, Snell wrote to Commissioner of Education Frank L. West, "If we make our institutes religious centers, centers for character building through instruction, leisure-time social contacts (which should comprehend conversation, reading, etc., as well as 'parties'), meditation, and public worship, the institutes are eminently worth while. If we turn them in the direction of mere worldliness they are not. They should help build the 'great society,' the Kingdom of God."[77] These were heady times at the institutes, reflecting evolving Mormon mentalities.

Inscribing Separate Spheres of Science and Religion

In the 1930s, Mormons continued to chart the shifting boundaries between religion and science, the life of the mind and the life of the spirit. For many, whether theologically liberal or conservative, the two "spheres" became increasingly difficult—even impossible—to reconcile. Of those who argued for separate spheres, L. John Nuttall Jr., dean of the BYU College of Education, was perhaps the most optimistic about how they might relate. As he formulated an educational mission for BYU in 1929, he proposed that BYU researchers and church leaders could join in a separate but harmonious quest for truth. He wrote, "The university work makes it more possible for the church to seek systematically for that new truth, 'that which is lovely, praiseworthy, and of good report,' for which it declares itself to be seeking. *Only by revelation and research can new truth be had.* The University can do for the Church the research work needed to carry on and keep abreast of the world so that the light of the Church may shine brightly in the portals of the learned as well as in the realms of the ever decreasing unlearned people of the earth."[78] Through the distinct vehicles of "revelation and research," Nuttall said, the university and the church could work together to discover God's unfolding truth.[79]

Others who embraced the notion of separate spheres did so with far more combativeness. In the heat of theological battle, they claimed supreme authority in their own province. In the early 1930s, a bitter debate between geology professor Sterling B. Talmage (son of James) and Apostle Joseph Fielding Smith (the church's official historian and the son of the late president Joseph F. Smith) exemplified this mentality of unyielding opposition.

The immediate occasion for the trouble between Talmage and Smith centered on Smith's explanation of Joshua 10:13, which he offered in an April 1930 genealogical conference address. Smith affirmed the literal, miraculous quality of the text's statement that "the sun stood still, and the moon stayed" during Joshua's battle with the Amorites. In an attempt to preserve the plausibility of such a unique cosmic event, Smith hazarded that the massive, spinning, orbiting earth must have slowed down gradually.

Smith's quasi-scientific reasoning infuriated Sterling Talmage. A Harvard-trained PhD in geology, Talmage openly questioned Smith's authority on such matters. In consultation with his father, who was also an apostle, Talmage drafted an "open letter" to Smith and the First Presidency, in which he pointed out that "If the earth were brought to a stop in several hours [the maximum allowable time given the parameters of the story, which confine it to a single afternoon], there would ensue worldwide west winds, ranging from a thousand miles an hour on the equator to nothing at the poles, but passing over Palestine at a rate *fully six times as great as in the most violent recorded hurricanes.*"[80] Like his Mormon colleagues trained in the academic study of religion at the University of Chicago, Talmage thought that the intellectual respectability of the church, and the church's ability to retain the faith and loyalty of the young, was at stake. He continued: "In your boyhood, and in mine, the statements of the General Authorities of the Church were considered to be final; nobody in good standing in the Church presumed to question them. Today this is not so, and I believe for only one reason, namely, that *some of the authorities have made statements that are not worthy of belief,* and I cite your explanation of the miracle at Joshua's battle as a conspicuous but by no means an isolated example of what I mean."[81] Talmage vowed an intellectual's revenge. For the sake of "the educated young people of the Church," he promised to take every opportunity to refute Smith, in order "to prove point by point by point that our faith is not founded on absurdity."[82]

Talmage told Smith to stick to what he knew—doctrine—and leave science to scientists. Smith could not countenance such a separation of expertise and authority. He wrote to Talmage in 1934:

I have not felt that I am under any obligation to accept the theories which are based on scientific research, but have the divine right to question them. I am, however, under obligation to accept revealed truth which comes through the opening of the heavens from the One who "comprehendeth all things," and when I find what I believe to be a conflict between the theories of men and the word of the Lord, I am bold to say that I accept the latter with full confidence that the theories must be changed. I live in the full confidence that when the Lord comes . . . many things accepted in the theories of men today will be found to be untrue and these theories will have to be discarded or reconstructed to conform to the revelations which are to come. There is nothing in all the world so dear to me as revealed truth—the Gospel with all its amplifications received through the word of the Lord to his prophets, even in our own day. When I think I find something which tends to destroy the faith of the youth in these revelations, or which is hurtful to this truth, I have opposed it with vigor and have freely expressed my views. I believe I am willing to modify my views if the evidence indicated that my interpretation has been wrong.[83]

Joseph Fielding Smith could hardly be expected to argue otherwise. Nor could Sterling Talmage accept Joseph Fielding Smith as an authority on much of anything. Smith's father had tried to block the emergence of a "theological scholastic aristocracy" back in 1911, and his son tirelessly performed a similar task.

J. Reuben Clark was feeling just as territorial as Talmage and Smith. He told BYU students in 1937 that "Religion is sovereign in its own territory; so is Science in its territory. Religion may no more rightfully or successfully invade the territory of Science, than Science may cross over its boundaries into the land of Religion."[84] The following year, he elaborated in a way that would have repercussions for decades. On August 8, 1938, he addressed the church's seminary and institute teachers at Aspen Grove with a speech entitled "The Charted Course of the Church in Education." In it Clark attacked teachers who, he thought, had drifted away from—or outright denied—the "fundamentals" of church doctrine. His speech, reminiscent of his 1933 remarks to the same body, mustered all the precision of his legal training. Yet his argument was anything but dispassionate.[85]

Clark delivered his address with the express consent of President Grant. "The Charted Course of the Church in Education" exhibited a familiarly foreboding tone. Its goal was "to restate some of the more outstanding and essential fundamentals underlying our Church school education."[86] Like Protestant fundamentalists, Clark viewed the "fundamentals" as essentially doctrinal affirmations. These included, according to Clark, basic Christian beliefs in Jesus as the only begotten son of God, the saving power of his atonement, and the literal fact of his resurrection. In addition to those historic Christian affirmations, Clark said, Mormons must add belief in: the veracity of Joseph Smith's visions and the Book of Mormon; the restoration, through Joseph Smith, of the true church, gospel, and priesthood; past and ongoing revelations to the church's rightful authorities; and the church's Articles of Faith. Clark designated all these core convictions as "positive facts" that "must stand unchanged, unmodified, without dilution, excuse, apology, or avoidance; they must not be explained away or submerged."[87]

It was not customary for Mormon authorities to speak in terms of "fundamentals." From the beginning, church members had ascribed to the thirteen Mormon articles of faith, but the language of "fundamentals" was of course borrowed. Clark appropriated the term from Protestant fundamentalists, it seems, because he thought that he and the fundamentalists had a shared enemy: "liberal" theologians who exalted the intellect above simple faith, the modern above the traditional, and the ethical above the supernatural. Clark said that students in the seminaries

J. Reuben Clark Jr. berated university-trained Mormon scholars in his landmark address "The Charted Course of the Church in Education," a document that still has a profoundly chilling effect on Mormon discourse about scholarship and higher education. Used by permission, L. Tom Perry Special Collections, Harold B. Lee Library, Brigham Young University, Provo.

and institutes "fully sense the hollowness of teachings which would make the Gospel plan a mere system of ethics, they know that Christ's teachings are in the highest degree ethical, but they also know they are more than this. . . . They know that the Gospel teachings not only touch this life, but the life that is to come, with its salvation and exaltation as the final goal."[88] Like his high-ranking predecessors who condemned the Chamberlins and Petersons, Clark imported fundamentalism to attack imported liberalism.

Clark's address reinforced the new Mormon populism. His message carried all the more force coming from an educated man. "No amount of learning, no amount of study, and no number of scholastic degrees," Clark warned, could substitute for a "living, burning, honest testimony . . . that Jesus is the Christ and that Joseph was God's prophet."[89] Clark excoriated an emerging caste of theological "experts," whose imported ideas threatened to undermine church authority. Allowing their own "philosophy," rather than the teachings of church authorities, to govern their instruction, the teachers threatened to introduce a "chaos" of subjectivity and fragmentation into the church school system.[90] Clark identified Mormon education abroad as a main source of the problem. He wrote, "On more than one occasion our Church members have gone to other places for special training in particular lines; they have had the training which was supposedly the last word, the most modern view, the ne plus ultra of up-to-dateness; then they have brought it back and dosed it upon us without any thought as to whether we needed it or not. I refrain from mentioning well-known and, I believe, well-recognized instances of this sort of thing. I do not wish to wound any feelings."[91]

Although Clark found fault with the "Latter-day Saint psychologist, chemist, physicist, geologist, archeologist, or any other scientist" who fit his profile of the consummately arrogant church school teacher, he reserved special ire for Mormon religious educators like those who had attended the University of Chicago's Divinity School. Clark alleged that many of their teachings tried to answer theological questions that Mormon youth simply did not have. Clark said, "Before effort is made to inoculate us with new ideas, experts should kindly consider whether the methods, used to spur community spirit or build religious activities among groups that are decadent and maybe dead to these things, are quite applicable to us, and whether their effort to impose these upon us is a rather crude, even gross anachronism."[92] Such misguided and dangerous pedagogy only aroused doubt in students, and, as he had in 1933, Clark prophesied judgment upon those who abused a position of trust by troubling the waters of a young person's faith. "Great is the burden and the condemnation of any teacher who sows doubt in a trusting soul," Clark declared.[93]

Conclusion

To defend Mormon fundamentals, J. Reuben Clark departed from traditional Mormon teaching about the church's ability to incorporate all truth, regardless of its source. Clark reduced religious truth to its own narrow sphere. Church school teachers, Clark insisted, "are not to teach the philosophies of the world, ancient or modern, pagan or Christian, for this is the field of the public schools. Your sole field is the Gospel, and that is boundless in its own sphere."[94] How something could be "boundless in its own sphere" doubtless perplexed even the most philosophically minded Mormons. In any case, Clark said that the truth, as possessed and known only by Latter-day Saints, would inevitably conflict with "the findings of human research," and the Saints needed to have the "intellectual courage" to embrace the truth.[95]

Clark's address worried a number of teachers in the seminary and institute system. Supervisor of LDS seminaries and institutes M. Lynn Bennion, who had a PhD in education from Berkeley, called it "alarming, to say the least."[96] Some in the LDS Department of Education, like Chicago divinity school graduate Vernon F. Larsen, cited Clark's hostility as a reason for leaving the Department in the early 1940s.[97]

Clark's influence was powerful and enduring, but not thoroughgoing. Institute directors continued to teach courses—like "The Prophets and Modern Social Problems," "Religion and Literature in the Apostolic Age," "Social and Religious Teachings of Jesus," and "Survey of World Religions"—that used the scholarly apparatus of the broader academic study of religion. BYU also continued to promote the academic study of religion, organizing its own division of religion in 1939, which received the approval of the BYU Board of Trustees in 1940.[98] Three of the four division faculty—Sidney Sperry, Russel Swensen, and Wesley Lloyd—had earned the PhD at the University of Chicago. And powerful undercurrents of intellectual independence were stirring in the likes of Sterling McMurrin, a theologically liberal LDS Institute teacher who would soon earn a PhD in philosophy from the University of Southern California and go on to become John F. Kennedy's commissioner of education; Obert Tanner

(Joseph Marion's son), who taught religion and philosophy at Stanford in the late 1930s and 1940s and, like McMurrin, would challenge the church's practices of racial discrimination; and Columbia University–trained Juanita Brooks, whose immersions in professional historiography would culminate in a courageous, monumental history of one of Mormonism's darkest hours, the 1857 Mountain Meadows Massacre.[99]

The intellectual and theological debates of the 1930s would limit the influence, and determine the destiny, of the likes of McMurrin, Tanner, and Brooks, who were fated to become prophetic outliers in the shifting landscapes of modern Mormonism. In that pivotal decade, Mormon academics and ecclesiastics took hard-line positions that Joseph Smith and Brigham Young had long tried to avoid. Strident voices on both sides now embraced irreconcilable ideas of how to arrive at truth, how to formulate the essence of the faith, and how to instruct the young. This accumulating rigidity made a middle ground increasingly difficult to occupy. The old confidence of Ellis Reynolds Shipp—who declared in 1874 that "*all truth*, all knowledge comes from God"—had become untenable.

Conclusion

Mormonism Uncharted

· ·

Scholars studying the Mormon past have documented the manifold ways in which external pressure—economic, political, and legal—forced Mormons to abandon their isolated quest for purity and their deep hostility toward the outside world. The power of those forces cannot be denied. Yet more subtle eroding influences were also long at work among Mormons themselves. As Mormon students gravitated to the growing universities of the United States, they began to develop extra-ecclesial and transregional loyalties to their schools, their mentors, and their disciplines. Those loyalties, wide-ranging and difficult for theologically conservative authorities to control, became engines for institutional conflict and change. Other Mormon activities—proselytizing, secular business affairs, and increasing contact with non-Mormons in the Intermountain West—encouraged a certain anti-parochialism, but nothing nourished strong, competing loyalties like studying in the American university.

Mormons' new educational interests and influences reflected the orientations of an emerging, postpioneer Mormon society and culture. New ideas did not always meet with the approval of the pioneers, who had never intended for the church to have much of a history in these latter days. Rescuing the Christian gospel, church, and priesthood from a corrupt past, the early Saints expected the imminent dawn of a new millennium. As that day receded into an unknown future, Mormons had to reckon with the vagaries of time and chance. It was natural for them to disagree about how to proceed. Long before President Woodruff issued his Manifesto, in fact, the Saints' populist distrust of "learned" non-Mormons had already begun to weaken. Romania Pratt's plea for "cultivated skill" in medicine in 1879 was an especially clear rejection of that rhetorical and cultural posture. Periodically, though, the Saints reasserted their old populism and a related anti-intellectualism. Hannah Sorenson begged Mormon women not to study medicine in the wicked cities of the East, Joseph F. Smith tried to root out a growing "theological scholastic aristocracy" in the church, and J. Reuben Clark Jr. railed against influence of the social sciences in Mormon religious education. Then and now, the challenge for the Saints has been to advance in wisdom and understanding while holding fast to what endures.

In his classic sociological analysis of religion, *The Sacred Canopy*, Peter Berger argued that "every human society is an enterprise of world-building."[1] For the enterprise to succeed and perpetuate itself, Berger says, it has to "hide, as much as possible, its *constructed* character."[2] Likewise, Pierre Bourdieu has maintained that religious authority works most effectively when a representative of that authority seems "not [to] act in his own name and on his own authority, but in his capacity as a delegate."[3] Mormonism has not varied from the pattern. It has been the task—some would say the great success—of Mormon leaders to preserve their aura of unique authority through the twentieth century and into the postmodern twenty-first. Maintaining that authority has involved periodic, forceful denunciations of "the theories of men."

In such an environment, Mormon scholars and educators still have minefields to navigate. Even after decades of professional, academic Mormon history and the emergence of Mormon Studies as a vibrant field in its own right,[4] church leaders routinely use J. Reuben Clark's "The Charted Course of the Church in Education" as shorthand and code to ensure that teachers in the church's educational system stay within carefully prescribed boundaries. Occasional, blunt declarations like "The Mantle [of church authority] is Far, Far Greater Than the Intellect" have also reinforced Clark's ideas.[5] In that 1981 address, Apostle Boyd K. Packer said that "a member of the Church ought always, particularly if he is pursuing extensive academic studies, to judge the professions of man against the revealed word of the Lord."[6] A scholarly position of "objectivity" or "neutrality," in deference to the professional standards of non-Mormons, Packer stated, is anathema for a true Latter-day Saint, who must always wage war against "the adversary."[7]

Packer's apocalyptic portrait of the battle between Saints and scholars reveals how much has been at stake in twentieth-century debates over the role of academic scholarship in the evolution of Mormonism. It was no accident or surprise, then, that in the 1990s, the simmering tensions finally erupted over issues of academic freedom and tenure at Brigham Young University.[8] The affair offered some of the clearest evidence of the lingering rivalries between ecclesiastical and scholarly authority.

As a result, an official, tortuous eight-page policy statement on academic freedom now governs the faculty at BYU, whose motto, derived from scripture, is "The glory of God is intelligence." Implemented in 1993, the statement strains to uphold a vision of BYU as a university that is world-class and yet has the "institutional freedom" to be "openly and distinctively LDS."[9] Raising the specter of assimilation and institutional extinction in "an overwhelmingly secular modern academia," the statement aligns itself with once (and sometimes still) bitter enemies—conservative Catholics and evangelical Protestants—in raising concerns about a secularist turn in American higher education.[10] It affirms "the individual's freedom to ask genuine, even difficult questions" in an environment of "untrammeled inquiry," but it cites J. Reuben Clark Jr. with approval and states that the expected "faculty posture is one of loyalty."[11] It adds that academic freedom at BYU cannot include the freedom to "harm . . . the University mission or the Church." Specifically, faculty ought not engage in "expression with students or in public that:

- contradicts or opposes, rather than analyzes or discusses, fundamental Church doctrine or policy;
- deliberately attacks or derides the Church or its general leaders; or
- violates the Honor Code because the expression is dishonest, illegal, unchaste, profane, or unduly disrespectful of others."[12]

The controversy reflects an ambivalence within Mormonism—now one hundred and fifty years old—about the American university. Hospitable to Mormon principles of intelligence, freedom, and growth, the American university has offered a relatively "safe space" to Mormons beyond their cultural borders. Yet the university has also rivaled the church in its power to form and transform individual consciousness and identity, fostering commitments and loyalties that can extend beyond the church.[13] Perhaps most important, the American university has maintained its position as a national (and now global) arbiter of intellectual and cultural achievement.[14] This matters as much to Mormons today as it did a century and a half ago.[15] The BYU of the twenty-first century represents the legacy of a very complicated Mormon and American past.

With a policy like BYU's statement on academic freedom firmly in place, one can expect the cultural and intellectual firestorms of twenty-first-century Mormonism to match, and even surpass, those of the twentieth. Indeed, Mormonism's long institutional adolescence—its struggle to come into its own in a diverse, often hostile world—continues. Since World War II alone, the church has experienced explosive international growth, and internal theological and intellectual conflicts have multiplied. As the church's reach and influence expand, its encounters and dialogues with diverse interlocutors grow increasingly complex. As one might predict, the church has at times struggled to maintain a clear, steady voice in a turbulent culture that often forcefully challenges its claims.

In the arena of race, for example, the church has disavowed its past racism, but questions remain about whether LDS authorities will go so far today as to say that past leaders, like Brigham Young, had confused their own racism with God's will.[16] In the arenas of gender and authority, Jean Stevens (in 2013) became the first woman to lead a prayer during the church's semiannual General Conference, while in 2014 Kate Kelly was excommunicated for persistently advocating for the ordination of women.[17] In the area of sexuality, the church's 2015 endorsement of antidiscrimination legislation in Utah paralleled its opposition to same-sex marriage when the issue came before the Supreme Court.[18]

In such a climate, Mormonism's dormant feminist tradition has been slow to reemerge, and courageous intellectual and spiritual reflection about the church's history has been rare, notwithstanding a recent admission by a member of the First Presidency that church leaders have indeed "made mistakes" in the past.[19] Accordingly, after a century and a half of immersion in American higher education, genuine reconciliation between Mormon scholars and the Mormon hierarchy seems destined to elude the church until the millennium, indefinitely postponed, comes at last.

Appendices

Appendices A–E represent five ways of understanding broad patterns in Mormon academic migration from the 1860s through the 1930s. By themselves, they do not tell the full story of Mormon academic migration in the late nineteenth and early twentieth centuries, nor do they represent the full extent of my research, but they have helped frame my narrative and may offer scholars opportunities for further research. They derive from my examination of relevant archives and university alumni directories, histories of the professions and higher education in Utah, Mormon periodicals, the Journal History of the Church of Jesus Christ of Latter-day Saints, and the published and unpublished correspondence of Mormons who pursued higher education beyond the borders of the Intermountain West.

Appendix A

Mormons Studying "Abroad" before the Woodruff Manifesto (1890)

Name	Birthplace/Childhood	School, Dates, Degree	Subsequent Career
Elvira S. Barney (1832–1909)	Chautauqua Co. NY, Nauvoo IL, Salt Lake City (hereafter SLC) by 1848	Wheaton Coll. 1864–66, Woman's Medical Coll. 1879–80, Univ. of Michigan 1880–81 nongrad. Add'l training in WI, MD, and PA ca. 1882	SLC doctor
Heber J. Richards (1840–1919)	England; Nauvoo IL, SLC	Bellevue Hospital Medical Coll. 1867–MD ca. 1869	SLC, Provo UT doctor
Willard Young (1852–1936)	SLC	West Point 1871–grad 1875	Pres. of Latter-day Saints' Univ., General Church Board of Education member
Seymour B. Young (1837–1924)	Kirtland OH, SLC	Coll. of Physicians and Surgeons, NYC 1872–73, 1873–MD 1874	SLC doctor; LDS General Authority (First Council of Seventies)
Joseph S. Richards	SLC (brother of Heber J. Richards)	Bellevue Hospital Medical Coll. 1873–MD 1875	SLC doctor
H. C. Longmore	Nephi UT	Coll. of Physicians and Surgeons, Keokuk IA ca. 1873–MD ca. 1877	
LeGrand Young (1859–1921)	SLC	Univ. of Michigan Law School 1873–LLB 1874	SLC lawyer, judge

Name	Birthplace/Childhood	School, Dates, Degree	Subsequent Career
Romania Pratt [Penrose] (1839–1932)	IN, Nauvoo IL, IA, SLC by 1855	Woman's Medical Coll. early 1874–spring 1875, fall 1875–MD 1877; Bellevue Hospital Medical Coll. summer 1874; New York Eye and Ear Infirmary late 1873, 1881–82	SLC doctor
Feramorz L. Young (1858–81)	SLC	U.S. Naval Academy 1874–resigned 1876; Rensselaer Polytech. Inst. 1877–grad 1879	Died 1881 on church mission to Mexico
Ellis R. Shipp (1847–1939)	Davis Co. IA; Battle Creek (Pleasant Grove) UT by 1852	Woman's Medical Coll. 1875–MD 1878; postgrad work Univ. of Michigan 1892–93	SLC doctor, founder of School of Nursing and Obstetrics; member of Relief Society and YLMIA General Boards
Joseph D. C. Young (1855–1938)	SLC	Rensselaer Polytech. Inst. 1875–grad 1879	SLC architect
William G. Sharp (1857–1919)		Rensselaer Polytech. Inst. 1875–grad 1879	Superintendent, Pleasant Valley Coal Co.; pres., U.S. Smelting and Refining Co.
Alfales Young (1853–1920)	SLC	Univ. of Michigan Law 1875–LLB 1877	SLC lawyer, editor

(continued)

Name	Birthplace/Childhood	School, Dates, Degree	Subsequent Career
Arthur Bruce Taylor (b. 1853)	SLC	Univ. of Michigan Law 1875–LLB 1877	Little known—moved to Oregon shortly after returning to Utah
John T. Caine Jr. (b. 1854)	SLC	Cornell 1876–77 (returned because of illness)	Territorial congressional rep.; history professor, Ag. Coll. of Utah
Maggie C. Shipp [Roberts] (d. 1926)		Woman's Medical Coll., 1875, 1877–MD 1883	SLC doctor, head of Relief Society's nursing school
Richard W. Young (1858–1919)	SLC	West Point 1878–grad 1882; Columbia Law School 1882–LLB 1884	SLC lawyer; LDS stake pres.; SLC Board of Education; Univ. of Utah regent, BYU and BYC trustee
Martha P. Hughes [Cannon] (1857–1932)	Wales; SLC by 1861	Univ. of Michigan 1878–MD 1881; Univ. of Pennsylvania 1881–BS 1882 (Medicine); National School of Elocution and Oratory, Philadelphia, bachelor's in oratory 1882	SLC doctor; first female state senator in U.S.; California doctor
Samuel R. Thurman (1850–1941)	Larue County KY, UT by 1870	Univ. of Michigan Law LLB 1880	SLC, Provo UT lawyer; Utah territorial legislature; appointed U.S. attorney for Utah territory by Pres. Cleveland; member of 1895 Constitutional Convention

Name	Birthplace/Childhood	School, Dates, Degree	Subsequent Career
Milford Bard Shipp (1836–1918)	Edinburg IN	Jefferson Medical Coll. 1880–MD 1882	LDS Missionary, publishes *The Sanitarian* with Ellis and Maggie Shipp 1888–91
John W. "Will" Clawson (1858–1936)	SLC	National Acad. of Design (NYC) 1881–84; Add'l art study in Europe 1891–96	SLC artist, first secretary of Society of Utah Artists; artist in SF, LA, NYC before retiring in SLC
James E. Talmage (1862–1933)	England; SLC by 1876	Lehigh Univ. 1882–83, BS 1891; The Johns Hopkins Univ. 1883–84; Wesleyan Univ. PhD (nonres. work 1896)	BYA and Univ. of Utah professor; pres. of Univ. of Utah; LDS apostle
James H. Moyle (1858–1946)	SLC	Univ. of Michigan 1882–83, Law LLB 1885	SLC lawyer, U.S. senator, assistant sec. of Treasury under Pres. Wilson; pres. of Eastern States Mission 1929–
Henry Rolapp (1860–1936)	Denmark; SLC by 1880	Univ. of Michigan Law LLB 1884	Ogden UT lawyer, 2nd district judge; Univ. of Utah regent; LDS Sunday School General Board 30 years; pres. Eastern States Mission 1927–29

(continued)

Name	Birthplace/Childhood	School, Dates, Degree	Subsequent Career
David Evans	Provo UT	Univ. of Michigan Law 1883–84, nongrad	U.S. attorney, Utah Territory 1887–92
Milton H. Hardy (1844–1905)	Groveland MA, SLC	NYU Medical School 1883–MD 1885	SLC doctor, Provo UT hospital administrator
George Q. Coray (1857–1929)	Provo UT	Cornell 1883–86, nongrad	Univ. of Utah sociology and anthropology professor; Columbia 1903–AM 1904
Joseph M. Romney		Cornell BS 1886	SLC publisher (briefly w/ Coray)
Parley P. Pratt Jr.	Kirtland OH; then SLC	New York School of Pharmacy ca. 1884–expected graduation 1885	Husband of Romania Pratt before she divorced him and married Apostle Charles Penrose
Hiram S. Laney		Univ. of Michigan Law LLB 1885	
Waldemar Van Cott (b. 1859)	SLC	Univ. of Michigan Law LLB 1885	SLC lawyer; Univ. of Utah regent
Benjamin W. Driggs (1858–1930)	Pleasant Grove UT	Univ. of Michigan Law 1884–LLB 1886	Provo UT, SLC, and Driggs ID lawyer
William Henry King (1863–1949)	Fillmore UT	Univ. of Michigan Law LLB 1887	Provo UT, SLC lawyer; U.S. congressman, U.S. senator

Name	Birthplace/Childhood	School, Dates, Degree	Subsequent Career
Thomas Adams		Univ. of Michigan Law LLB 1887	
Benjamin Cluff Jr. (1858–1948)	Provo UT	Univ. of Michigan College 1887–BS 1890, 1893–MS 1894	Pres. of Brigham Young Academy; manager, Utah–Mexico Rubber Plantation
John A. Bagley		Univ. of Michigan Law 1887–LLB 1888	Montpelier ID lawyer
Noble Warrum		Univ. of Michigan Law 1887–88, nongrad	Utah historian, author of *Utah Since Statehood* (1919)
Emma Atkin		Woman's Medical Coll. MD by 1887	Juab County UT doctor
Charles H. Hart (1866–1934)	Bear Lake ID	Univ. of Michigan College 1887–grad 1889	Logan UT lawyer, 1st distr. judge; LDS general authority (First Council of the Seventy)
Oscar W. Moyle (b. 1868)	SLC	Univ. of Michigan College 1888–PhB 1890, LLB 1892	SLC lawyer, pres. of SLC Board of Education
Thomas D. Lewis (b. 1865)	SLC	Univ. of Michigan College 1888–89, Law LLB 1891	Utah state senator, 3rd distr. judge
Julia A. MacDonald [Place]		Univ. of Michigan Medicine 1888–91, nongrad	Utah doctor, writer

(continued)

Name	Birthplace/Childhood	School, Dates, Degree	Subsequent Career
Daniel B. H. Richards (b. 1853)	Mill Creek UT	Univ. of Michigan Law 1888–LLB 1890, LLM 1891	Univ. of Geneva LLD 1894; SLC lawyer; LDS mission
Orrice Abram Murdock (b. 1866)		Univ. of Michigan Law 1888–LLB 1890	Beaver UT lawyer, 5th distr. judge
Alfred Osmond (1862–1938)		Univ. of Michigan Law 1888–89	Harvard AB 1903, Columbia AM 1921; BYU English professor
John Mousley Cannon (1856–1917)	St. George UT	Univ. of Michigan Law 1888–LLB 1890	SLC lawyer
George Quayle Rich		Univ. of Michigan Law 1888–LLB 1890	
B. Howell Jones (1869–1939)	Box Elder County UT	Univ. of Michigan Law 1888–89, nongrad	Brigham City UT lawyer, newspaper publisher; Republican party leader after statehood
Ferdinand Ericksen (1863–1927)	Mt. Pleasant UT	Univ. of Michigan Law 1889–90, nongrad	Mt. Pleasant UT, SLC lawyer; 7th distr. judge

Appendix B

Mormons at the University of Michigan, 1874–1913

Name	Birthplace	School, Dates, Degree	Subsequent Career
LeGrand Young (1849–1921)	Salt Lake City (hereafter SLC)	Law LLB 1874	SLC lawyer
Alfales Young (1853–1920)	SLC	Law 1875–LLB 1877	SLC lawyer, journalist
Arthur Bruce Taylor		Law LLB 1877	Little known—moved to Oregon shortly after returning to Utah
Dr. Martha Hughes [Cannon] (1857–1932)	Wales; SLC by 1860	Medicine 1878–MD 1880	SLC doctor, state senator
Samuel R. Thurman (b. 1850)	Larue County KY, Utah by 1870	Law LLB 1890	SLC, Provo UT lawyer; Utah territorial legislature; appointed U.S. attorney for Utah territory by Pres. Cleveland; member of 1895 Constitutional Convention
Elvira S. Barney (1832–1909)	Chautauqua Co. NY, Nauvoo IL, SLC by 1848	Medicine 1880–81 nongrad	SLC doctor
James H. Moyle (1858–1946)	SLC	College 1882–83, Law LLB 1885	SLC lawyer, U.S. senator, assistant sec. of Treasury under President Wilson; pres. Eastern States Mission 1929–

Name	Birthplace	School, Dates, Degree	Subsequent Career
Henry Rolapp (1860–1936)	Denmark; to SLC 1880	Law LLB 1884	Ogden UT lawyer, 2nd district judge; Univ. of Utah regent; LDS Sunday School General Board 30 years; pres. of Eastern States Mission 1927–29
David Evans	Provo UT	Law 1883–84 nongrad	U.S. attorney, Utah Territory 1887–92
Hiram S. Laney		Law LLB 1885	
Waldemar Van Cott (b. 1859)	SLC	Law LLB 1885	SLC lawyer, Univ. of Utah regent
Benjamin W. Driggs (1858–1930)	Pleasant Grove UT	Law 1884–LLB 1886	Provo UT, SLC, and Driggs ID lawyer
William Henry King (1863–1949)	Fillmore UT	Law LLB 1887	Provo UT, SLC lawyer; U.S. congressman, U.S. senator
Thomas Adams		Law LLB 1887	
"Cactus"		Medicine 1887–MD 1889	
Benjamin Cluff Jr. (1858–1948)	Provo UT	College 1887–BS 1890, 1893–MS 1894	Brigham Young Academy president; manager, Utah–Mexico Rubber Plantation
John A. Bagley		Law 1887–LLB 1888	Montpelier ID lawyer

(continued)

Name	Birthplace	School, Dates, Degree	Subsequent Career
Noble Warrum		Law 1887–88 nongrad	
Charles H. Hart (1866–1934)	Bear Lake ID	Law 1887–LLB 1889	Logan UT lawyer, 1st distr. judge; LDS General Authority (First Council of the Seventy)
Alfred Osmond (1862–1938)		Law 1888–89 nongrad	Harvard AB 1903, Columbia AM 1921, BYU English professor
Oscar W. Moyle (b. 1868)	SLC	College 1888–PhB 1890, LLB 1892	SLC lawyer; pres. SLC Board of Education
Thomas D. Lewis (b. 1865)	SLC	College 1888–89, Law LLB 1891	Utah state senator, 3rd district judge; Univ. of Utah lecturer in law 1907–21
Julia A. MacDonald [Place]		Medicine 1888–91 nongrad	Utah doctor, writer
Daniel Brigham Hill Richards (b. 1853)	Mill Creek UT	Law 1888–LLB 1890, LLM 1891	Univ. of Geneva LLD 1894; SLC lawyer
Orrice Abram Murdock (b. 1866)		Law 1888–LLB 1890	Beaver UT lawyer, 5th distr. judge
John Mousley Cannon (1856–1917)	St. George UT	Law 1888–LLB 1890	SLC lawyer
George Quayle Rich		Law 1888–LLB 1890	

Name	Birthplace	School, Dates, Degree	Subsequent Career
B. Howell Jones (1869–1939)	Box Elder County UT	Law 1888–89 nongrad	Brigham City UT lawyer, newspaper publisher; Republican party leader after statehood
Ferdinand Ericksen (1863–1927)	Mt. Pleasant UT	Law 1889–90 nongrad	Mt. Pleasant UT, SLC lawyer; 7th distr. judge
Garrie van Schoonhoven (b. ca. 1870)		Pharmacy 1890–PhC 1891	Denver CO news agent with Moffatt RR
Mary van Schoonhoven (1844–1908)	Nauvoo IL, to SLC ca. 1854	Homeopathic Med. 1890–grad 1891	SLC doctor
Joseph F. Merrill (1868–1952)	Richmond UT	College 1889–BS 1893	Univ. of Utah engineering professor; LDS commissioner of education 1928–33; pres. European Mission 1933–
Daniel Harrington (1860–1943)	American Fork UT	Law 1890–LLB 1891	SLC lawyer, judge
Willard Weston Maughan (1854–1924)	Tooele UT	Law LLB 1891	
Libbie Almira Merrill [Hendricks]		College 1890–91 nongrad	

(continued)

Name	Birthplace	School, Dates, Degree	Subsequent Career
Hiram Alma Smith (b. 1865)	Draper UT	Law 1890–LLB 1892	SLC lawyer
Samuel White Stewart (1867–1955)	Draper UT	Law at least 1890–LLB 1892	SLC lawyer, 3rd distr. judge
Isaac John Stewart (1855–1911)	Salt Lake County UT	Law at least 1890–LLB 1892	Richfield UT and Rexburg ID lawyer
Richard A. Shipp (b. 1869)	SLC	College at least 1890–BL 1893 Law LLB 1893	Harvard AM 1894; SLC, in real estate
Samuel A. King (b. 1868)	Fillmore UT	Law LLB 1893	Provo, SLC lawyer
Charles B. Stewart	Draper UT	Law LLB 1893	SLC lawyer
Alice Louise Reynolds (1873–1938)	SLC	College 1892–94 nongrad	BYA/BYU English professor; Relief Society General Board
Robert Harris		Law 1892–93 nongrad	With Gunnison Valley Sugar Co.
Emil Isgreen		Law 1893–94 nongrad	Rush Medical College MD 1897
Ezra Clark Robinson (b. 1872)	Farmington UT	Law/College 1893–94 nongrad	Bountiful UT lawyer
George Halverson (b. 1868)	Weber County UT	Law LLB 1894	Ogden UT lawyer, 3rd distr. DA
Joseph Alma Harris		Law LLB 1894	

Name	Birthplace	School, Dates, Degree	Subsequent Career
Hyrum Smith Harris (1860–1937)		Law LLB 1894	
Nathan Harris (1864–1936)	Harrisville UT	Law 1892–LLB 1894	Ogden UT lawyer, 2nd distr. judge
James H. McDonald (b. 1866)	Heber City UT	Law LLB 1894	Heber City UT lawyer; 4th distr. DA
Joseph E. Page (d. 1904)		Law LLB 1894	
James Z. Stewart Jr. (1873–1915)	Draper UT	Law LLB 1894	Logan UT lawyer
Joseph McGregor		Law LLB 1894	Illinois Medical Coll. MD 1905; Beaver UT physician and surgeon
Richard R. Lyman (1870–1963)	Fillmore UT	College 1892–BS 1895	Cornell PhD 1905; Univ. of Utah engineering professor; LDS apostle; excommunicated 1943, rebaptized 1954
Josiah E. Hickman (1862–1937)	Salem UT	College 1892–BL 1895	BYA education, psychology professor; Columbia AM 1907; principal, Beaver Branch of BYU and Murdock Academy; BYC education prof.; Logan UT insurance salesman

(continued)

Name	Birthplace	School, Dates, Degree	Subsequent Career
Edwin S. Hinckley (1868–1929)	Fillmore UT	College BL 1895	BYU geology, education professor; supt. of State Industrial School, Ogden UT
Robert Anderson (b. 1871)	Moroni UT	Law LLB 1895, LLM 1896	Mt. Pleasant UT, Provo UT lawyer
James L. Brown (1860–1921)	Lehi UT	College 1893–BS 1897	BYU physical sciences, elementary educ. professor
Arthur Dalley		College 1894–97 nongrad	Aberdeen ID farmer
Jedediah Foss Woolley		College BL 1897	SLC businessman
Henry N. Hayes (b. 1867)	Pleasant Grove UT	Law LLB 1897	Sevier County UT supt. of schools
Grant C. Bagley (1872–1916)	Cottonwood UT	Law LLB 1897	Provo UT lawyer, Masonic Order
Joseph Erickson (1864–1948)	Norway; to Utah 1866	Law LLB 1898	Richfield UT lawyer, 6th distr. judge
Ephraim Hanson (1872–1952)	Ephraim UT	Law LLB 1898	Ephraim UT, SLC lawyer; Utah Supr. Ct. justice
James A. Melville (1870–1942)	Fillmore UT	Law LLB 1898	Millard County UT county attorney; 5th distr. judge; SLC lawyer
Henry C. Lund (b. 1873)	Ephraim UT	Law LLB 1899	SLC lawyer
Henry S. Tanner (b. 1869)	Payson UT	Law LLB 1899	SLC lawyer

Name	Birthplace	School, Dates, Degree	Subsequent Career
O. P. Soule (b. 1872)	Hooper UT	Law LLB 1899	SLC lawyer
A. B. Christenson (1869–1931)	Gunnison UT	College ca. 1897–AB 1901	Principal of Beaver Branch of BYU and Ricks Academy, Rexburg ID
William F. Ward	Parowan UT	College 1897–1900 nongrad	BYU math professor
Jesse R. S. Budge (1878–1967)	Paris ID	Law 1897–LLB 1900	Bear Lake County ID prosecuting attorney; SLC, Pocatello ID lawyer
Culbert L. Olson (1876–1962)	Fillmore UT	Law 1899–1900 nongrad	Columbian Univ. (now George Washington Univ.) LLB 1901; SLC lawyer
Peter Carlos Evans (1870–1941)	Coalville UT	Law LLB 1900	SLC lawyer, 3rd distr. judge
William Rydalch	Grantsville UT	Law LLB 1900	Provo UT lawyer
Bernard J. Stewart (b. 1873)	Draper UT	Law LLB 1900	SLC lawyer
Mathoniah Thomas (b. 1872)	South Wales; to Utah 1878	Law LLB 1900	SLC lawyer; trustee and lecturer, Utah Agricultural College of Utah; Salt Lake City Board of Education
Elias Hyrum Beckstrand	Meadow UT	College BS 1900	Cornell MME 1901; Univ. of Utah engineering professor

(continued)

Name	Birthplace	School, Dates, Degree	Subsequent Career
James Ingebretsen (b. 1876)	Norway; to Utah 1891	Law LLB 1901	SLC lawyer
Ashby Snow (b. 1867)	St. George UT	Law LLB 1901	SLC lawyer
J. W. Stringfellow	SLC	Law LLB 1901	SLC lawyer
Annie Pike [Greenwood]		College 1901–02 nongrad	Briefly taught at Agricultural College of Utah
Willard Hanson (b. 1874)	Fillmore UT	Law LLB 1902	SLC lawyer; Masonic Order
Alonzo Blair Irvine (b. 1875)	SLC	Law LLB 1902	SLC lawyer
Daniel H. Thomas (b. 1874)	Franklin ID	Law LLB 1902	Provo UT, SLC lawyer
Stephen L. Richards (1879–1959)	Mendon UT	Law 1902–03 nongrad	University of Chicago LLB 1904; SLC lawyer; LDS apostle
John Charles Davis (1878–1951)	Willard UT	Law LLB 1904	Malad ID and Ogden UT lawyer
Nathaniel H. Tanner (b. 1876)	Payson UT	Law LLB 1904	SLC lawyer; Salt Lake County deputy county clerk; City Judge
Don Byron Colton (1876–1952)		Law LLB 1905	Vernal UT lawyer
Benjamin Carlos Call (1877–1962)	Willard UT	Law 1904–05 nongrad	Brigham City UT lawyer

Name	Birthplace	School, Dates, Degree	Subsequent Career
Francis W. Kirkham (1877–1972)	Lehi UT	College AB 1906	Univ. of Utah LLB 1913; Berkeley PhD 1931; BYU history professor; director of National Child Welfare Association
Erastus D. Woolley (b. 1880)	St. George UT	Law LLB 1906	Manti UT lawyer
Claude T. Barnes (b. 1884)	Kaysville UT	Law 1906–07 nongrad	SLC lawyer; Masonic Order
George B. Hancock (b. 1877)	Pine Valley UT	Law LLB 1907	SLC lawyer
Gustave A. Iverson (1871–1945)	Norway; to UT 1875	Law LLB 1907	Price UT lawyer; Carbon UT stake president; Utah state senator 1911–15, UT asst. state attorney general 1915–18; pres. of LDS Eastern States Mission
Royal Eccles (1884–1963)	Ogden UT	Law LLB 1908	Ogden UT lawyer
Fred Waldo Crockett (1876–1938)	Logan UT	Law LLB 1908	Logan UT lawyer; pres. of Ogden, Lewiston, & Northern Railroad Company
Dr. Clarence Snow	St. George UT	Medicine MD 1908	Previous AB degree from Harvard; SLC doctor; SLC Board of Education
William J. Lowe (1881–1948)	Willard UT	Law LLB 1909	Brigham City, Ogden UT lawyer
William E. Davis (b. 1883)	Harrisville UT	Law LLB 1910	Brigham City UT lawyer
George P. Parker (b. 1884)	American Fork UT	Law LLB 1911	Provo UT lawyer

Appendix C

Mormons at Harvard, 1891–1913

Name	Birthplace	School, Dates, Degree	Subsequent Career
Joseph M. Tanner (1859–1927)	Payson UT, in Provo UT by age 2	Law 1891–1894 nongrad	Pres. of Brigham Young College and Agricultural Coll. of Utah; supt. of LDS Church Schools
John A. Widtsoe (1872–1952)	Norway, in Logan UT by 1883	Lawrence Scientific School 1891–SB 1894	1900 PhD Goettingen; pres. of Agricultural Coll. of Utah and Univ. of Utah; LDS apostle; LDS church commissioner of education
George L. Swendsen	Richmond UT	Lawrence Scientific School 1891–SB 1894	Agricultural Coll. of Utah civil engineering professor; Utah, Boise ID, Fresno CA civil engineer
George Thomas (1866–1951)	Hyde Park UT, Benson UT	College 1892–AB 1896, 1900–AM 1901	1903 PhD Friedrich Wilhelm Univ, Halle; pres. of Univ. of Utah
Moses C. Davis (1869–1946)	Malad ID	College 1892–94 nongrad	Brigham Young Academy professor (1895–98); Provo UT lawyer
Susa Young Gates (1856–1933)	SLC	Summer School 1892	LDS Relief Society president; BYU, Agricultural Coll. of Utah trustee
Leah Dunford [Widtsoe] (1874–1965)	SLC	Summer School 1893	Student in domestic science at Pratt Institute 1896–97; founder of Utah League of Women Voters; co-author with husband, John A. Widtsoe, of *The Word of Wisdom; a Modern Interpretation* (1937)

Name	Birthplace	School, Dates, Degree	Subsequent Career
Mae Taylor [Nystrom] (1871–1959)		Summer School 1893	
Belle Salmon [Ross] (1867–1947)		Summer School 1893	Educator associated with Utah schools for the deaf and blind
Kate Thomas (1871–1950)	SLC	Summer School 1893	NYC writer; Utah writer, patron of arts and theater
Arthur F. S. Thomas	SLC	Lawrence Scientific School, 1893–94, College 1894–96, AB conferred 1897	Washington, DC lawyer
Caleb Tanner (1868–1960)	Provo UT	Lawrence Scientific School 1891–95, SB earned 1894	Utah state engineer
Clarence Snow	St. George UT	Lawrence Scientific School 1893–SB 1897	Agricultural Coll. of Utah math and physics professor; 1908 MD Univ. of Michigan; SLC doctor; pres. of Univ. of Utah Board of Regents
Richard A. Shipp (b. 1869)	SLC	Graduate School 1893–AM 1894	SLC attorney, in real estate
Hyrum A. Anderson		Medical School 1893–MD 1896	BYU professor; Rigby ID doctor

(continued)

Name	Birthplace	School, Dates, Degree	Subsequent Career
Levi Edgar Young (1874–1963)	SLC	College 1898–1899 nongrad	Univ. of Utah professor; 1910 AM Columbia Univ.; LDS general authority (First Council of the Seventy)
Walter W. Little (b. 1876)	SLC	Law 1899–1902 nongrad	SLC, Los Angeles lawyer
Alfred Osmond (1862–1938)		College 1900–AB 1903	BYU English professor
J. W. Jensen		Lawrence Scientific School 1900–SB 1901	Agricultural Coll. of Utah civil engineering professor
Joseph Jenson (1867–1936)	St. Charles ID	Lawrence Scientific School 1901–SB 1902	Previously at MIT; Agricultural Coll. of Utah physics and mechanical engineering professor; Utah state engineer, Klamath Co. OR engineer
J. C. Thomas		Lawrence Scientific School 1901–SB 1903	Latter-day Saints' University, Agricultural Coll. of Utah chemistry professor
George B. Hendricks	Richmond UT	Graduate School 1903–1905, 1907–AM 1908	Agricultural Coll. of Utah economics, commerce professor
Freeman Tanner		Lawrence Scientific School 1903–1906, College 1906–1907 nongrad	Utah, Oregon civil engineer
Chester Snow		College 1903–AB 1906	BYU math and physics professor, government research in Chevy Chase MD

Name	Birthplace	School, Dates, Degree	Subsequent Career
Osborne J. P. Widtsoe (1877–1920)	Norway, in Logan UT by 1883	Graduate School 1904–AM 1905	LDSU, Univ. of Utah English professor
Isaac Blair Evans (b. 1885)	Ogden UT	College 1904–AB 1908, Law LLB 1913	SLC lawyer
LeGrand R. Humpherys		Lawrence Scientific School 1905–1906 nongrad	Agricultural Coll. of Utah engineering professor, administrator
Henry Peterson (1868–1957)	Huntsville UT	Graduate School 1905–1907, AM conferred 1906	LDSU, BYU, and Agricultural Coll. education and psychology professor
Christian Larsen		College 1903–1904, Graduate School 1905–AM 1906	LDSU, Agricultural Coll. of Utah modern languages professor
George Christian Jensen		Graduate School 1905–AM 1906	Agricultural Coll. of Utah modern languages professor
W. H. Chamberlin (1870–1921)	SLC	College 1906–1907, Graduate School 1916–1917	BYU, Univ. of Utah, Agricultural Coll. of Utah philosophy and theology professor
Christen Jensen		Graduate School 1907–AM 1908	1921 PhD Univ. of Chicago; pres. of Utah State Board of Education; BYU government, history, and economics professor; BYU dean of Graduate School

(continued)

Name	Birthplace	School, Dates, Degree	Subsequent Career
Franklin D. Daines		Graduate School 1908–1909, 1910–AM 1912	Agricultural Coll. of Utah history and political science professor
Lyman Martineau Jr. (b. 1886)	Logan UT	College AB 1909, Law LLB 1912	SLC, Los Angeles lawyer
Parley Erastus Peterson		Business 1909–1910 nongrad	Agricultural Coll. of Utah accounting teacher
Alma L. Merrill		Law 1909–LLB 1912	Pocatello ID lawyer
Alma N. Sorenson		Graduate School 1910–11, 1915–16, AM conferred 1917	Agricultural Coll. of Utah English professor
James M. Carlson (b. 1884)	SLC	Law LLB 1912	SLC lawyer
Asa Bullen		Law 1910–LLB 1913	Agricultural Coll. of Utah lecturer and instructor in law
Melvin C. Merrill		Graduate School 1912–AM 1913	PhD horticulture Washington Univ. (St. Louis); Agricultural Coll. of Utah, BYU horticulture professor; work with USDA in Washington DC
Waldemar Q. Van Cott	SLC	Law 1911–LLB 1914	SLC lawyer

Appendix D

Mormons at Columbia, 1882–1921

Name	Birthplace	School, Dates, Degree	Subsequent Career
Richard W. Young (1858–1919)	SLC	Law 1882–LLB 1884	SLC lawyer; LDS stake pres.; SLC Board of Education; BYU, Univ. of Utah trustee
James L. Gibson (b. 1873)	Kamas UT	1897–AM 1898	1903 AM Cambridge Univ.; Univ. of Utah dean of School of Arts and Sciences; 1921 PhD Univ. of Vienna
Milton Bennion (1870–1953)	Taylorsville UT	AM 1901	Univ. of Utah philosophy and education professor, dean; editor of *Utah Educational Review*
George Q. Coray (1857–1929)	Provo UT	1903–AM 1904	Univ. of Utah sociology and anthropology professor
J. Reuben Clark Jr. (1871–1961)	Grantsville UT	Law 1903–LLB 1906	Lawyer with U.S. State Dept.; U.S. ambassador to Mexico; member of LDS First Presidency
Aquila C. Nebeker		1903–EM (Mining Engineering) 1906	Prescott AZ engineer
Alfales B. Young		EM 1906	With International Smelting Co. in SLC
Gustavus E. Anderson		AM 1906	Lehi UT
Frederick J. Pack (1875–1938)	West Bountiful UT	1904–AM 1905, PhD 1906	Univ. of Utah geology professor; author of *Science and Faith in God* (1924)

Name	Birthplace	School, Dates, Degree	Subsequent Career
Susa Talmage (1879–1908)	Provo UT	Teachers Coll. 1904–06, 1907 nongrad	BYU Training School professor, died shortly after return from Columbia
Ella Larson Brown (1871–1962)	Pleasant Grove UT	Teachers Coll. 1905–06 nongrad	BYU Training School professor
Josiah Hickman (1862–1937)	Salem UT	1906–AM 1907	BYA education, psychology professor; Columbia AM 1907; principal, Beaver Branch of BYU; principal, Murdock Academy; BYC education professor; Logan UT insurance salesman
Ellis Shipp Musser	SLC	Teachers Coll. AM 1907	
Ida Smoot Dusenberry (1873–1955)	SLC	Teachers Coll. 1907–08 nongrad	BYU education professor; delegate to meetings of International Council of Women
Blanche Caine	Logan UT	Teachers Coll. ca. 1907–08 nongrad	
Lottie Harris		Teachers Coll. (one year before 1910) nongrad	BYU domestic science professor
Preston D. Richards (1881–1952)	Mendon UT	Law 1908–09 nongrad	1911 LLB Univ. of Chicago; assistant solicitor for U.S. Dept. of State; SLC law partnership with J. Reuben Clark Jr.

(continued)

Name	Birthplace	School, Dates, Degree	Subsequent Career
Levi E. Young (1874–1963)	SLC	AM 1910	Univ. of Utah history professor, LDS general authority (First Council of the Seventy)
Thomas A. Beal		AM 1910, Business MS 1919	Univ. of Utah dean of Business
Willard S. Langton		AM 1911	Logan UT (not known what field)
L. John Nuttall Jr. (1887–1944)	SLC	Teachers Coll BS 1911, AM 1912, PhD 1930	BYU, Univ. of Utah education professor, SLC superintendent of schools
Adam S. Bennion (1886–1958)	Taylorsville UT	1911–AM 1912	1923 PhD Berkeley (studied literature and educational administration); superintendent of LDS Church Schools
F. F. Hintze Jr. (1881–1973)	Big Cottonwood UT	ca. 1909–PhD 1913	Univ. of Utah geology professor
Albert C. Boyle (1880–1951)		Columbia AM 1910, PhD 1913	Columbia, Univ. of Wyoming geology professor; chief geologist for Union Pacific RR; Donated 10,000+ volumes to BYU science library named after him
Arthur V. Watkins (1886–1973)	Midway UT	Law 1910–LLB 1912	Utah lawyer, rancher, editor; U.S. senator
Warren A. Colton		Medicine MD 1913	Castle Point NY doctor
Joseph A. Geddes (b. 1884)		AM 1913, PhD 1924	Agricultural Coll. of Utah sociology professor

Name	Birthplace	School, Dates, Degree	Subsequent Career
Dean Brimhall	Provo UT	1913–AM 1915, PhD 1920	With Psychological Corporation in NYC
Jean Cox		Teachers Coll. BS 1915	Manti UT (not known what field)
Mary Anna Ward Hunt		Teachers Coll. AM 1915	St. George UT librarian
Niels K. Nielsen		Teachers Coll. AM 1917	Springville UT (not known what field)
Milton Hyrum Harris		AM 1917	Agricultural Coll. of Utah agricultural economics professor
Herond Sheranian (b. 1892)	Turkey; in Utah by age 10	Medicine 1917–18 nongrad	1920 PhD State University of New York; founder of Murray UT hospital
William G. Barton		AM 1918	In Ephraim UT (not known what field)
Newton E. Noyes		Teachers Coll. AM 1918	Ephraim UT school principal
Frederick R. Taylor		Medicine MD 1918	Provo UT doctor
Irene Tolton		AM 1921	Beaver UT (not known what field)
Alfred Osmond (1862–1938)		1920–AM 1921	BYU English professor
John C. Swenson (1869–1953)	Pleasant Grove UT, Springville UT	1920–AM 1921	BYU economics, sociology professor

Appendix E

Advanced Degrees Earned by Mormons in Religion, History, and the Social Sciences, 1920–1940

Name	School, Dates, Degree	Thesis
E. E. Ericksen (1882–1967)	Univ. of Chicago PhD Philosophy 1918	"The Psychological and Ethical Aspects of Mormon Group Life"
Andrew L. Neff (1878–1936)	Berkeley PhD History 1918	"The Mormon Migration to Utah, 1830–1947"
Dean Brimhall (1886–1972)	Columbia Univ. PhD Psychology 1920	"Family Resemblances among American Men of Science"
Kimball Young (1893–1972)	Univ. of Chicago AM Sociology 1918; Stanford Univ. PhD Psychology 1921	"A Sociological Study of a Disintegrated Neighborhood" (1918); "Mental Differences in Certain Immigrant Groups; Psychological Tests of South Europeans in Typical California Schools with Bearing on the Educational Policy and on the Problems of Racial Contacts in This Country" (1921)
Arthur L. Beeley (b. 1890)	Univ. of Chicago AM Social Psychology 1918, PhD 1925	"The Bail System in Chicago"
Christen Jensen (1881–1961)	Univ. of Chicago PhD History 1921	"The Pardoning Power in the American States"
Adam S. Bennion (1886–1958)	Berkeley PhD Literature 1923	"An Objective Determination of Materials for a Course of Study in Biblical Literature"
LeRoy Hafen (b. 1893)	Berkeley PhD History 1923	"The Overland Mail to the Pacific Coast, 1848–1869, a Pioneer for Settlement, the Precursor of Railroad"
William James Snow (1869–1947)	Berkeley PhD History 1923	"The Great Basin before the Coming of the Mormons"
Joseph A. Geddes (b. 1884)	Columbia Univ. PhD Sociology 1924	"The United Order among the Mormons (Missouri Phase)"
Leland Creer (b. 1895)	Berkeley PhD History 1926	"Utah and the Nation, 1846–1861"

Name	School, Dates, Degree	Thesis
Thomas C. Romney (b. 1876)	Berkeley AM History 1924, PhD 1929	"The State of Deseret" (1924 and 1929)
Lowry Nelson (b. 1893)	Univ. of Wisconsin PhD Sociology 1929	"The Mormon Village: A Study in Social Origins"
Nels Anderson (1889–1986)	Univ. of Chicago AM Sociology 1925, NYU PhD 1930	"The Hobo: The Sociology of the Homeless Man" (published 1923, accepted for master's degree 1925)
Joel E. Ricks (1889–1974)	Univ. of Chicago AM History 1920, PhD 1930	"The Early Land System of Utah, 1847–1870" (1920); "Forms and Methods of Early Mormon Settlement in Utah and the Surrounding Region, 1847–1877" (1930)
T. Lynn Smith (1903–76)	Univ. of Minnesota PhD Sociology 1932	"A Sociological Analysis of Some of the Aspects of Rural Religious Culture as Shown by Mormonism" (1929 MA Thesis)
Milton R. Hunter (b. 1902)	Berkeley PhD History 1935	"Brigham Young the Colonizer"
Sidney B. Sperry (1895–1977)	Univ. of Chicago Divinity AM 1926, PhD 1931	"The Text of Isaiah in the Book of Mormon" (1926); "The Scholia of Bar Hebraeus to the Books of Kings" (1931)
George S. Tanner (1897–1992)	Univ. of Chicago Divinity AM 1931	"The Religious Environment in Which Mormonism Arose"
Lowell Bennion (b. 1908)	Univ. of Strasbourg PhD Sociology 1933	"Max Weber's Methodology"
Russel B. Swensen (b. 1902)	Univ. of Chicago Divinity AM 1931, PhD 1934	"New Testament Sources of the Eschatology of the Church of Latter Day Saints" (1931); "The Rise of the Sects as an Aspect of Religious Experience" (1934)
Daryl Chase (1901–84)	Univ. of Chicago Divinity AM 1931, PhD 1936	"Sidney Rigdon—Early Mormon" (1931); "The Early Shakers, an Experiment in Religious Communism" (1936)

(continued)

Name	School, Dates, Degree	Thesis
T. Edgar Lyon (1903–78)	Univ. of Chicago Divinity AM 1932	"Orson Pratt, Early Mormon Leader"
Carl J. Furr (b. 1903)	Univ. of Chicago Divinity PhD humanities division 1937 (began 1931)	"The Religious Philosophy of Brigham Young"
Waldemer P. Read	Univ. of Chicago AM Humanities Division 1933, PhD 1947	"Practical Value as a Criterion of Truth in the Philosophy of William James" (1933); "John Dewey's Conception of Intelligent Social Action" (1947)
Heber C. Snell (1883–1974)	Univ. of Chicago Divinity PhD 1940 (began 1932)	"The Background and Study of the Teaching-of-Jesus Literature in America"
Vernon F. Larsen (1906–)	Univ. of Chicago Divinity PhD 1942 (began 1933)	"Development of a Religious Inventory for a Specific Study in Higher Education"
Wesley P. Lloyd (1904–77)	Univ. of Chicago Divinity PhD 1937	"The Rise and Development of Lay Leadership in the Latter-day Saint Movement"
Therald N. Jensen (1908–)	Univ. of Chicago Divinity PhD 1938	"The Mormon Theory of Church and State"
Anthon S. Cannon (1906–76)	Univ. of Chicago Divinity PhD 1938	"A Socio-Psychological Interpretation of Religious Vocation"
John C. Moffitt (b. 1896)	Univ. of Chicago PhD History 1940	"The Development of Centralizing Tendencies in Educational Organization and Administration in Utah"
Harold T. Christensen (b. 1909)	Univ. of Wisconsin PhD Sociology 1941 (enrolled 1938–40)	"Population Pressure among Wisconsin Farmers"
Asahel D. Woodruff (b. 1904)	Univ. of Chicago PhD Sociology 1941	"A Study of Directive Factors in Individual Behavior"

Notes

Introduction

1. The (debatable) claim that Mormons, as late as 1893, were "the most despised large group" in America is Martin Marty's. Marty, *Modern American Religion, Volume 1*, 301. Some notable scholarship on the historical evolution of Mormonism includes: Hansen, *Mormonism and the American Experience*; Shipps, *Mormonism*; Alexander, *Mormonism in Transition*; Barlow, "Shifting Ground"; and Yorgason, *Transformation*. The late Leonard J. Arrington characterized this process of evolution perhaps too charitably, playing down strong elements of social control, when he described the church as handling its historical moments of crisis with "minimal adjustment and pragmatic compromise." Arrington, "Crisis in Identity," 169.

2. On nineteenth-century persecution and migration as crucibles for the formation of Mormon identity and peoplehood, see Shipps, *Mormonism*. On Mormonism's distinctive conceptions of apostasy, see Wilcox and Young, *Standing Apart*.

3. Judge James B. McKean, President Ulysses S. Grant's notoriously anti-Mormon appointee to the post of Utah's territorial chief justice, used the memorable phrase "polygamic theocracy" in 1871 when Brigham Young stood before him facing the charge of "lascivious cohabitation." Protestant preacher, politician, and social reformer Josiah Strong, in his widely read nativist book *Our Country*, wrote that "Mormon despotism . . . has its roots in the superstition of the people; and this Congress cannot legislate away. The people must be elevated and enlightened through . . . the preaching of the gospel." Strong, *Our Country*, 120.

4. In his history of the modern American university, Lawrence Veysey writes: "Talk about 'citizenship-training' as a purpose of the university was eventually to become cheap coin indeed, but in the nineteenth century such affirmations still possessed something of the power of innocence. . . . Higher education, it was hoped, might affect the conduct of public affairs in at least three ways. First, the university would make each of its graduates into a force for civic virtue. Second, it would train a group of political leaders who would take a knightly plunge into 'real life' and clean it up. Finally, through scientifically oriented scholarship, rational substitutes could be found for political procedures subject to personal influence." Veysey, *The Emergence of the American University*, 72.

5. On the ways that a kind of nonsectarianism, rather than full-fledged secularism, characterized the universities of the late nineteenth century, see Reuben, *The Making of the Modern University*.

6. See, for example, Hansen, *Mormonism and the American Experience*; Shipps, *Mormonism*; and Alexander, *Mormonism in Transition*.

7. For a history of Mormon polygamy, see Daynes, *More Wives Than One*. Edward Leo Lyman's *Political Deliverance* provides the best account of how post-Manifesto political realignment in Utah (shifting from mainly Mormon and anti-Mormon alliances to Democratic and Republican ones) strengthened the case for statehood. On the economic history of the Mormons, see Arrington, *Great Basin Kingdom*. For the major changes in religious practice, see Shipps, *Mormonism*.

8. Leone, *Roots of Modern Mormonism*.

9. Moore, *Religious Outsiders*, 42.

10. Shipps, *Mormonism*, 139.

11. Joseph F. Smith, "Philosophy and the Church Schools," 209.

12. Hatch, *The Democratization of American Christianity*, 5.

13. Book of Mormon, 2 Nephi 26:20. Hatch aptly describes the Book of Mormon as "a document of profound social protest." Hatch, *Democratization*, 116.

14. Ibid. 2 Nephi 9:29.

15. J. Reuben Clark Jr., "The Charted Course of the Church in Education," 251.

16. Dunford, "Students Leave Zion."

17. On the question and evolution of Mormon ethnicity, see, for example, Shipps, *Mormonism*, and Limerick, "Peace Initiative."

18. On the experiences of Progressive Era women with coeducation at American colleges and universities, see Lynn Gordon, "From Seminary to University."

19. For this fascinating episode from the history of Catholics in American higher education, see Mahoney, *Catholic Higher Education*.

20. See Klingenstein, *Jews in the American Academy*, and Levine, "Discrimination in College Admissions." Levine concludes, "In the 1920s and 1930s, American institutions of higher education engaged in egalitarian rhetoric, but their performance was a mockery of American ideals" (469).

21. On Mormons' evolving conceptions of race, see Mauss, *All Abraham's Children*, and Fluhman, *"A Peculiar People,"* 110–17. On evolving American conceptions of race, ethnicity, and whiteness in America, see Roediger, *Working Toward Whiteness*. For a comparative analysis of "group repulsion" and struggle in the history of American higher education in terms of class, race, gender, and ethnicity, see Wechsler, "An Academic Gresham's Law," as well as Wang, "Asian Americans in Higher Education," and MacDonald and García, "Historical Perspectives on Latino Access."

22. Tweed, *Crossing and Dwelling*, 13.

23. Bitton, *Guide to Mormon Diaries and Autobiographies*.

24. In using the term "intellectual genealogy," I am, of course, hinting at Mormons' own consuming devotional passion for genealogy. I am also, however,

drawing directly on the thought of Cornel West, whose book *The American Evasion of Philosophy: A Genealogy of Pragmatism* has had an enduring influence on my thinking about American intellectual history. There, he describes his work as a "social history of ideas" that "conceives of the intellectual sphere of history as distinct, unique, and personal sets of cultural practices intimately connected with concomitant developments in the larger society and culture." Cornel West, *The American Evasion of Philosophy,* 6.

25. In *The Great American University,* former Columbia provost Jonathan R. Cole makes an impassioned argument for taking bold, concerted action to preserve the historic, global "preeminence" of American universities. "Nothing less than the economic and social health of the nation is at stake," he writes, but he worries that "The dream of creating research universities that provide both access to economically disadvantaged students and world-class research may be fading with the choices taken by shortsighted state legislators." Cole, *The Great American University,* 471, 481.

Chapter One

1. *Doctrine and Covenants* 93:36, 90:15.

2. This sparse information about Dr. Barney's time at Wheaton comes from Crocheron, *Representative Women of Deseret,* 80. In the 1870s and 1880s, Elvira Stevens Barney would study at the Woman's Medical College and the University of Michigan, eventually earning an MD.

3. Brigham Young, "Intelligence, Etc.," in *Discourses of Brigham Young,* 7:283–84.

4. Brigham Young, "Diversity among Men as to their Capacity for Receiving Truth, &c," in *Discourses,* 8:160.

5. Brigham Young to Theodore W. Curtis, July 24, 1866. Arrington Papers, Brigham Young Letter Books, Series 9, Box 6, Folder 3.

6. In 1850, the general assembly of the provisional state of Deseret had provided for a "University of Deseret" in Salt Lake City, but financial troubles dogged that institution until its revival and reorganization in 1869. Deseret (the "t" is pronounced) is a word that comes from the Book of Mormon (Ether 2:3). It denotes "a honey bee," and it symbolized an industrious, close-knit society. (Before Utah became a territory in 1850, Mormons had proposed a massive state of Deseret that would have extended from western Colorado to the southern California coast. It would have included all of modern-day Utah, most of what is now Nevada and Arizona, and sections of what became New Mexico, Colorado, Wyoming, Idaho, Oregon, and California. The Utah territory, organized in 1850, covered a significantly smaller area, but it still included most of what became Nevada, as well as portions of modern-day Colorado and Wyoming. Utah assumed its current borders in 1868. For maps of the proposed territory of Deseret and the territory of Utah, see Gaustad and Barlow, *New Historical Atlas of Religion in America,* 300.)

7. Brigham Young to Thomas L. Kane, November 9, 1867. Arrington Papers, Brigham Young Letter Books, Box 6, Folder 5.

8. *Doctrine and Covenants* 66:9, 42:43. Spurning professional medicine, Mormons joined other Americans in embracing the teachings of Samuel Thomson, an untrained but popular nineteenth-century promoter of "botanic" natural remedies. Divett, "Medicine and the Mormons," 2–3. As Nathan Hatch has explained, Thomson struck a chord with Mormons and other "democratizing" Christian movements in postrevolutionary America by calling on them to "throw off the oppressive yoke of clergymen, lawyers, and physicians." Hatch, *The Democratization of American Christianity,* 29.

9. Brigham Young to Heber John Richards, undated letter written between December 25 and 30, 1867. Arrington Papers, Brigham Young Letter Books, Box 6, Folder 6.

10. Ibid.

11. Brigham Young to Heber John Richards, November 10, 1867. Arrington Papers, Brigham Young Letter Books, Box 6, Folder 5. Young also allowed for Heber's brother Joseph to study at Bellevue at the same time, but Joseph would not study at Bellevue until 1873. He graduated in 1875.

12. Brigham Young's letters do not provide evidence that Richards had the church's financial support, but Claire Noall's history of Mormons and medicine claims that Richards went to Bellevue "at Church expense." Noall, *Guardians of the Hearth,* 97.

13. Brigham Young to Heber John Richards, November 10, 1867.

14. Taylor blessing upon Heber John Richards, November 10, 1867. Heber John Richards Papers.

15. Stewart, Letter to the Editor of the *Deseret News,* May 8, 1868.

16. Stewart, Letter to the Editor of the *Deseret News,* January 25, 1869.

17. "Dr. Heber John Richards Dies at Provo," *Deseret Evening News,* May 12, 1919.

18. Arrington, *Brigham Young,* 342.

19. Brigham Young had twenty-five wives during his life (two additional wives died in the winter of 1845–46 shortly after being "sealed" to Brigham) and sired fifty-seven children. Arrington, *Brigham Young,* 420–21.

20. Blessing cited in Brigham Young, *Letters of Brigham Young to His Sons,* 163.

21. Brigham Young to Willard Young, June 17, 1871, in Young, *Letters,* 166–68.

22. Willard Young to Brigham Young, June 19, 1871, in Young, *Letters,* 169; Brigham Young to Willard Young, July 25, 1871, in Young, *Letters,* 171; Willard Young to Brigham Young, December 9, 1871, in Young, *Letters,* 172.

23. Editorial, with text of interview included, the *Deseret News,* June 8, 1871. Journal History of the Church of Jesus Christ of Latter-day Saints (hereafter referred to as "Journal History"), June 8, 1871.

24. "Return of Utah's West Point Cadet," *Deseret Evening News,* July 2, 1875.

25. Yet after sending Willard to West Point in 1871, Brigham continued to support educational missions only in cases that promised immediate, practical ben-

efit for the Mormon kingdom. In 1872 Brigham sent just one student east to study: his thirty-five-year-old nephew, Seymour Young. Seymour studied at the medical college of New York University during the winters of 1872–73 and 1873–74. After earning his MD in February 1874, Seymour felt that he had "succeeded in my studies beyond my most sanguine expectations." He returned to Salt Lake City, where he opened his own practice and attended personally to the ailing Brigham Young. Seymour B. Young Journal, entry dated October 30, 1872 (but written February 1874 or later), Seymour B. Young Papers.

26. Backman, "Attitudes within the Mormon Church toward the Study of Law," in *BYU Education Week Lectures on the History of Mormon Lawyers*, 15; and Noall, *Guardians of the Hearth*, 100.

27. Dean C. Jessee, introduction to October 21, 1875, letter from Brigham Young to Don Carlos Young, in Brigham Young, *Letters*, 265. Brigham had supported the revival of the University of Deseret in the late 1860s. His able ally in resurrecting the university was its president, John R. Park, a native of Ohio and a trained doctor who had come to Salt Lake City in 1861. The school was not parochial; the curriculum was broad, and eastern-trained, non-Mormon faculty directly contributed to the university's early success. See Chamberlin, *The University of Utah*, and Arrington, *Brigham Young*, 353–54.

28. Backman, "The Pioneer Lawyer," in *BYU Education Week Lectures on the History of Mormon Lawyers*, 28.

29. Backman, "Attitudes within the Mormon Church toward the Study of Law," in *BYU Education Week Lectures on the History of Mormon Lawyers*, 15.

30. Brigham Young to Alfales Young, August 17, 1876, in Brigham Young, *Letters*, 232.

31. Backman has noted that "up until the 1870s the Mormon lawyers with very few exceptions had become involved in the legal profession through their own reading or they had been thrust into a quasi-legal position as probate judges because they were leading authorities and citizens in the community. By the mid-1870s a number of gentile lawyers had come into the city, some of them had been trained at law schools in the east and some had prior experience in other communities. In general there were two types of attorneys coming from the outside to practice law in Utah. First were the federally appointed officials in the territory who continued to live in Utah and to conduct a private practice of law. These included Judge Robert N. Baskin, Judge Orlando Powers and Judge Charles Zane. The other development that brought many gentile lawyers to Utah was the completion of the railroad and the increasing importance of the mining industries in Utah. Many ambitious young lawyers followed businesses into the territory hoping to become successful." Backman, "The Pioneer Lawyer," in *BYU Education Week Lectures on the History of Mormon Lawyers*, 17.

32. Brigham Young, October 1873 General Conference address, cited in Noall, *Guardians of the Hearth*, 105.

33. Arrington, *Brigham Young*, 367. The Relief Society, the LDS women's humanitarian organization with origins in Nauvoo, Illinois, in the 1840s, was revived in the late 1860s as part of Brigham Young's drive to protect the Mormon kingdom. According to Arrington, "Their objectives were to prevent or diminish female extravagance; inform themselves on political matters so they could lobby effectively against anti-Mormon legislation; establish a woman's commission store as an outlet for their handicraft and home manufacturing; and direct the education of their daughters." The Young Ladies' Retrenchment Society, organized by Brigham Young in the late 1860s, encouraged young women to cultivate simplicity and independence from the outside world in their manner of living. In 1878, the group changed its name to the Young Ladies' Mutual Improvement Association (later the Young Women's Mutual Improvement Association), marking a shift in purpose toward self-improvement. Arrington, *Brigham Young*, 351–53. See also Derr, Cannon, and Beecher, *Women of Covenant*.

34. Report on young ladies' meeting in Ogden, *The Ogden Junction*, August 15, 1873. Article reprinted in the *Deseret News*, August 16, 1873, and typed into Journal History, August 15, 1873.

35. Noall, *Guardians of the Hearth*, 105–6.

36. T. A. Larson notes, "In the [U.S.] territories . . . woman suffrage could be adopted without a popular vote, and, indeed, woman suffrage bills came close to being passed by the legislatures of Washington and Nebraska territories in 1854 and 1856, respectively. A simple majority, either in Congress or in a territorial legislature, with the approval of the executive in each case, was all that was necessary." Wyoming's legislature approved woman suffrage in 1869, and Utah followed in 1870. Under the terms of Utah's amendment, however, women could not hold office. Larson, "Woman Suffrage in Western America," 9, 10.

37. The political divisions remained intact until the 1890s, when realignment into democratic and republican parties served as a preface to Utah's admission into the union. See Lyman, *Political Deliverance*.

38. Arrington, *Brigham Young*, 363, 365.

39. Louisa Lula Greene, a grandniece of Brigham Young, started the magazine, which, according to Leonard Arrington, was just the second magazine "by and for women west of the Mississippi." The official motto of the magazine was "The Rights of the Women of Zion, and the Rights of Women of all Nations." The magazine ran under its original name until 1914, when the name was changed to the *Relief Society Magazine*. Arrington, *Brigham Young*, 366.

40. "Lady Lawyers," *Woman's Exponent* 1.9 (October 1, 1872): 68.

41. "Educate Yourself," *Woman's Exponent* 1.9 (October 1, 1872): 69.

42. Beechwood, "A Mormon Woman's Views of Marriage," 54.

43. "Women in Reform," *Woman's Exponent* 6.12 (November 15, 1877): 92.

44. Arrington, *Brigham Young*, 367; "Home Affairs," *Woman's Exponent* 3.22 (April 15, 1875): 173. The latter account in the *Woman's Exponent* states that Pratt had studied at the Free Medical College for Women and the Eye and Ear Infirmary

in New York City during her fourteen-month absence. That information does not square with Noall, *Guardians of the Hearth*, but Pratt may have studied at the New York schools while she was with Parley there.

45. Noall, *Guardians of the Hearth*, 107.

46. That fall Eliza R. Snow was planning to ask the Utah legislature for funds for a women's medical college in Utah, and she hoped Pratt's eastern training would qualify her to preside over the school. "R.S., Y.L.M.I.A., and P.A. Reports," *Woman's Exponent* 14.9 (October 1, 1885): 70. The plans for the medical college never materialized, but the Relief Society would succeed in establishing the Deseret Hospital in Salt Lake City in 1882, and Romania Pratt would play a leading role in the operation of the hospital.

47. Shipp, undated 1875 diary entry. *While Others Slept*, 172.

48. Shipp Diary, November 13, 1872. *While Others Slept*, 110.

49. Shipp Diary, November 10, 1875. *While Others Slept*, 172.

50. Noall, *Guardians of the Hearth*, 121.

51. Shipp Diary, January 20, 1876. *While Others Slept*, 184.

52. Shipp Diary, January 20, 1874. *While Others Slept*, 151. Emphasis in original.

53. Shipp Diary, February 3, 1876, and March 28, 1876. *While Others Slept*, 189; 204–5.

54. Sanction for plural marriage is found in Section 132 of the *Doctrine and Covenants*. Joseph Smith and close associates practiced "the principle," but it became more widespread following Brigham Young's public endorsement of it in Utah in 1852. Estimates of how many Mormons actually practiced polygamy range from about 9 percent to 20 percent. More accurate numbers are difficult to produce because of incomplete historical records.

55. Shipp Diary, February 17, 1873. *While Others Slept*, 78.

56. Shipp Diary, June 28, 1872. *While Others Slept*, 103.

57. Maggie Curtis Shipp, Letter to Ellis Reynolds Shipp, January 2, 1876. Ellis Reynolds Shipp Papers. Emphasis in original.

58. Shipp Diary, April 14, 1877. *While Others Slept*, 252–53. Emphasis in original.

59. Shipp Diary, March 12, 1877. *While Others Slept*, 251.

60. In the fall of 1877, Ellis received an unexpected comfort when Maggie arrived. Maggie had been working to save money to come to the Woman's Medical College, but by August she had been ready to give up, thinking that it would be too expensive for the family to have Ellis and Maggie in school at the same time. In late September, Maggie suddenly appeared at the home where Ellis was boarding, and they "sprang into each other's arms while tears of joy fell thick and fast." Shipp Diary, August 6 and September 25, 1877. *While Others Slept*, 264, 275.

61. "Women Physicians," *Woman's Exponent* 5.22 (April 15, 1877): 171.

62. Barney, "Correspondence."

63. Ibid.

64. Brigham Young to Feramorz Young, October 15, 1874. Brigham Young, *Letters*, 298.

65. Brigham Young to Alfales Young, September 21, 1875. Brigham Young, *Letters*, 221. Alfales thought that fellow Mormon law student A. B. Taylor was too prone to provoking arguments with non-Mormons. Taylor, the son of John Taylor (the counselor of Brigham Young who succeeded him as prophet), also studied law at Michigan from 1875–77, earning the LLB. His fascinating story is fleshed out in chapter 2.

66. Brigham Young to Alfales Young, October 6, 1875. Brigham Young, *Letters*, 223.

67. In his concerns about intellectual and spiritual corruption, Brigham surely saw the specter of contemporary, free-thinking Utah dissidents like William Godbe and Elias Harrison, who challenged and annoyed Young to no end. On Young's clash with them and other Mormon dissidents late in his life, see Turner, "The Monster in the Vale," chap. 12 in *Brigham Young, Pioneer Prophet*.

68. Brigham Young to Willard Young, October 19, 1876. Brigham Young, *Letters*, 199.

69. Brigham Young to Alfales Young, August 23, 1877. Brigham Young, *Letters*, 315. See also Brigham Young to Alfales Young, December 26, 1876. Brigham Young, *Letters*, 238.

Chapter Two

1. Sarah Barringer Gordon notes that as early as 1856, members of the new Republican Party began waging rhetorical war on the "twin relics of barbarism," slavery and polygamy, in U.S. territories. Sarah Barringer Gordon, *The Mormon Question*, 55.

2. On Christian populism in America, see Hatch, *The Democratization of American Christianity*, 5. See also Hatch, "The Populist Vision of Joseph Smith," 123–36.

3. "Utah's Lady Professional," *Deseret News*, September 20, 1877. Journal History, September 20, 1877.

4. Editorial, *Deseret News*, April 5, 1878. Journal History, April 5, 1878.

5. Taylor was the senior member of the Council of Twelve Apostles; he would ultimately succeed Brigham Young as president in 1880, when the church officially reorganized its First Presidency to clarify lines of succession. Cannon, a junior member of the Twelve, was likewise sustained at the October 1880 General Conference of the church as one of two counselors to Taylor. (Cannon also served as Utah's delegate to Congress during this period. Elected in 1872, he served from late 1873 until 1882.) The other counselor to President Taylor was Joseph F. Smith.

6. Journal History, August 13, 1878.

7. See Peckham, *The Making of the University of Michigan, 1817–1992*, 64. Historian Ruth Bordin calls the 1870s "a golden decade for women students at Michigan," when they enjoyed "a degree of acceptance that in later years proved almost impossible to duplicate." (Women began to enroll in the school's Medical Department in 1871, and after a year of keeping classes segregated by sex, the depart-

ment began to allow women to attend classes with men. The women, however, still sat apart from men and worked in separate laboratories.) Bordin, *Women at Michigan*, 12, 14–15.

8. "About Women," *Woman's Exponent* 1.2 (June 15, 1872): 15.

9. Marsden notes that "Michigan was often mentioned hopefully [by Christians] as a model for the future of religion in higher education. The Ann Arbor example showed not only that a state school could be openly sympathetic to Christianity—the same could be said of most state universities—but also that such sympathy was in fact displayed by a leader among the new research universities." Marsden, *The Soul of the American University*, 167.

10. Pratt, "Work for Women," *Woman's Exponent* 7.21 (April 1, 1879): 217.

11. Joseph F. Smith, blessing upon Romania B. Pratt, August 16, 1881. Esther Romania Bunnell [Pratt] Penrose Papers.

12. As late as 1890, Susa Young Gates, one of Brigham's daughters and the editor of the church periodical the *Young Woman's Journal*, prefaced one of Pratt's published articles by assuring the magazine's readers that the learned Dr. Pratt will not "desert us," since "her heart is in the work of aiding and benefiting the young women of Zion. Although a physician with a large and increasing practice, she says she longs to see the time when we can have faith to enter our temples and be healed instantly. Her whole soul is filled with the love of this gospel." Gates, "The Editor's Department." Gates was not ideologically opposed to higher education; she would attend a summer school session at Harvard in 1893.

13. For years, members of the church's women's organization, the Relief Society, had promoted the building project and raised funds for it. When the hospital was finally dedicated in the summer of 1882, the *Woman's Exponent* exulted to see a hospital "where the sick of the Lord's people could be attended and have the benefit of the ordinances of the Church as well as skillful treatment." "Deseret Hospital," *Woman's Exponent* 11.5 (August 1, 1882): 36.

14. Ibid.

15. Wilkinson, ed., *Brigham Young University*, 1:394–95. In the early twentieth century, as the head of the church's educational system, Cummings would become powerfully suspicious of university-trained Mormon faculty, whom Cummings perceived to be too liberal in their embrace of scientific evolution and modern biblical scholarship. Cummings found strong support for his emerging anti-intellectualism in Joseph F. Smith, who by then had become the church's president and prophet.

16. James E. Talmage Journal, August 26, 1882. Talmage Papers, Brigham Young University.

17. Moyle, *Mormon Democrat*, cited in Backman, "The Pioneer Lawyer," in *BYU Education Week Lectures on the History of Mormon Lawyers*, 22–24.

18. Arthur Bruce Taylor accompanied Alfales Young to the University of Michigan in 1875 and earned his LLB degree in 1877. On the alleged confession, see O'Donavan, "'The Abominable and Detestable Crime Against Humanity'."

19. James E. Talmage Journal, June 17, 1882.

20. Ibid., May 4, 1884.

21. For an analysis of the fundamentalist–modernist debate in a Mormon key, see chapters 3 and 4.

22. Legal pressure on Mormon polygamists and their families had been intensifying steadily since 1884, when Charles Zane, the chief justice of Utah's territorial supreme court, introduced innovations to the war on barbarism. In selecting juries, determining bonds, dealing with witnesses who would not testify, and sentencing, Zane vigorously attacked his Mormon enemies. Apostle Rudger Clawson came under arrest in 1884, and the rest of the decade saw some 1,300 Mormons arrested in the ensuing federal "raid" on Mormon polygamists. By early 1885, President Taylor and his counselor George Cannon had gone to the Mormon underground, helping order the church's affairs in secret. Taylor would remain in exile until his death in July 1887.

23. This phrase was penned by the exiled Martha Hughes Cannon, MD, plural wife, from Paris, France, in 1885. Cited in Crall, " 'Something More'," 37.

24. The author ("Wandering Boy") had to have been either Richard W. Young, the only Utah Mormon at West Point at the time, or his wife, Minerva, who could have been writing pseudonymously about Richard's experiences for fellow Relief Society women at home. Young was not the first Mormon to attend the prestigious military academy; Brigham Young had sent one of his own sons, Willard, there in 1871 to make a quiet but clear display of Mormon discipline, manhood, and intelligence, while acquiring practical expertise as an engineer.

25. Wandering Boy, "College Evils," *Woman's Exponent*, January 1, 1885, and March 1, 1885. It is no accident that the school in question, West Point, was not one of the universities or professional schools Mormons far more frequently attended. In the late nineteenth century, West Point had Protestant religious affiliations and an established student culture that could easily make a Mormon cadet feel that he was in enemy territory.

26. Ibid., January 1, 1885.

27. James Henry Moyle Diary, March 31, 1885. James H. Moyle Collection, Archives of the Church of Jesus Christ of Latter-day Saints. Transcription in Moyle, *A View of James Henry Moyle*.

28. Moyle Diary, September 18, 1882.

29. This group of Mormon law students at Michigan was the first sizeable contingent of Mormons to study "abroad" together. The group included Rolapp (LLB 1884); Moyle, Hiram Laney, and Van Cott (LLB 1885); Benjamin Driggs (LLB 1886); William H. King (LLB 1887); and Evans, who enrolled for the year 1884–85 but did not graduate. The University of Michigan, *Catalogue of Graduates*. Of all the students, only Moyle conceived of his studies as a form of church mission, as had been customary in Brigham Young's lifetime. Individual aspirations for a career in law were now just as likely to motivate Mormons as any desire to defend and

expand the Mormon kingdom, and the University of Michigan was the school that offered them the best combination of affordability, proximity, and prestige.

30. Moyle Diary, March 8, 1884.

31. Ibid., March 26, 1884. Rolapp did much more than "keep up appearance" in his subsequent church activity. He was a member for the LDS Sunday School General Board for thirty years. "Judge Rolapp Dies on Coast."

32. Moyle Diary, October 26, 1884.

33. Ibid., May 24, 1885. Van Cott also ended up using his training to serve the interests of Latter-day Saints, as an attorney for Mormon apostle and U.S. senator Reed Smoot. As a regent for the University of Utah, he helped John A. Widtsoe, a Mormon, assume the presidency of the school in 1916 after a bitter controversy over academic freedom had engulfed it.

34. Ibid., August 11, 1884.

35. In 1882, in his first semester at Michigan, Moyle had to contend with the argument that if Congress left polygamy unchecked, religious freedom would logically have to extend to "heathens" who "believed in murdering or killing or sacraficing [sic] human beings as a religious duty." Ibid., October 12, 1882. Even though Mormons were used to hearing Gentiles label polygamy as a primitive, barbaric institution—the Supreme Court had done so when it justified abridging religious freedom for polygamists in *Reynolds v. United States* (1879)—Moyle bristled at the association of Mormons and "heathens." As evidence of Mormons' "enlightened" character, he cited their Christ-like devotion and faith, which left them willing to "leave home, friends, relatives, even wives or husbands and children and father and mother and face a scorning world, and suffer martyrdom, imprisonment or anything else for their religion." Ibid., October 12, 1882. For analysis of the importance of the *Reynolds* case in American legal and religious history, see Sarah Barringer Gordon, *The Mormon Question*, esp. chap. 4.

36. Henry Rolapp, October 21, 1883, letter to William Budge, printed in the November 10, 1883, *Bear Lake Democrat*. Journal History, October 21, 1883.

37. Ibid.

38. Karl G. Maeser to John Taylor, December 8, 1886. BYU President's Records, 1879–92.

39. Maeser to Taylor, January 24, 1887. BYU President's Records. Benjamin Cluff Jr., twenty-eight, had been serving as an instructor at the Brigham Young Academy since 1882. During his tenure there, Cluff had earned Maeser's trust as "a very faithful Latterday [sic] Saint." Maeser told President Taylor that Cluff "possesses that firmness of character and integrity of heart which entitles him to all confidence possible, that he will maintain his integrity before God, in case you should permit him to go to some eastern College." Maeser to Taylor, April 19, 1886. BYU President's Records. Granted that permission, Cluff received an official blessing from Taylor before departing to study civil engineering in December 1886. Benjamin Cluff Jr. Diaries, December 19, 1886.

40. Cluff Diaries, June 16, 1889. In this case, Cluff referred to Orrice Abram Murdock, an 1890 law graduate, who apparently gave an uninspiring address at a Sunday meeting.

41. Ibid., October 21, 1888.

42. Ibid., June 30, 1889. Garrie Green van Schoonhoven studied pharmacy at Michigan beginning in 1889. He graduated in 1891. Still a teenager when he commenced his studies, Garrie was accompanied by his mother, Mary Emma, who studied homeopathic medicine. She also graduated in 1891 with her Pharmaceutical Chemistry (PhC) degree, awarded after completion of a two-year course. She practiced medicine in Salt Lake City for fifteen years after graduating. She died in 1907. See Noall, "Utah's Pioneer Women Doctors," in *Guardians of the Hearth*, 1974.

43. Ferdinand Ericksen studied law at Michigan from 1889 to 1890 but did not graduate.

44. Cluff Diaries, January 7, 1890.

45. Ibid., January 12, 1890. Joseph Hart, according to Cluff, began studying law at Michigan in 1888, but Michigan alumni and nongraduate records do not corroborate Hart's enrollment.

46. The measure provided for the seizure of all church property holdings valued over $50,000; rendered illegitimate the children of polygamous households; and took away Utah women's right to vote.

47. My greatest frustration with this project is that the identity of this enormously important figure has so far eluded me. The dates of her enrollment (1887) and graduation (1889) do not match any information I have gathered from university alumni records and Mormons' private and published writings. According to university alumni records, the likeliest match, Julia A. MacDonald [Place], was an enrolled student from 1888 to 1891, but the university records say clearly that she did not graduate, while "Cactus" notes that she herself earned the MD in 1889. MacDonald went on to be a doctor and writer in Utah. The diary entries of "Cactus" were published in the *Young Woman's Journal* in 1889 and 1890.

48. "Cactus," diary entry for September 22, 1887, published in "Leaves from the Journal of a Medical Student," *Young Woman's Journal* 1.8 (May 1890): 266.

49. "Cactus," diary entry for December 21, 1887, published in "Leaves," *Young Woman's Journal* 1.12 (September 1890): 474.

50. Sorenson, "Letters to the Young Women of Zion," *Young Woman's Journal* 2.3 (December 1890): 142.

51. Sorenson, "Letters to the Young Women of Zion," *Young Woman's Journal* 1.12 (September 1890): 471.

52. Sorenson, "Letters to the Young Women of Zion," *Young Woman's Journal* 2.2 (November 1890): 91; 2.4 (January 1891): 188; 2.3 (December 1890): 141.

53. "Cactus," "Hygiene of Student Life," 59.

54. Cluff's father-in-law and uncle, respectively.

55. Maeser to Cluff, March 17, 1889. BYU President's Records.

56. Ibid.

57. Maeser to Cluff, May 16, 1889. BYU President's Records. Emphasis mine.

58. Maeser told Cluff, "It is the intention of President Woodruff and his brethren [sic] of the General Authorities to avail themselves of the best educational talent among the Latterday [sic] Saints that is willing to cooperate with us in the line indicated, that our churchschool-service [sic] may reach a standard by and by worthy of Zion's destiny." Maeser to Cluff, June 7, 1889, BYU President's Records. Historian Thomas G. Alexander has noted that the three "colleges" were still "basically high schools" through the end of the nineteenth century, even though BYA and BYC were offering some college degrees. Alexander, *Mormonism in Transition*, 157.

59. Maeser to Woodruff, June 12, 1889. BYU President's Records.

60. Cluff to Maeser, April 21, 1890. BYU President's Records.

61. Since Tanner had married his three wives before the 1890 Manifesto, he was not subject to prosecution. Only Tanner's third wife, Josephine Snow Tanner, would accompany him all the way to Cambridge. Joseph—his family and friends called him "Marion"—planned to have his second wife, Annie Clark Tanner, take Josephine's place in 1892, while Jennie, his first wife, would travel with the group only as far as Akron, New York. Ward, *A Life Divided*, 28–29.

62. The others were Joseph Jenson, George Swendsen, Moses Davis, and George F. Thatcher. Widtsoe and Thomas were two of the first Mormons to earn the PhD. Both served as president of the University of Utah, and Widtsoe would become an apostle and head of the church's educational system.

63. Maeser to Woodruff, March 21, 1891. BYU President's Records.

64. Despite Tanner's departure, BYC still had its best years ahead of it during the administrations of W. J. Kerr (1894–1900) and J. H. Linford (1900–13). Garr, "A History of Brigham Young College," 32–34.

65. Jennie Tanner to Daniel Harrington, December 12, 1890. Daniel Harrington Papers, Brigham Young University. By "another" two-year period of separation, Jennie alluded to a previous separation while Marion proselytized. As one can imagine, not every sentiment of Tanner's wives was this gracious and self-denying. On the occasion of Marion's third marriage, to Josephine Snow, Marion's second wife, Annie Clark Tanner, wrote, "So, within six months of my wedding day [December 27, 1883], he married again and was off to Europe. I had not seen the third wife, but I did wonder wherein I lacked that so soon he should take another wife. Then I remembered the doctrine of the Trinity as taught by the Church—that if one wanted to attain the very pinnacle of glory in the next world there must be, at least, three wives." Annie Clark Tanner, *A Mormon Mother*, 63–64, cited in Ward, *A Life Divided*, 18–19.

66. Widtsoe, *In a Sunlit Land*, 28.

67. Ibid., 37.

68. For a more detailed analysis of Eliot's reforms, see Marsden, *The Soul of the American University*, 186–89.

69. Widtsoe, *In a Sunlit Land*, 34.

70. Erickson, "The Life and Educational Contributions of Dr. George Thomas," 13.

71. Ibid.

72. Eliot's ultimate destination was California, but he made time for a short stay in Utah. The LDS General Board of Education received Eliot as its guest, inviting him to speak to a public assembly in the Salt Lake Tabernacle. During his stay in Salt Lake City, Eliot met with LDS president Wilford Woodruff; addressed audiences of students at the Fourteenth Ward School and the University of Utah; and took a short train ride, courtesy of the General Board, to see the Great Salt Lake. "President Eliot Entertained," *Deseret Evening News*, March 17, 1892.

73. "President Eliot Replies," *Deseret Evening News*, March 26, 1892.

74. Ibid.

75. Reprint of March 26, 1892, San Francisco *Call* article in "President Eliot's Visit," March 29, 1892.

76. "President Eliot's Visit."

77. March 25, 1892, Associated Press dispatch from Boston, printed in "President Eliot's Visit."

78. The summer schools signified the increasing importance of teacher training, or "normal" school work, at the BYA. With the (forced) emergence of a public school system in 1890, Utah's teaching corps had seen a dramatic influx of non-Mormons, many of them trained outside Utah. In the Salt Lake City public schools in 1890, 88 percent of teachers had been trained outside Utah. The rate fluctuated dramatically throughout the decade, however, so that by 1894 only half of the teachers had been trained outside Utah. Buchanan, *Culture Clash and Accommodation*, 38–39.

79. Swenson, "Autobiography of John Canute Swenson," 12–13.

80. "Educational Ideas." Reprint of August 10, 1892, *Boston Transcript* article in the *Deseret Evening News*, August 12, 1892.

81. "Col. Parker's Lecture," *Deseret Evening News*, August 8, 1892.

82. "Provo Teachers' Institute," *Deseret Evening News*, August 15, 1892.

83. "B.Y. Summer School," *Deseret Evening News*, August 8, 1893.

84. "Provo Summer School," *Deseret Evening News*, August 7, 1894.

85. "Pedagogical History of the Brigham Young University Class of 1893." Another member of the class, Clinton D. Ray, enrolled at Stanford in the mid-1890s, but I have found no evidence that he graduated. Stanford Alumni Association, *Stanford Alumni*. George H. Brimhall also earned the BPd in 1893. Brimhall would serve as BYU president from 1903–21. A key administrator at the BYA for much of the 1890s, he never got the chance to pursue university training outside Utah. His resulting ambivalence about modern scholarship left a lasting mark on BYU, especially during a 1911 crisis over evolution and biblical criticism, discussed in the next chapter, which led to the firing of a number of faculty with advanced degrees from elite American universities.

86. He left the BYA in the care of his trusted colleagues Brimhall and Joseph Keeler, with whom he regularly corresponded. Cluff continued some of the mathematical studies he had undertaken as an undergraduate, but he concentrated most of his attention in the field of education, taking general psychology, physiological psychology, school supervision, and "general pedagogics." Cluff to Brimhall, October 9, 1893. BYU President's Records.

87. Ibid.

88. Benjamin Cluff, address to the students of the Brigham Young Academy, December 16, 1893. Enclosed in an undated letter to Brimhall. BYU President's Records.

89. Cluff to Brimhall, November 5, 1893. BYU President's Records. To promote "self culture" among his faculty, Cluff planned to adopt Michigan's furlough policy, which granted faculty a year of paid leave on a rotating basis. He hoped that Brimhall and Keeler would be the first to take advantage, using the opportunity to study somewhere in the East for a year or more, if possible. Although Cluff successfully introduced sabbatical leaves in the 1890s, they would not become regular at BYU until the 1920s. For Cluff, such a policy would instill a sense of pride and professionalism in the faculty, allowing the Academy "to take her proper position among the schools of the United States" in just "a few years." Cluff to Brimhall and Joseph Keeler, November 12, 1893. BYU President's Records.

90. Cluff Diary, December 25, 1894. Cluff's tour of normal schools and universities took him from Michigan through Toronto, upstate New York, Boston, New York City, and Chicago before he finally returned to Utah.

91. Cluff to Brimhall, February 27, 1894. BYU President's Records.

92. Over the course of their conversation, William James gave Cluff the opportunity of a Mormon lifetime. James, who less than a decade later would deliver his massively influential lectures on "the varieties of religious experience," asked Cluff to describe Joseph Smith's first revelatory experience. Cluff recalled the exchange: "After I had [offered an account of the vision], a student—postgraduate—asked the Doctor how he would explain the vision scientifically. James replied[,] 'On the theory of hallucination.' 'Joseph Smith had an hallucination.' He then went on to say that if others had seen the angel or the plates it would have been different. I corrected him by informing him that others, three witnesses had seen the angel and the plates and eight had seen the plates. 'That changes it then.' The Dr[.] wanted a set of our books from which he could read up on this subject. I wrote to the [first] presidency and they kindly sent him a full set of works." Cluff Diary, December 25, 1894. Cluff's "correction" of Dr. James could have amounted to an unprecedented proselytizing success for the church, since James apparently conceded that Smith's vision involved something objectively verifiable by witnesses, something manifest outside the Smith's interior, subjective consciousness. Yet in *The Varieties*, James's brief treatment of Joseph Smith varied little from his original estimation. James judged Smith's first vision

to have been "predominantly sensorial," that is, on the order of a private hallucination. William James, *The Varieties of Religious Experience*, 472.

93. Maeser to Wilford Woodruff, December 29, 1894. BYU President's Records.

94. Starting in 1890, a small group of Mormon students—John Hafen, John B. Fairbanks, Lorus Pratt, Edwin Evans, and Will Clawson—began studying in the art schools of Paris, with the direct support of George Q. Cannon and the goal of acquiring training that would help beautify LDS temples.

95. Richard R. Lyman, "The University of Michigan, Ann Arbor," *Juvenile Instructor* 29.14 (July 15, 1894): 427.

96. Ibid., 428. Mormon doctrine situated the original Garden of Eden closer to Independence, Missouri.

97. Richard R. Lyman, "My College Days," *Contributor* 17.1 (November 1895): 56.

98. Richard R. Lyman, "My College Days," *Contributor* 17.3 (January 1896): 138. After Angell's warm welcome, Lyman felt secure and confident enough to take his rightful place among his non-Mormon classmates, as Henry Rolapp and James Henry Moyle had done a decade earlier. Like them, he would also be a high achiever; he went on to be elected president of the university's class of 1895 and an apostle in the church. Josiah Hickman, "Journal of J. E. Hickman," October 27, 1894.

99. "Cornell University," *Juvenile Instructor* 29.8 (April 15, 1894): 236; Lyman, "The University of Michigan," 426; Arthur Thomas, "Harvard College," 531.

100. Lewis T. Cannon, "The Massachusetts Institute of Technology," 468.

101. Richard R. Lyman, "The University of Michigan, Ann Arbor," *Juvenile Instructor* 29.9 (May 1, 1894): 265.

102. Ellis Reynolds Shipp, "Woman's Progress," *Woman's Exponent* 21.13 (January 1, 1893): 102. Articles in the men's periodicals also highlighted opportunities for Mormon women to study abroad. Lewis T. Cannon took care to note that MIT was a coeducational institution, and the *Juvenile Instructor's* piece on Cornell made the same point. Lewis T. Cannon, "The Massachusetts Institute of Technology," 469; Anonymous, "Cornell University," 235.

103. Ellis Reynolds Shipp, "Woman's Progress," 102.

104. Josiah Hickman, "Journal of J. E. Hickman," July 26, 1893.

105. Ibid., March 17 and 24, 1895. Hickman acknowledged the merit of the first- and second-place orations, but he took solace in hearing from some students and professors that his third-place finish was a "rank injustice." For a fuller account of the oratorical contest, see Martin B. Hickman, "Josiah Hickman," 99–103.

106. Hickman, "Journal of J. E. Hickman," March 10, 1895.

107. Ibid., October 27, 1894.

108. Ibid., February 17, 1895.

109. Ibid., October 1, 1893. Hickman reported that during a meeting Benjamin Cluff had said that the Seventies, the authorities who oversaw church missions, "expected . . . that the gospel would soon be preached to the rich and learned instead of the poor and ignorant."

110. Ibid., June 10, 1894.

111. Ibid., August 6, 1894.

112. James Brown to Benjamin Cluff, May 4, 1897. BYU President's Records.

113. Both Martha and Angus could have won, since they were vying for a number of available seats.

114. Crall, "'Something More'," 32.

115. "A Training School for Nurses," *Woman's Exponent* 17.15 (January 1, 1889): 117.

116. Swenson to Cluff, February 7, 1896. BYU President's Records.

117. President Joseph F. Smith would warn of a "theological scholastic aristocracy" in 1911, in "Philosophy and the Church Schools," 209.

Chapter Three

1. Donnette Smith to Benjamin Cluff, November 4, 1896. BYU President's Records.

2. Leah Dunford to Benjamin Cluff, April 2, 1897. BYU President's Records.

3. Aretta Young to Benjamin Cluff, May 5, 1897. BYU President's Records. Charles B. Scott, head of the Oswego State Normal School, gave high praise to the Mormon women who had attended his school. He said that Lillian Cannon's teaching was "as good . . . as has been done in our school since I have been connected with it." He added that Cannon and Aretta Young "have both been a credit to their State and will be a credit to our school. We hope you can send us many more like them." Scott to Benjamin Cluff, April 25, 1898. BYU President's Records.

4. Yorgason's *Transformation of the Mormon Culture Region* has an excellent chapter called "Moderating Feminist Imaginations," which offers the best explanation I have read for these complex, surprising developments. Lola van Wagenen has also keenly observed that after statehood, "Utah's politically active women continued to engage in partisan politics, and a small number continued to win elective office. But the extraordinary era of woman suffragism in Utah was the zenith of political activism among women." She adds that "Mormon women's political aspirations were of increasingly less interest to their brethren. . . . [T]he nineteenth-century brethren who had been visible and vocal supporters of women's political activism appear not to have reproduced themselves[.]" Van Wagenen, *Sister-Wives and Suffragists*, 151.

5. The gendering of Mormon intellectual discourse also reflected the broader American gendering of academic expertise and elite higher education. In their quest to establish themselves as intellectual, scientific, and progressive at the dawn of the twentieth century, male Mormon scholars had mainly male models to imitate.

6. The phenomenon of Roman Catholic modernism will be discussed in further detail later in the chapter.

7. When Benjamin Cluff surveyed the country for the best educational theory and methods in 1894, he looked not only to the East, but to the West as well. The

pioneering educational work at Stanford University drew Cluff's particular attention. "They are doing some original work" at Stanford, Cluff wrote to George Brimhall, "and if you read of their ideas and desires you can better understand mine." Cluff to Brimhall, December 26, 1893. BYU President's Records.

8. Swenson, "Autobiography," 19.

9. Ibid., 20.

10. Ibid.

11. Ibid., 21.

12. Swenson to Cluff, December 28, 1895. BYU President's Records.

13. Swenson to Cluff, February 7, 1896.

14. Ibid.

15. Jensen to Brimhall, November 5, 1900. BYU President's Records.

16. Jensen to Brimhall, November 5, 1900, and January 20, 1901. BYU President's Records. Emphasis in original.

17. Jensen could be referring here to Stanford education professor Ellwood R. Cubberley, who strongly recommended Bullock for a teaching position at the Brigham Young Academy. Cubberley wrote, "This I take much pleasure in doing, as Mr. Bullock was one of our strongest students. . . . He has done as careful and earnest work as any student we have ever had." Cubberley to Brimhall, June 28, 1900. BYU President's Records.

18. Jensen to Brimhall, January 20, 1901. BYU President's Records.

19. After graduating from Stanford, Jensen taught at the Latter-day Saints' College in Salt Lake City for ten years. I have not been able to locate any additional information about his subsequent career. In 1903, the church organized a Stanford Branch. Charles Maw, a student in chemistry and pedagogy, was its first presiding elder. In disposition Maw was loyal to the church, without displaying either Swenson's veneration of the university or Jensen's disgust. Early in his studies, Maw remarked simply, "I care not what science *may seem* to indicate the word of God is sufficient for me." That was sufficient for church authorities to place Maw at the head of a new and increasingly important outpost for the labors of the church. Maw to Brimhall, January 10, 1901. BYU President's Records. Emphasis in original.

20. Levi Edgar Young, Harvard Diary, January 21, 1899. Levi Edgar Young Papers, Utah State Historical Society.

21. The expedition was undertaken in the wake of an inconclusive BYA conference on "Book of Mormon Geography." Swenson, "Autobiography," 26.

22. Cluff to Brimhall, February 24, 1901. BYU President's Records.

23. Cluff, "Education from the Latter-day Saint Point of View," 7.

24. Ibid.

25. Ibid., 11.

26. For an account of the Smoot hearings, see Flake, *The Politics of American Religious Identity.*

27. Tanner had married twice since the Manifesto. After leaving his post at the helm of the church school system in 1906, he retreated to a farm in Alberta, Can-

ada, where he cultivated land originally secured by Mormons seeking refuge from the Raid in the late 1880s. He continued to write articles for church periodicals and lecture in the Intermountain West, but he would never occupy a position of prominence in the church again. Tanner died in Alberta in 1927. Ward, *A Life Divided*, 45–51, 58–62.

28. Josiah Hickman deserves mention here as well. The polygamist and former prize-winning orator at the University of Michigan continued to advocate polygamy, but he stayed in the good graces of the church long enough to teach for four years at Brigham Young University's branch in Beaver, Utah. After further earning a master's degree at Columbia and conducting additional work toward a PhD, he spent seven years at the head of the education department at the Brigham Young College in Logan. After that, Hickman became an insurance salesman, which paid better than teaching. His increased salary allowed him to realize a dream: to provide some college education for each of his sixteen children. Hickman, "Autobiography."

29. Tanner's biographer, Margery Ward, offers no explanation for his early departure, but Benjamin Cluff implied in late 1893 that Tanner had run himself ragged. Cluff wrote of his former BYA colleague, "I regret to hear that Tanner has failed. I do not think the failure is at all to his credit. I can study as hard as anyone, but I must be careful of my diet and habits." Cluff to Brimhall, December 3, 1893. BYU President's Records.

30. Ward, *A Life Divided*, 36–38. The appropriations committee, it turned out, was right to worry. A 1900 congressional appropriations bill for agricultural colleges in the United States carried with it an amendment stipulating "that no money should be paid to the college in Utah until the Secretary of Agriculture was satisfied that no trustee or teacher in the institution practiced polygamy." *Deseret News*, January 30, 1900, cited in Ward, *A Life Divided*, 38.

31. Church of Jesus Christ of Latter-day Saints Board of Education, General Board of Education Minutes, March 27, 1903. Excerpts extracted by staff of the church archives.

32. The board would gradually clarify some of the details that were hazy at first. In October 1903, the board set the interest rate for the loans at 6 percent, and in April 1904, the board recommended that the church contribute funds that matched the teachers' contributions, not the fixed amount of $1,000 originally requested. General Board Minutes, October 9, 1903, and April 29, 1904.

33. Ibid., February 20, 1907.

34. Ibid., March 4, 1907.

35. Ibid., March 4, 1907. I was unable to secure an exhaustive list of loan recipients. Financial Records for the education fund are held at the church archives, but access to them is restricted. The register for the collection (call number CR 102 51) lists loan recipients' names, but the roster is incomplete and includes no information about the schools recipients attended and when.

36. Historian Merrill Singer has written that "By the 1930s [Baldwin's] innovative skills had helped Utah become a leading manufacturer of radio loudspeakers

and headsets. His products were marketed worldwide, being especially sought by the United States Navy in the First World War." Singer, "Nathaniel Baldwin," 42–43.

37. Alexander, *Mormonism in Transition*, 192.

38. Like its counterpart for young women, the YMMIA emerged in the 1870s. It offered the church's young men a chance to develop their skills in public speaking and encouraged them to develop an appreciation for education and culture.

39. John Widtsoe, *Joseph Smith as Scientist*, 2.

40. Ibid., 7.

41. Other major books followed: some of the best known among Mormons were *Rational Theology; As Taught by the Church of Jesus Christ of Latter-day Saints* (1915), *The Word of Wisdom; a Modern Interpretation* (1937, co-authored by John's wife, Leah); and *Evidences and Reconciliations; Aids to Faith in a Modern Day* (1943).

42. John Widtsoe, *Joseph Smith as Scientist*, 8.

43. Ibid., 1.

44. Ibid.

45. John Widtsoe's abilities in research, teaching, and administration propelled him to the presidencies of the Agricultural College of Utah (1907–16) and the University of Utah (1916–21). His skillful apologetics, however, would ultimately entice the First Presidency to call Widtsoe away from his work in the state colleges and universities of Utah. In 1921, Widtsoe became one of the church's twelve apostles, and in the 1920s and 1930s, he would spend much of his time overseeing the work of the church educational system.

46. Osborne Widtsoe, "The Mormon Boy at College," 17.

47. Ibid., 18.

48. Ibid.

49. Ibid., 19.

50. West, "How Knowledge Comes," 493.

51. Editors' note preceding West, "How Knowledge Comes," 489.

52. West, "How Knowledge Comes," 490.

53. Ibid., 491.

54. Ibid., 492.

55. Ibid., 493.

56. Milton Bennion, "The Modern Skeptic," 523.

57. Ibid., 526.

58. Ibid., 525.

59. See chapter 2, note 92.

60. Bennion, "The Modern Skeptic," 525–26.

61. The church history examination at BYU for the school year 1909–10 reflected this emerging concern over the nature of religious experience. Question 7 read, "Do you look upon the first vision of Joseph Smith as a mental state with-

out a corresponding external reality, or a mental state accompanied by a corresponding external or objective reality?" BYU President's Records.

62. Hutchison, *The Modernist Impulse*, 2.

63. Fogarty, *The Vatican and the American Hierarchy*, 193.

64. Wilkinson, ed., *Brigham Young University*, 1:394–95.

65. In a 1908 letter to BYU President George H. Brimhall, Cummings wrote, "We are sadly in need of better qualified teachers and this fund is our chief hope to supply the deficiency." Cummings to Brimhall, December 20, 1908. BYU President's Records. In his early history of Teachers College, Franklin T. Baker wrote that "A graduate of a secondary school, able to pass the College entrance examination, may enter upon a four years' College course and receive at the end of it the degree of Bachelor of Science, and according to his elections, a diploma to teach in either art, manual training, kindergarten, elementary schools, or some one or more subjects in high schools." Baker, "Teachers College," in *A History of Columbia University*, 415.

66. Wilkinson, ed., *Brigham Young University*, 1:396.

67. The decision to consolidate normal and other college-level work at BYU had a devastating effect on the Brigham Young College in Logan, which had been conferring college degrees since 1894. In 1908, eighteen of the forty-five BYC faculty boasted eastern training from schools like Chicago, Harvard, Cornell, Columbia, and the University of Wisconsin. The transfer of college work to BYU precipitated inexorable decline at the BYC, which continued to function as a normal school until it finally closed in 1926. A number of faculty members left for positions with the Agricultural College, the University of Utah, or BYU; others left the academic world entirely for ventures in private business. Garr, "A History of Brigham Young College," 35, 46–47.

68. Brimhall to Ellis R. Shipp, May 9, 1907. BYU President's Records.

69. Joseph Peterson, reporting to President Brimhall after a summer student recruitment trip for the university, regretted to convey that he had discovered "considerable objection to our 'farmer' teachers." Peterson concluded that "the best way to advertise our College is to become professional and devote our entire time to education." Joseph Peterson to George Brimhall, August 30, 1910. BYU President's Records. Ralph Chamberlin's summer recruitment tour left him with the same impression. He wrote, "The opinion seems quite widely to prevail that we are lacking in genuine scholarship, the son of one of the leading men in the church saying that he regarded the main body of my associates here as a 'bunch of farmers' who gave their leisure only to teaching and who lacked any genuine devotion to the profession. It will be important for us to remove grounds for such criticisms as this, as in the face of them many students whom we might rightly expect to attend our College turn elsewhere." Ralph Chamberlin to George Brimhall, September 3, 1910. BYU President's Records.

70. Wilkinson, ed., *Brigham Young University*, 1:412.

71. Cummings to Brimhall, February 27, 1908. BYU President's Records.

72. Horace Hall Cummings report to President Joseph F. Smith and members of the General Church Board of Education, January 21, 1911. Hereafter cited as Cummings Report. Included in minutes for the February 20, 1911, meeting of the BYU Board of Trustees. Henry Peterson Papers, Utah State University.

73. Hutchison, *The Modernist Impulse*, 116.

74. Abbott, *The Evolution of Christianity*, iv.

75. Ibid., 5, 258.

76. Ibid., vi.

77. "The Origin of Man" was originally published in the November 1909 issue of *The Improvement Era* (13:75–81) and has been reprinted in full in Clark, ed., *Messages of the First Presidency*, 4:205.

78. "B.Y.U. Teachers Put on Carpet," *Salt Lake Tribune*, February 19, 1911. The president of the Utah Stake at the time was J. B. Keeler, one of George Brimhall's counselors in the presidency of BYU and himself an outspoken critic of evolution.

79. Cummings Report.

80. Henry Peterson, typed autobiographical notes, 96-B. Henry Peterson Papers.

81. Cummings Report.

82. Ibid.

83. The other five members were Heber J. Grant, Hyrum M. Smith, George F. Richards, Anthony W. Ivins, and George H. Brimhall. Apparently, no transcript of the hearing exists.

84. "Special committee report to President Joseph F. Smith and Members of the Board of Trustees of the Brigham Young University." Included in minutes for the February 20, 1911, meeting of the BYU Board of Trustees. Henry Peterson Papers.

85. BYU Board of Trustees Minutes, February 20, 1911. Henry Peterson Papers.

86. *The Fundamentals: A Testimony to the Truth.*

87. Marsden, *Fundamentalism and American Culture*, 118–21. The earliest Protestant fundamentalists were apolitical and more rhetorically moderate than their militant successors in the 1920s. Marsden, *Fundamentalism*, 119.

88. "The Book of Jonah," *Deseret Evening News*, February 8, 1911.

89. Wellhausen, *Prolegomena to the History of Israel.*

90. "True Philosophy," *Deseret Evening News*, February 25, 1911.

91. Roberts, "Higher Criticism and the Book of Mormon," *The Improvement Era* 14:9 (July 1911): 774. Roberts delivered the lecture on April 2, 1911. *The Improvement Era* published it in two parts in its June and July issues.

92. Roberts, "Higher Criticism and the Book of Mormon," 781.

93. See Roberts, *Studies of the Book of Mormon.*

94. "The B.Y. School Controversy," *Salt Lake Tribune*, February 22, 1911.

95. "The Evolution Ruction," *Salt Lake Tribune*, March 13, 1911.

96. "On Evolution," *The Deseret Evening News*, March 11, 1911. The same argument appeared verbatim in the *Deseret Evening News* editorial "True Philosophy," which appeared two weeks earlier.

97. "Evolution God's Creative Scheme," Salt Lake City *Herald–Republican*, February 23, 1911.

98. "W.H. Chamberlain [*sic*] Offers Views on Evolution," *Deseret News*, March 11, 1911.

99. BYU Presidency to Henry Peterson, March 16, 1911. Henry Peterson Papers.

100. "B.Y.U. Students Destroy Reply of [University] Presidency," *Salt Lake Tribune*, March 16, 1911.

101. Ibid.

102. "Evolution God's Creative Scheme," Salt Lake City *Herald*, Republican, February 23, 1911.

103. Milton Bennion, "The 'Evolution' and 'Higher Criticism' Controversy," 9–10.

104. Brimhall to Joseph F. Smith, December 3, 1910. BYU President's Records.

105. "The Facts in the Trouble at Provo," *Deseret Evening News*, March 17, 1911. On the growing tensions in American higher education between faculty and administration, labor and management, and autocracy and democracy in the twentieth century, see Newfield, "The Rise of University Management."

106. In a letter to BYU English professor Alice Reynolds, who was studying in London at the time, Brimhall wrote, "I think we can keep our reputation as an educational institution and still strictly follow in the line of the school following the Church." Brimhall to Reynolds, February 21, 1911. BYU President's Records. Some two weeks later, Brimhall told Senator Reed Smoot that "The school cannot go off and leave the Church in any line of activity without *perishing in the desert*. . . . I would rather the Maeser Memorial [the new college building at BYU] remain a sealed tomb containing our college hopes and ambitions until the day of a new educational resurrection than to have its doors thrown open to influences antagonistic to the heroism, inspiration and revelation of those who have made the school and who have the right to say, 'Thus far shalt thou go and no farther.' The school follows the Church, or it ought to stop." Brimhall to Smoot, March 8, 1911. BYU President's Records. Emphasis in original.

107. Cummings to Brimhall, April 11, 1911. BYU President's Records.

108. Brimhall to Victor Bean, March 27, 1912. BYU President's Records.

109. Joseph F. Smith, "Theory and Divine Revelation," 550.

110. Joseph F. Smith, "Philosophy and the Church Schools," 208.

111. Henry Peterson to Joseph F. Smith, April 3, 1911. Henry Peterson Papers. Emphasis in original.

112. In some important ways, the Mormon debate echoed the relevant one between W. E. B. Du Bois and Booker T. Washington about, in Du Bois's words, "the training of black men." Although Mormons and African Americans were emerging from incomparably different historical circumstances, they shared some concerns about education. Many Mormons found much to admire in Washington's

insistence that education be, above all else, "practical"—some even pointed directly to Washington's ideas as models for Utah—while others would have shared Du Bois's passion for giving students every possible opportunity for intellectual growth. (In February 1911, just as the investigation of the BYU professors was reaching fever pitch, Salt Lake City's superintendent of public schools, D. H. Christensen, a Mormon, visited Dr. Washington at the Tuskegee Institute in Alabama. In 1913, Washington came to Salt Lake City to address the annual convention of the National Education Association. He seemed to hold Mormons in high regard for their industriousness and their perseverance through persecution.) See Buchanan, *Culture Clash and Accommodation*, 57 and 80, and W. E. B. Du Bois, *The Souls of Black Folk*. Du Bois, incidentally, had conducted his PhD work at Harvard in the early 1890s, when the first group of Mormons enrolled there. There is no evidence that the Mormon students had any contact with Du Bois.

113. Smith, "Philosophy and the Church Schools," 209.

114. "Circular of Instructions of the General Board of Education of the Church of Jesus Christ of Latter-day Saints" (Salt Lake City, 1911): 1, 8.

115. James Harris, introduction to Talmage, *The Essential James E. Talmage*, xxii.

116. Talmage Journal, September 30, 1909, cited in Harris, Introduction, xxv.

117. Talmage Journal, March 16, 1884, also see citation in chapter 2.

118. Some reports suggest that when the situation demanded it, Talmage could play the monkey card. When Henry Peterson secured a job teaching in the Box Elder County public schools after being fired from BYU, Talmage appeared in Brigham City, where Peterson was just beginning his work, to give an address on evolution. A friend of Peterson reported that Talmage stirred up sentiment against Peterson by telling the audience that evolutionists believe "that man sprang from the monkey." (Henry Peterson, handwritten autobiographical notes, Box 2, Folder 5, Henry Peterson Papers.) What seemed like an attempt to sabotage Peterson's career, even after he had lost his job at BYU, caused Peterson to despise Talmage for the rest of his life. Others shared the opinion. Joseph T. Kingsbury, the non-Mormon president of the University of Utah who had succeeded Talmage in that office, told Peterson that the BYU "heretics" were responsible for Talmage's rise in the church ranks. Kingsbury told Henry Peterson that Talmage's ordination as an apostle led Talmage "to believe that his appointment meant by implication that he, being the educated man of the church, had the great responsibility of combating Evolution [*sic*]." (Henry Peterson, typed autobiographical notes, 112 B. Henry Peterson Papers.) According to Kingsbury, Talmage had immediately begun delivering "hypocritical" public attacks on evolution in Salt Lake City and beyond.

119. Brimhall to Victor Bean, March 27, 1912. BYU President's Records. The biblical metaphor is chilling; see 1 Kings 18:40.

120. Fletcher returned to BYU for a brief stint in the 1950s. While he was in New York, he remained active in the church.

121. Complaints from teachers prompted the General Board to make contributions voluntary starting in the school year 1911–12. Board of Education Minutes, December 27, 1911, and January 23, 1912.

122. Dean Brimhall earned his master's degree at Columbia in 1915 and his PhD there in 1920.

123. George Brimhall to Horace Hall Cummings, December 16, 1912. BYU President's Records. Brimhall had hoped that L. John Nuttall Jr., a beneficiary of the Education Fund, would help BYU in its college work after he earned his BS degree from Columbia's Teachers College in 1911, but Nuttall had somehow "failed as a man," according to Brimhall. Brimhall to Cummings, December 16, 1912. BYU President's Records. Nuttall resigned late in 1911, immediately returning to Columbia to earn his master's degree there. He came back to BYU in the 1920s as dean of its College of Education before finishing his career as Salt Lake City's superintendent of public schools, a position he held from 1932 until his death in 1944.

124. Ericksen, *Memories and Reflections: The Autobiography of E. E. Ericksen*, 41–42.

125. Scott G. Kenney provides an outline of Ericksen's coursework in Ericksen, *Memories and Reflections*, 39–40.

126. Ericksen, *Memories and Reflections*, 40.

127. Ibid. 59.

128. Ericksen to Cummings, March 18, 1911. BYU President's Records.

129. Cummings to Brimhall, March 23, 1911. BYU President's Records.

130. Brimhall to Ericksen, March 25, 1911. BYU President's Records.

131. Ericksen to Brimhall, March 30, 1911. BYU President's Records.

132. Brimhall to Ericksen, May 5, 1911. BYU President's Records.

133. Ericksen, *Memories and Reflections*, 60.

134. "Public Statement by the Board of Regents of the University of Utah," pamphlet of statement adopted March 17, 1915. Part of Ralph Chamberlin scrapbook on the controversy of 1915. Ralph Chamberlin Papers.

135. Carol S. Gruber notes that in American universities of the early twentieth century, "the position of the faculty was insecure; its dual professional-employee status created tensions that could and did lead to confrontations and conflict. . . . Professional consciousness too was rudimentary; the AAUP had just been founded in 1915 and commanded neither widespread support in the profession nor influence in the infrastructure of university politics." Gruber, "Backdrop," 274.

136. "Statue of Moroni Used by Utonian," *Salt Lake Tribune*, May 21, 1915, in Ralph Chamberlin scrapbook, Ralph Chamberlin Papers.

137. "R. W. Young Discusses Issues at University," *Salt Lake Tribune*, May 27, 1915, in Ralph Chamberlin scrapbook, Ralph Chamberlin Papers.

138. Ericksen, *Psychological and Ethical Aspects*, 7.

139. Ibid., 59.

Chapter Four

1. Another two of the twelve apostles at this time, James Talmage and Stephen L. Richards, had gone east to study. Talmage's training has already been discussed; Richards was the first Latter-day Saint to graduate from the University of Chicago's law school. He earned the LLB cum laude in 1904.

2. Alexander, *Mormonism in Transition*, 165.

3. In 1919, the First Presidency and the General Board of Education had created a Commission of Education to determine the policy and oversee the operations of the church school system. David O. McKay was appointed as the first commissioner of education. He had two assistant commissioners, Stephen L. Richards and Richard Lyman. Also appointed was a "Superintendent of Church Schools," Adam S. Bennion, who dealt with the "day-to-day operations of the schools." President Grant remained a member of the General Board of Education. Sometime in the mid-1920s, the office of the superintendent became known as the Department of Education, a designation common by the time Joseph Merrill became commissioner in 1928. Westwood, "Administrative History of the Church Educational System," 12, 13.

4. That organization had been established in 1908 to "give an impetus to scientific studies in the State and . . . bring the Scientific men of the State together." Minutes of the Utah Academy of Arts, Sciences, and Letters, January 3, 1908. Records of the Utah Academy of Arts, Sciences, and Letters, 1908–. The organization adopted its current name in 1933.

5. Franklin Harris to M. L. Harris, July 8, 1921. BYU President's Records.

6. Franklin Harris to Eyring, May 5, 1921. BYU President's Records.

7. The faculty member with a PhD at BYU in 1920 was Martin P. Henderson, a botany professor, who earned his doctorate at the University of Wisconsin in 1914 and became head of the botany department at BYU in 1915. The figure for the University of Utah comes from Chamberlin, *The University of Utah*, 385.

8. Remarks of Heber J. Grant at meeting of the BYU Board of Trustees, April 26, 1921. BYU President's Records.

9. Further evidence of Grant's support for higher education in general came when he invited non-Mormon educators to speak at the LDS general conferences of 1921 and 1922. It was unusual for non-Mormons to speak at general conference. Those invited were: Perry G. Holden of Iowa State College; Thomas Nixon Carver of Harvard; Walter Ernest Clark, president of the University of Nevada; and Charles A. Lory, president of the Colorado Agricultural College. Wilkinson, ed., *Brigham Young University*, 2:48.

10. Ibid., 2:125.

11. Ibid., 2:39.

12. Fletcher to Harris, January 7, 1922, and Harris to Fletcher, January 31, 1922. BYU President's Records.

13. Lyman to Harris, January 14, 1922. BYU President's Records. The introduction to the Ralph Chamberlin papers at the Utah State Historical Society notes that Chamberlin's first marriage fell apart in 1910 (soon before his career at BYU was engulfed by the modernism controversy), and he remarried in 1922. Ralph Vary Chamberlin Papers.

14. Ralph Chamberlin to Lyman, excerpted in Lyman to Harris, May 16, 1922. BYU President's Records.

15. Chamberlin, *Life and Philosophy of W. H. Chamberlin*, 144–45.

16. Ibid., 284.

17. Ibid., 288.

18. Ibid., 287.

19. Anonymous, typescript biography of Vasco M. Tanner. Filed in "Life History" folder of the Vasco M. Tanner Collection, Brigham Young University.

20. In a 1981 oral history interview with Mark K. Allen, Tanner reaffirmed that he never felt any pressure to modify his instruction about evolution. A transcript of the interview is available in the L. Tom Perry Special Collections, Harold B. Lee Library, Brigham Young University (call number UA OH 135).

21. Swensen, "Mormons at the University of Chicago Divinity School," 39.

22. Wilkinson, ed., *Brigham Young University*, 2:287.

23. Merrill to Harris, May 2, 1929. BYU President's Records. Cited in Wilkinson, ed., *Brigham Young University*, 2:219.

24. The tensions that would emerge in relation to the academic study of religion in Mormonism reflected broader debates in American higher education. Jurgen Herbst notes that in the late nineteenth century university presidents like Charles Eliot were already wondering, "Can divinity schools claim their teaching to be scientific when they are asked to endorse and abide by the creeds and prayer books of their sponsoring denominations, churches, or sects? Can they belong to the world of scholarship only when they divest themselves of any ties to [a] particular confession?" Herbst, "Rethinking American Professional Education," 416.

25. For another history of this movement, see Griffiths, "The Chicago Experiment."

26. For the Mormon students, it also helped that enrolling in the divinity school was relatively inexpensive. LDS Commissioner of Education Joseph F. Merrill thought that it was "probably the cheapest place" besides BYU itself to conduct work in religious education. George Tanner, a southern Idaho seminary teacher who enrolled at Chicago in 1930, found that registering in the divinity school allowed him and his two Mormon colleagues to "get most of our tuition free." On top of that, the university afforded Tanner status as a missionary student, which cut his housing costs in half. George S. Tanner, typescript autobiography (1979), 30. George S. Tanner Papers. The Mormon students at the University of Chicago Divinity School during this period were: Sidney B. Sperry (AM 1926, PhD 1931), George S. Tanner (AM 1931), Russel B. Swensen (AM 1931, PhD 1934), Daryl Chase

(AM 1931, PhD 1936), T. Edgar Lyon (AM 1932), Carl J. Furr (enrolled in the Divinity School in 1931 and earned his PhD in the humanities division in 1937), Wesley P. Lloyd (PhD 1937), Therald N. Jensen (PhD 1938), Anthon S. Cannon (PhD 1938), Heber C. Snell (PhD 1940), and Vernon F. Larsen (PhD 1942).

27. Joseph Merrill to Russel Swensen, March 10, 1930. Russel B. Swensen Papers, L. Tom Perry Special Collections, Harold B. Lee Library, Brigham Young University. Swensen, "Mormons at the University of Chicago Divinity School," 40.

28. Merrill to Tanner, June 19, 1930. George S. Tanner Papers.

29. Merrill to Tanner, July 27, 1931. George S. Tanner Papers.

30. Goodspeed to Sperry, August 5, 1930. Sidney B. Sperry Collection, Brigham Young University.

31. George S. Tanner typescript autobiography (1979, hereafter cited as "Tanner Autobiography"), 30. George S. Tanner Papers.

32. Russel B. Swensen to S. L. Swenson, July 26, 1930. Russel B. Swensen Papers, Brigham Young University. Russel and his father, S. L. Swenson, consistently spell their last name differently for reasons that are unclear. Russel was the nephew of BYU professor and Stanford alumnus John C. Swenson, who, like S. L., always spelled his last name "Swenson." Incidentally, Russel was also the nephew of LDS apostle and Cornell PhD Richard R. Lyman.

33. Tanner Autobiography, 31.

34. Sweet, *The Story of Religion in America*, 396.

35. George S. Tanner, transcript of oral history interview with Davis Bitton, August 24, 1972, 13. Tanner Papers.

36. Russel B. Swensen to George S. Tanner, December 31, 1931. Swensen Papers.

37. Tanner Oral History, 12.

38. Russel Swensen to S. L. Swenson, June 13, 1931. Swensen Papers.

39. "L.D.S. Department of Education," *Deseret News* Church Department, August 29, 1931.

40. Russel Swensen to S. L. Swenson, March 23, 1933. Swensen Papers.

41. S. L. Swenson to Russel Swensen, April 2, 1933. Swensen Papers. S. L. wrote, "Of course [the Chicago professors] cant [sic] comprehend our point of view, or no doubt they would believe as we do."

42. Russel Swensen to S. L. Swenson, September 21, 1930. Swensen Papers.

43. Russel Swensen to S. L. Swenson, December 10, 1931. Swensen Papers.

44. Russel Swensen to S. L. Swenson, March 23, 1933. Swensen Papers.

45. Russel Swensen to S. L. Swenson, January 28, 1933, and October 31, 1932. Swensen Papers.

46. Russel Swensen to S. L. Swenson, February 15, 1933. Swensen Papers.

47. Russel Swensen to S. L. Swenson, December 19, 1932. Swensen Papers.

48. Lyon's life is chronicled in Lyon, *T. Edgar Lyon: A Teacher in Zion*.

49. T. Edgar Lyon to David Lyon, August 21, 1931.

50. Ibid.

51. Ibid. Born in 1903, Lyon would not have had detailed, firsthand knowledge of the modernist controversy of 1911. His comment thus offers another indication of how large the Petersons and Chamberlins loomed in Mormon academic circles.

52. Tanner Oral History, 13.

53. T. Edgar Lyon to David and Mary Lyon, April 18, 1932. T. Edgar Lyon Collection, Brigham Young University.

54. Ibid.

55. The Mormons at Chicago were not the only Mormon students trained in academic approaches to the study of history. After World War I, a number of Mormons studied the history of the western United States under Herbert Bolton at Berkeley, and they wrote theses on Utah history. Those who earned the PhD included Andrew L. Neff, LeRoy Hafen, William James Snow, Leland H. Creer, Thomas C. Romney, and Milton H. Hunter. Joel E. Ricks also wrote on Utah history for his 1930 PhD from the University of Chicago. Neff and Creer taught history at the University of Utah; LeRoy Hafen spent thirty years as Colorado State Historian before accepting a position in history at BYU in the 1950s; Snow taught history at BYU; Romney and Hunter were directors of the LDS Institute in Logan, Utah; and Ricks taught history at the Utah State Agricultural College.

56. Oaks, *Medical Aspects*, 10.

57. Poulson, draft of letter to Joseph F. Merrill, March 2, 1932. M. Wilford Poulson Papers, Brigham Young University.

58. Poulson to Russel B. Swensen, March 10, 1930. Poulson Papers.

59. "L.D.S. Department of Education," *Deseret News* Church Department, October 24, 1931.

60. T. Edgar Lyon to David Lyon, August 21, 1931. Lyon Collection.

61. T. Edgar Lyon to David and Mary Lyon, April 18, 1932. Lyon Collection.

62. Lyman to Harris, June 14, 1932. Copy in Lyman–Swensen correspondence, Swensen Papers.

63. Lyman to Swensen, June 15, 1932. Swensen Papers.

64. Tanner to Swensen, April 21, 1932. Swensen Papers.

65. Lyon to Merrill, March 1 and June 20, 1932. Lyon Collection.

66. Lyon to Merrill, June 20, 1932. Lyon Collection. After one year at Ricks College, Lyon received a call to become the president of the LDS Netherlands Mission. When he returned to Salt Lake City in 1937, he was able to secure an appointment that made better use of his Chicago training: a position as director of the LDS Institute at the University of Utah.

67. Chase to Swensen, November 1933 (date unspecified). Swensen Papers.

68. Furr to Swensen, April 3, 1934. Swensen Papers.

69. Ibid.

70. Clark earned his LLB from Columbia in 1906. There, he served on the editorial board of the *Columbia Law Review*. His term as ambassador lasted from 1930 to 1933.

71. Clark gave these remarks on October 8, 1933. The regular "Department of Education" column in the weekly "Church News" section of the *Deseret News* published a transcript of the remarks on November 18, 1933.

72. Grant, "Teach That Which Encourages Faith," 3–4. Emphasis mine.

73. Lowry Nelson, *In the Direction of His Dreams*, 249.

74. Ibid., 258, 259. In the 1940s, Nelson would begin to raise critical questions about Mormonism and race, becoming a forerunner for those who would challenge the church's priesthood ban later in the twentieth century. The ban would not be lifted until 1978.

75. Lowell Bennion Oral History, cited in Bradford, *Lowell L. Bennion: Teacher, Counselor, Humanitarian*, 65.

76. Bradford, *Lowell L. Bennion*, 66.

77. Snell to West, March 17, 1937. Heber C. Snell Papers, Utah State University.

78. L. John Nuttall Jr., October 1929 statement of BYU's educational objectives, cited in Wilkinson, ed., *Brigham Young University*, 2:220. Emphasis mine.

79. Nuttall's delineation of the boundaries is similar to Stephen Jay Gould's, encapsulated in the notion of "non-overlapping magisteria." See, for example, Gould, *Rocks of Ages*.

80. Sterling B. Talmage, "An Open Letter to Joseph Fielding Smith," June 28, 1931, 4. Sterling B. Talmage Papers, University of Utah. Bracketed material and emphasis in original.

81. Ibid., 10. Emphasis in original.

82. Ibid., 13.

83. Joseph Fielding Smith to Sterling B. Talmage, September 29, 1934. Sterling B. Talmage Papers.

84. J. Reuben Clark Jr., June 1937 BYU Commencement Address, cited in Wilkinson, ed., *Brigham Young University*, 2:245.

85. Clark's biographer, D. Michael Quinn, has written that Clark's "distrust of Mormon intellectuals was a result of his own spiritual-intellectual crisis earlier in life. In the attempt to rationalize and intellectualize the LDS gospel, he found himself heading toward absolute skepticism. In letters to non-LDS friend Cloyd Marvin, he said that he avoided atheism only by refusing to question fundamental gospel principles." Quinn, *Elder Statesman*, 206.

86. Clark, "The Charted Course of the Church in Education," 244.

87. Ibid., 245.

88. Ibid., 248.

89. Ibid., 249, 248.

90. Ibid., 253.

91. Ibid., 250–51.

92. Ibid., 252.

93. Ibid., 246.

94. Ibid., 254.

95. Ibid., 250.

96. M. Lynn Bennion, *Recollections of a School Man*, 106.

97. Larsen, "The Life and Times of Vernon F. Larsen volume V," 60.

98. Wilkinson, ed., *Brigham Young University*, 2:293–94.

99. See, for example, McMurrin, Sterling, and Jackson, eds., *Matters of Conscience*; Tanner, *One Man's Journey*; and Brooks, *The Mountain Meadows Massacre*.

Conclusion

1. Peter Berger, *The Sacred Canopy*, 3.

2. Ibid., 33. Emphasis in original.

3. Bourdieu, *Language and Symbolic Power*, 115.

4. See, for example, Quinn, ed., *The New Mormon History*; Bowman, "Context and the New-New Mormon History"; and Barlow, "Jan Shipps." The scholarly Mormon History Association celebrated its fiftieth anniversary in 2015, and endowed chairs in Mormon Studies have been established recently at Utah State University, Claremont Graduate University, and the University of Virginia.

5. Packer, "The Mantle."

6. Ibid., 259.

7. Ibid., 267, 268.

8. For an overview of these controversies, see Nussbaum, *Cultivating Humanity*, chap. 8; Helen Whitney's important PBS documentary *The Mormons*; and the retrospectives of Lavina Fielding Anderson ("The Church and Its Scholars") and Armand Mauss ("Seeing the Church as a Human Institution") in the July 2003 issue of *Sunstone*.

9. Brigham Young University, "Academic Freedom Policy," 3.

10. Ibid., 1. On page 4, the statement cites the magazine *First Things* and John Paul II's "Apostolic Constitution on Catholic Universities" (*Ex Corde Ecclessiae*) with approval, as well as the work of leading evangelical Protestant scholar George Marsden.

11. Ibid., 6, 2, 5, 8.

12. Ibid., 7.

13. For an analysis of how higher education tends to foster "ecumenism" in student worldviews, see Astin, Astin, and Lindholm, *Cultivating the Spirit*, which is based on the recent UCLA Higher Education Research Institute study "Spirituality in Higher Education."

14. In *The Great American University*, Jonathan Cole has expressed increasingly common fears of the decline of the American university and a plea for its continued preeminence. More recent works like Deresiewicz's *Excellent Sheep* have intensified the debates. Chad Wellmon's review of the latter in the *Hedgehog Review* offers important historical context and correctives.

15. A 2011 *Deseret News* article noted with pride that BYU is one of the top five universities in the nation at producing students who go on to earn the PhD at other universities. Askar, "BYU Is Top-5 Launching Pad for PhDs."

16. See Turner, "Why Race Is Still a Problem for Mormons."

17. See Berkes, "A Woman's Prayer," and Bailey, "Kate Kelly."

18. A brief moment in the spring of 2015 was revealing: on the same day, major media outlets disseminated praise for the church's role in supporting Utah's antidiscrimination legislation, along with criticism for the amicus brief it filed with the Supreme Court in opposition to same-sex marriage. See Chokshi, "Gay Rights," and Guion, "Mormon Church."

19. Joanna Brooks made waves in the summer of 2013 with a call for serious discussion of women's ordination at http://askmormongirl.com/, and a group of blogging "FeministMormonHousewives" (http://www.feministmormonhousewives .org/) could also get an ironic laugh from a fairly wide following in the twenty-first century. See also Goodstein, "A Leader's Admission."

Bibliography

Archival Collections

Logan, Utah

    Special Collections and Archives, Merrill-Cazier Library, Utah State University

        Leonard J. Arrington Papers, 1839–1999.

        Henry Peterson Papers.

        Heber Cyrus Snell Papers, 1899–1974.

Provo, Utah

    L. Tom Perry Special Collections, Harold B. Lee Library, Brigham Young University

        Brigham Young University President's Records, Karl G. Maeser, 1879–92.

        Brigham Young University President's Records, Benjamin Cluff Jr., 1903–21.

        Brigham Young University President's Records, George H. Brimhall, 1903–21.

        Brigham Young University President's Records, Franklin S. Harris, 1921–45.

        John Hafen Papers, Correspondence, and Memorabilia 1879–1918

        Daniel Harrington Papers, 1850–1905.

        T. Edgar Lyon Collection, 1915–91.

        Joseph Frances Merrill Papers, ca. 1887–1963.

        M. Wilford Poulson Papers, 1808–1965.

        Sidney B. Sperry Collection, 1837–1958.

        Russel B. Swensen Papers, 1897–1953.

        James E. Talmage Papers, 1876–1933.

        Vasco M. Tanner Collection.

Salt Lake City, Utah

    Church History Library, Church of Jesus Christ of Latter-day Saints.

        Education Fund Financial Records, 1904–40 (access restricted).

        General Board of Education Minutes, 1888–1987 (access restricted).

        Journal History of the Church of Jesus Christ of Latter-day Saints ("Journal History" in the notes and bibliography).

        James H. Moyle Collection.

        Esther Romania Bunnell Penrose [Pratt] Papers, 1875–98.

        Heber John Richards Papers, 1863–1902.

        Seymour B. Young Papers, 1857–1924.

    International Society Daughters of Utah Pioneers.

    Special Collections, J. Willard Marriott Library, University of Utah.

        Sterling B. Talmage Papers, 1878–1955.

George S. Tanner Papers, 1912–92.

LeGrand Young Diaries, 1859–1921.

Richard W. Young Papers, 1858–1919.

Utah State Historical Society

Ralph Vary Chamberlin Papers, 1940–67

Ellis Reynolds Shipp Papers, 1875–1955.

Levi Edgar Young Papers, 1898–1959.

Primary Sources

"About Women." *Woman's Exponent* 1:2 (June 15, 1872): 15.

"An Address by Miss Eliza R. Snow." *Woman's Exponent* 2:8 (September 15, 1873): 62–63.

Arrington, Leonard J. Papers, 1839–1999. Merrill-Cazier Library, Utah State University. Logan, Utah.

Barney, Elvira Stevens. "Correspondence." *Woman's Exponent* 9:4 (July 15, 1880): 29.

———. "On the Wing." *Woman's Exponent* 8:21 (April 1, 1880): 162.

Beechwood, Blanche. "A Mormon Woman's Views of Marriage." *Woman's Exponent* 6:7 (September 1, 1877): 54.

Bennion, Milton. "The 'Evolution' and 'Higher Criticism' Controversy at the Brigham Young University." *Utah Educational Review* 4:7 (March 1911): 9–10.

———. "The Modern Skeptic." *Improvement Era* 11:7 (May 1908): 523–26.

Bennion, M. Lynn. *Recollections of a School Man: The Autobiography of M. Lynn Bennion.* Salt Lake City: Western Epics, 1987.

"The Book of Jonah." *Deseret Evening News*, February 8, 1911. Journal History of the Church (hereafter "Journal History").

Brigham Young University. Academic Freedom Policy. Accessed May 1, 2015. https://policy.byu.edu/content/managed/9/AcademicFreedomPolicy.pdf.

Brigham Young University Pedagogy Class of 1893. "Pedagogical History of the Brigham Young University." Lee Library, Brigham Young University. Provo, Utah.

Brimhall, George H. Brigham Young University President's Records, 1903–21. Lee Library, Brigham Young University. Provo, Utah.

"The B.Y. School Controversy." *Salt Lake Tribune*, February 22, 1911. Journal History February 22, 1911.

"B.Y. Summer School." *Deseret Evening News*, August 8, 1893. Journal History August 7, 1893.

"B.Y.U. Students Destroy Reply of Presidency and Make Public Protest They Formulated." *Salt Lake Tribune.* March 16, 1911. Journal History March 16, 1911.

"B.Y.U. Teachers Put on Carpet." *Salt Lake Tribune*, February 19, 1911. Journal History February 19, 1911.

"Cactus." "Hygiene of Student Life." *Young Woman's Journal* 1:2 (November 1889): 59–62.

——. "Leaves from the Journal of a Medical Student." *Young Woman's Journal* 1:8 (May 1890): 265–68; 1:10 (July 1890): 380–83; 1:12 (September 1890): 472–74; 2:1 (October 1890): 43–45; 2:3 (December 1890): 438–40; 2:6 (March 1891): 280–83; 2:8 (May 1891): 369–72.

California Alumni Association. *Directory of Graduates of the University of California, 1864–1916*. Berkeley: University of California, 1916.

Cannon, Annie W. "The Women of Utah, Part IV: Women in Medicine." *Woman's Exponent* 17:7 (September 1, 1888): 49–50.

Cannon, Lewis T. "The Massachusetts Institute of Technology." *Juvenile Instructor* 29:15 (August 1, 1894): 468–72.

Chamberlin, Ralph Vary. *Life and Philosophy of William H. Chamberlin*. Salt Lake City: The Deseret News Press, 1926.

——. Papers, 1940–67 [collection also covers material much earlier than 1940]. Utah State Historical Society. Salt Lake City, Utah.

——. *The University of Utah: A History of Its First Hundred Years, 1850–1950*. Salt Lake City: University of Utah Press, 1960.

"Church News." *The Deseret News*, November 18, 1933.

Church of Jesus Christ of Latter-day Saints. Journal History of the Church of Jesus Christ of Latter-day Saints ("Journal History" in the notes and bibliography). Church History Library. Salt Lake City, Utah.

Church of Jesus Christ of Latter-day Saints Board of Education. Education Fund Financial Records, 1904–40. Access Restricted. (A register for the collection is available and has a partial list of the fund's beneficiaries.)

——. General Board of Education Minutes, 1888–1987. Church History Library. Salt Lake City, Utah. Access Restricted. Portions extracted by Church History Library staff.

Church of Jesus Christ of Latter Day Saints General Church Board of Education. "Circular of Instructions of the General Board of Education of the Church of Jesus Christ of Latter-day Saints." Salt Lake City, 1911.

Clark, James R., ed. *Messages of the First Presidency of the Church of Jesus Christ of Latter-day Saints*. 5 vols. Salt Lake City: Bookcraft Inc., 1970.

Clark, J. Reuben, Jr. "The Charted Course of the Church in Education." In *J. Reuben Clark: Selected Papers on Religion, Education, and Youth*, edited by David H. Yarn Jr., 243–56. Provo: Brigham Young University Press, 1984.

Cluff, Benjamin, Jr. Diaries, 1881–1909. Lee Library, Brigham Young University. Provo, Utah.

——. Brigham Young University President's Records, 1892–1903. Lee Library, Brigham Young University. Provo, Utah.

——. "Education from the Latter-day Saint Point of View, 1898." Church History Library, Salt Lake City, Utah.

"Col. Parker's Lecture." *Deseret Evening News*, August 8, 1892. Journal History
August 7, 1892.

Columbia University Committee on General Catalogue. *Columbia University
Alumni Register, 1754–1931*. New York: Columbia University Press, 1932.

"Cornell University." *Juvenile Instructor* 29:8 (April 15, 1894): 233–36.

"Correspondence." *Woman's Exponent* 6:4 (July 15, 1877): 30.

Crocheron, Augusta Joyce. *Representative Women of Deseret*. Salt Lake
City: J. C. Graham and Company, 1884.

"Deseret Hospital." *Woman's Exponent* 11:2 (June 15, 1882): 12; 11:5 (August 1,
1882): 36.

"Dr. Heber John Richards Dies at Provo." *Deseret Evening News*, May 12, 1919.
Journal History May 12, 1919.

Du Bois, W. E. B. *The Souls of Black Folk*. New York: Penguin Books, 1989. First
published 1903 by A. C. McClurg & Co.

D. W. P. "Some of Our Educators." *Utah Educational Review* 19:9 (May 1926):
367–68, 409–13.

Editorial. *Deseret News*, June 8, 1871. Journal History June 8, 1871.

Editorial. *Deseret News*, April 5, 1878. Journal History April 5, 1878.

"Editorial Notes." *Woman's Exponent* 15:17 (February 1, 1887): 133.

"Educate Yourself." *Woman's Exponent* 1:9 (October 1, 1872): 69.

"Educational Ideas." Reprint of August 10, 1892, *Boston Transcript* article in the
Deseret Evening News, August 12, 1892. Journal History August 12, 1892.

Ericksen, E. E. *Memories and Reflections: The Autobiography of E. E. Ericksen*.
Edited by Scott G. Kenney. Salt Lake City: Signature Books, 1987.

———. *The Psychological and Ethical Aspects of Mormon Group Life*. Chicago:
University of Chicago Press, 1922.

"Evolution God's Creative Scheme." Salt Lake City *Herald–Republican*,
February 23, 1911. Journal History February 23, 1911.

"The Evolution Ruction." *Salt Lake Tribune*, March 13, 1911. Journal History
March 13, 1911.

"The Facts in the Trouble at Provo." *Deseret Evening News*, March 17, 1911.
Journal History March 17, 1911.

First Presidency of the Church of Jesus Christ of Latter-day Saints. "The Origin
of Man." *Improvement Era* 13:1 (November 1909): 75–81.

Gates, Susa Young. "The Editor's Department." *Young Woman's Journal* 1:12
(September 1890): 474–75.

Grant, Heber J. "Teach that which Encourages Faith." Salt Lake City: Deseret
News Press, 1934.

Hafen, John. "An Art Student in Paris." *Contributor* 15:8 (June 1894): 485–87;
15:9 (July 1894): 546–48; 15:10 (August 1894): 599–600; 15:11 (September
1894): 690–92; 15:12 (October 1894): 740–42.

———. Papers, Correspondence, and Memorabilia 1879–1918. Lee Library,
Brigham Young University. Provo, Utah.

Harrington, Daniel. Papers, 1850–1905. Lee Library, Brigham Young University. Provo, Utah.

Harris, Franklin S. Brigham Young University President's Records, 1921–45. Lee Library, Brigham Young University. Provo, Utah.

Harris, James P., ed. *The Essential James E. Talmage*. Salt Lake City: Signature Books, 1997.

Harvard Alumni Association. *Harvard Alumni Directory*. Cambridge, MA: Harvard University, 1910.

——. *Harvard Alumni Directory*. Boston: The Harvard Alumni Association, 1923.

Harvard University. *Harvard Alumni Directory*. Cambridge, MA: Harvard University, 1929.

——. *Harvard Alumni Directory*. Cambridge, MA: Harvard University, 1955.

Hickman, Josiah. "Autobiography." Posted to the Ancestry.com message board by Vivian Karen (Hickman) Bush, great granddaughter of Josiah E. Hickman. Accessed January 29, 2013, at http://boards.ancestry.co.uk /localities.northam.usa.states.utah.counties.cache/165.164/mb.ashx.

——. "Journal of J. E. Hickman." Published by the Hickman family online at www.hickmansfamily.homestead.com/JEHdiaries~ns4.html, accessed November 30, 2015.

Holmes, Frank R., and Lewis A. Williams Jr. *Cornell University: A History*. 4 vols. New York: University Publishing Society, 1905.

"Home Affairs." *Woman's Exponent* 3:22 (April 15, 1875): 173; 7:9 (October 1, 1878): 68–69; 9:3 (July 1, 1880): 20.

"Judge Rolapp Dies on Coast." *Deseret News*, January 8, 1936. Journal History January 8, 1936.

Keeler, Joseph B. "The Fallacy of Evolutionism." *Contributor* 9:9 (July 1888): 340–43.

"Lady Lawyers." *Woman's Exponent* 1:9 (October 1, 1872): 68.

Larsen, Vernon Fred. "The Life and Times of Vernon F. Larsen volume V 1994." Church History Library. Salt Lake City, Utah.

"L.D.S. Department of Education." *Deseret News*, August 29, 1931; October 24, 1931.

Lyman, Richard R. "My College Days." *Contributor* 17:1 (November 1895): 55–57; 17:2 (December 1895): 73–76; 17:3 (January 1896): 137–41; 17:4 (February 1896): 244–47; 17:5 (March 1896): 297–309; 17:6 (April 1896): 344–47; 17:7 (May 1896): 451–54; 17:8 (June 1896): 466–68; 17.9 (July 1896): 555–58.

——. "The University of Michigan, Ann Arbor." *Juvenile Instructor* 29:9 (May 1, 1894): 265–69; 29:12 (June 15, 1894): 36; 29:14 (July 15, 1894): 425–29.

Lyon, T. Edgar. Collection, 1915–1991. Lee Library, Brigham Young University. Provo, Utah.

——. *T. Edgar Lyon: A Teacher in Zion*. Provo: Brigham Young University Press, 2002.

Maeser, Karl G. Brigham Young University President's Records, 1879–92. Lee Library, Brigham Young University. Provo, Utah.

McMurrin, Sterling M., and L. Jackson Newell. *Matters of Conscience: Conversations with Sterling M. McMurrin on Philosophy, Education, and Religion.* Salt Lake City: Signature Books, 1996.

Merrill, Joseph Frances. Papers, ca. 1887–1963. Lee Library, Brigham Young University. Provo, Utah.

Moyle, James H. James H. Moyle Collection. Church History Library. Salt Lake City, Utah.

——. *A View of James Henry Moyle: His Diaries and Letters.* Edited by Gene A. Sessions. Salt Lake City, 1974.

"Mozo." "The United States Naval Academy." *Juvenile Instructor* 29:6 (March 15, 1894): 169–72; 29:7 (April 1, 1894): 201–5.

Nelson, Lowry. *In the Direction of His Dreams: Memoirs.* New York: Philosophical Library, 1985.

Oaks, Lewis Weston. *Medical Aspects of the Latter-day Saint Word of Wisdom.* Provo: Brigham Young University, 1929.

"On Evolution." *The Deseret Evening News*, March 11, 1911. Journal History March 13, 1911.

Pack, Frederick J. "The Creation of the Earth." *Improvement Era* 13:12 (October 1910): 1121–27.

Packer, Boyd K. "The Mantle Is Far, Far Greater Than the Intellect." *BYU Studies* 21:3 (Fall 1981): 259–78.

"Pedagogical History of the Brigham Young University Class of 1893." Typescript, 1942. Lee Library, Brigham Young University.

Penrose [Pratt], Esther Romania Bunnell. Papers, 1875–98. Church History Library. Salt Lake City, Utah.

Peterson, Henry. Papers Merill-Cazier Library, Utah State University. Logan, Utah.

Poulson, M. Wilford. Papers, 1808–1965. Lee Library, Brigham Young University. Provo, Utah.

Pratt, Romania. "Correspondence." *Woman's Exponent* 6:4 (July 15, 1877): 30.

——. "Work for Women." *Woman's Exponent* 7:21 (April 1, 1879): 217.

Pratt, Valton M. "From a College Youth." *Juvenile Instructor* 28:5 (March 1, 1893): 140–42.

"President Eliot Entertained." *Deseret Evening News*, March 17, 1892. Journal History March 17, 1892.

"President Eliot Replies." *Deseret Evening News*, March 26, 1892. Journal History March 26, 1892.

"President Eliot's Visit." *Deseret Evening News*, March 29, 1892. Journal History March 29, 1892.

"Provo Summer School." *Deseret Evening News*, August 7, 1894. Journal History August 6, 1894.

"Provo Teacher's Institute." *Deseret Evening News*, August 15, 1892. Journal History August 15, 1892.

"Return of Utah's West Point Cadet." *Deseret Evening News*, July 2, 1875. Journal History July 2, 1875.

Richards, Heber John. Papers, 1863–1902. Church History Library. Salt Lake City, Utah.

Roberts, B. H. "Higher Criticism and the Book of Mormon." *The Improvement Era* 14:8 (June 1911): 665–77; 14:9 (July 1911): 774–86.

———. *Studies of the Book of Mormon*. 2nd ed. Edited by Brigham D. Madsen. Salt Lake City: Signature Books, 1992.

Rolapp, Henry. October 21, 1883, Letter to William Budge, published in the November 10, 1883, *Bear Lake Democrat*. Journal History October 21, 1883.

"R.S. Reports." *Woman's Exponent* 4:10 (October 15, 1875): 74.

"R.S., Y.L.M.I.A. & P.A. Reports." *Woman's Exponent* 14:9 (October 1, 1885): 70.

Shipp, Ellis Reynolds. Papers, 1875–1955. Utah State Historical Society. Salt Lake City, Utah.

———. *While Others Slept: The Autobiography and Journal of Ellis Reynolds Shipp*. Salt Lake City: Bookcraft, 1985.

———. "Woman's Progress." *Woman's Exponent* 21:13 (January 1, 1893): 102.

Smith, Joseph F. "Philosophy and the Church Schools." *Juvenile Instructor* 46:4 (April 1911): 208–9.

———. "Theory and Divine Revelation." *Improvement Era* 14:6 (April 1911): 548–51.

Snell, Heber Cyrus. Papers, 1899–1974. Merrill-Cazier Library, Utah State University. Logan, Utah.

Sorenson, Hannah. "Letters to the Young Women of Zion. From a Graduated Obstetrician." *Young Woman's Journal* 1:12 (September 1890): 468–72; 1:13 (October 1890): 41–43; 2:2 (November 1890): 91–93; 2:3 (December 1890): 140–43; 2:4 (January 1891): 186–89; 2:5 (February 1891): 229–32; 2:7 (April 1891): 326–28; 2:11 (August 1891): 514–17.

Sperry, Sidney B. Collection, 1837–1958. Lee Library, Brigham Young University. Provo, Utah.

Stanford Alumni Association. *Stanford Alumni, 1891–1955*. Stanford, CA: Stanford University, 1956.

Stewart, David M. Letters to the Editor of the *Deseret News*, May 8, 1868, and January 25, 1869. Journal History May 8, 1868, and January 25, 1869.

Swensen, Russel B. Papers, 1897–1953. Lee Library, Brigham Young University. Provo, Utah.

Swenson, John C. Autobiography of John Canute Swenson. Lee Library, Brigham Young University. Provo, Utah.

Taggart, Spencer Laird. "The L.D.S. Institute in Thatcher, Arizona (1937–1939)." Church History Library. Salt Lake City, Utah.

Talmage, James E. Papers, 1876–1933. Lee Library, Brigham Young University. Provo, Utah.

Talmage, Sterling B. *Can Science Be Faith-Promoting?* Edited by Stan Larson. Salt Lake City: Blue Ribbon Books/Freethinker Press, 2001.

——. Papers, 1878–1955. Marriott Library, University of Utah. Salt Lake City, Utah.

Tanner, George S. Papers, 1912–92. Marriott Library, University of Utah. Salt Lake City, Utah.

Tanner, Obert C. *One Man's Journey: In Search of Freedom*. Salt Lake City: University of Utah Press, 1995.

Tanner, Vasco M. Collection (MSS SC 1515). Lee Library, Brigham Young University. Provo, Utah.

——. Oral History (transcript of interview with Mark K. Allen, July 8, 1981, call number UA OH 135). Lee Library, Brigham Young University. Provo, Utah.

Thomas, Arthur. "Harvard College." *Juvenile Instructor* 29:16 (August 15, 1894): 497–501; 29:17 (September 1, 1894): 529–32.

Torrey, R. A., and A. C. Dixon, eds. *The Fundamentals: A Testimony to the Truth.* Chicago: Testimony Publishing Company, 1910.

"A Training School for Nurses." *Woman's Exponent* 17:15 (January 1, 1889): 117.

"True Philosophy." *Deseret Evening News*, February 25, 1911. Journal History February 25, 1911.

University of Chicago. *General Register of the University of Chicago, 1892–1902.* Chicago: University of Chicago, 1903.

——. *University of Chicago Alumni Directory, 1973.* Chicago: University of Chicago, 1973.

University of Michigan. *Catalogue of Graduates, Non-graduates, Officers, and Members of the Faculties, 1837–1921.* Edited by H. L. Sensemann. Ann Arbor: University of Michigan, 1923.

Utah Academy of Arts, Sciences, and Letters. Records, 1908–. Utah State Historical Society. Salt Lake City, Utah.

"Utah's Lady Professional." *Deseret News*, September 20, 1877. Journal History September 20, 1877.

Wandering Boy. "College Evils." *Woman's Exponent* 13:15 (January 1, 1885): 118; 13:19 (March 1, 1885): 147.

Washington, Booker T. *Up from Slavery: An Autobiography*. New York: A. L. Burt Company, 1900.

West, Frank L. "How Knowledge Comes." *Improvement Era* 11:7 (May 1908): 489–93.

"W.H. Chamberlain [sic] Offers Views on Evolution." *Deseret News*, March 11, 1911. Journal History March 11, 1911.

Widtsoe, John A. *Evidences and Reconciliations: Aids to Faith in a Modern Day.* Salt Lake City: The Bookcraft Company, 1943.

——. *In a Sunlit Land: The Autobiography of John A. Widtsoe.* Salt Lake City: Deseret News Press, 1952.

——. *Joseph Smith as Scientist: A Contribution to Mormon Philosophy.* Grantsville, UT: Archive Publishers, 2000. First published by General Boards Young Men's Mutual Improvement Associations in 1908.

———. *Rational Theology: As Taught by the Church of Jesus Christ of Latter-day Saints.* Salt Lake City: Signature Books, 1997. First published by General Priesthood Committee of the Church of Jesus Christ of Latter-day Saints in 1915.

Widtsoe, John A., and Leah Widtsoe, *The Word of Wisdom; a Modern Interpretation.* Salt Lake City: Deseret Book Company, 1937.

Widtsoe, Osborne. "The Mormon Boy at College." *Improvement Era* 9:1 (1906): 15

"Women in Reform." *Woman's Exponent* 6:12 (November 15, 1877): 92.

"Women Physicians." *Woman's Exponent* 5:22 (April 15, 1877): 171.

Young, Brigham. *Discourses of Brigham Young, Second President of the Church of Jesus Christ of Latter-day Saints.* Edited by John A. Widtsoe. Salt Lake City: Deseret Book, 1925.

———. *Journal of Discourses by President Brigham Young, His Two Counsellors, The Twelve Apostles, and Others.* 26 vols. Salt Lake City: Deseret Book, 1974.

———. *Letters of Brigham Young to His Sons.* Edited by Dean C. Jessee. Salt Lake City: Deseret Book in Collaboration with the Historical Department of The Church of Jesus Christ of Latter-day Saints, 1974.

Young, LeGrand. Diaries, 1859–1921. Marriott Library, University of Utah. Salt Lake City, Utah.

Young, Levi Edgar. Papers, 1898–1959. Utah State Historical Society. Salt Lake City, Utah.

Young, Richard W. "'Mormons' Educationally." *Contributor* 1:2 (November 1879): 40–41.

———. Papers, 1858–1919. Marriott Library, University of Utah. Salt Lake City, Utah.

Young, Seymour B. Papers, 1857–1924. Church History Library. Salt Lake City, Utah.

Young, Willard. "Education." *Contributor* 12:10 (August 1891): 388–92.

Secondary Sources

Abbott, Lyman. *The Evolution of Christianity.* New York: Houghton, Mifflin, 1892.

Alexander, Thomas G. *All Things in Heaven and Earth: The Life and Times of Wilford Woodruff, a Mormon Prophet.* Salt Lake City: Signature Books, 1991.

———. *Mormonism in Transition: A History of the Latter-day Saints, 1890–1930.* Urbana: University of Illinois Press, 1986.

Allen, James B., and Glen M. Leonard. *The Story of the Latter-day Saints.* 2nd ed. Salt Lake City: Deseret Book, 1992.

Allen, James B., Ronald W. Walker, and David J. Whittaker. *Studies in Mormon History, 1830–1997: An Indexed Bibliography.* Urbana: University of Illinois Press, 2000.

Anderson, Lavina Fielding. "The Church and Its Scholars: Ten Years After." *Sunstone* 128 (July 2003): 13–19.

Arrington, Leonard J. *Brigham Young: American Moses*. New York: Alfred A. Knopf, 1985.

Askar, Jamshid Ghazi. "BYU Is Top-5 Launching Pad for PhDs." *Deseret News*, August 27, 2011. Accessed April 30, 2015, http://www.deseretnews.com /article/700174074/BYU-is-Top-5-launching-pad-for-PhDs.html?pg=all.

———. "Crisis in Identity: Mormon Responses in the Nineteenth and Twentieth Centuries." In *Mormonism and American Culture*, edited by Marvin S. Hill and James B. Allen, 168–69. New York: Harper and Row, 1972.

———. *Great Basin Kingdom: An Economic History of the Latter-day Saints, 1830–1900*. Cambridge, MA: Harvard University Press, 1958.

Astin, Alexander W., Helen S. Astin, and Jennifer A. Lindholm. *Cultivating the Spirit: How College Can Enhance Students' Inner Lives*. San Francisco: Jossey-Bass, 2011.

Backman, James H. *BYU Education Week Lectures on the History of Mormon Lawyers*. Provo: Brigham Young University Education Week, 1980.

Bailey, Sarah Pulliam. "Kate Kelly, Mormon Women's Group Founder, Excommunicated from Church." *Religion News Service*, June 23, 2014. Accessed December 1, 2015, http://www.religionnews.com/2014/06/23/kate -kelly-excommunicated-mormon-church/.

Barlow, Philip L. "Jan Shipps and the Mainstreaming of Mormon Studies." *Church History* 73:2 (June 2004): 412–26.

———. *Mormons and the Bible: The Place of the Latter-day Saints in American Religion*. New York: Oxford University Press, 1991.

———. "Shifting Ground and the Third Transformation of Mormonism." In *Perspectives on American Religion and Culture*. Edited by Peter W. Williams, 140–53. Oxford: Blackwell, 1999.

Berger, Peter. *The Sacred Canopy: Elements of a Sociological Theory of Religion*. New York: Anchor Books, 1990.

Berkes, Howard. "A Woman's Prayer Makes Mormon History." National Public Radio, April 8, 2013. Accessed April 30, 2015, http://www.npr.org/blogs /thetwo-way/2013/04/08/176604202/a-womans-prayer-makes-mormon -history.

Bitton, Davis. *George Q. Cannon: A Biography*. Salt Lake City: Deseret Book, 1999.

———. *Guide to Mormon Diaries and Autobiographies*. Provo: Brigham Young University Press, 1977.

Bordin, Ruth. *Women at Michigan: The "Dangerous Experiment," 1870s to the Present*. Ann Arbor: University of Michigan Press, 1999.

Bourdieu, Pierre. *Language and Symbolic Power*. Trans. Gino Raymond and Matthew Adamson. Cambridge, MA: Harvard University Press, 1991.

Bowman, Matthew. "Context and the New-New Mormon History." *Journal of Mormon History* 35:3 (Summer 2009): 208–13.

Bradford, Mary Lythgoe. *Lowell L. Bennion: Teacher, Counselor, Humanitarian.* Salt Lake City: Dialogue Foundation, 1995.

Brooks, Juanita. *The Mountain Meadows Massacre.* Stanford, CA: Stanford University Press, 1950.

Buchanan, Frederick S. *Culture Clash and Accommodation: Public Schooling in Salt Lake City, 1890–1994.* Salt Lake City: Signature Books, 1996.

Bushman, Claudia Lauper, and Richard Lyman Bushman. *Building the Kingdom: A History of Mormons in America.* Oxford and New York: Oxford University Press, 2001.

Chamberlin, Ralph V. *The University of Utah: A History of Its First Hundred Years, 1850–1950.* Edited by Harold W. Bentley. Salt Lake City: University of Utah Press, 1960.

Chokshi, Niraj. "Gay Rights, Religious Rights, and an Unlikely Compromise in an Unlikely Place: Utah." *The Washington Post*, April 12, 2015. Accessed April 30, 2015, http://www.washingtonpost.com/politics/gay-rights -religious-rights-and-a-compromise-in-an-unlikely-place-utah/2015/04/12 /39278b12-ded8-11e4-a500-1c5bb1d8ff6a_story.html.

Cole, Jonathan R. *The Great American University: Its Rise to Preeminence, Its Indispensable Role, and Why It Must Be Protected.* New York: Public Affairs (First Paperback Edition), 2012.

Crall, Shari Siebers. "'Something More': A Biography of Martha Hughes Cannon." Honors thesis. University Scholars Project, Brigham Young University, 1985.

Croce, Paul Jerome. *Science and Religion in the Era of William James, Volume 1: Eclipse of Certainty, 1820–1880.* Chapel Hill: University of North Carolina Press, 1995.

Culmsee, Carlton F. "Democracy Enrolls in College." *Utah Historical Quarterly* 30:3 (Summer 1962): 199–213.

Daynes, Kathryn M. *More Wives Than One: Transformation of the Mormon Marriage System, 1840–1910.* Urbana: University of Illinois Press, 2001.

Deresiewicz, William. *Excellent Sheep: The Miseducation of the American Elite and the Way to a Meaningful Life.* New York: Free Press, 2014.

Derr, Jill Mulvay, Janath Russell Cannon, and Maureen Ursenback Beecher. *Women of Covenant: The Story of Relief Society.* Salt Lake City: Deseret Book, 1992.

Divett, Robert T. "Medicine and the Mormons." *Bulletin of the Medical Library Association* 51 (January 1963): 1–15.

Dunford, John Parley. "Students Leave Zion: An Impetus in Twentieth Century Utah." Master's thesis, Utah State University, 1965.

Eliason, Eric A., ed. *Mormons and Mormonism: An Introduction to an American World Religion.* Urbana: University of Illinois Press, 2001.

Erickson, Joseph Glen. *The Life and Educational Contributions of Dr. George Thomas.* Master's thesis, University of Utah, 1954.

Evans, John Henry. *An Historical Sketch of the Latter-day Saints' University*. Salt Lake City: The Author, 1913.

Flake, Kathleen. *The Politics of American Religious Identity: The Seating of Senator Reed Smoot, Mormon Apostle*. Chapel Hill: University of North Carolina Press, 2004.

Fluhman, J. Spencer. *"A Peculiar People": Anti-Mormonism and the Making of Religion in Nineteenth-Century America*. Chapel Hill: University of North Carolina Press, 2012.

Fogarty, Gerald P. *The Vatican and the American Hierarchy from 1870 to 1965*. Wilmington, DE: Michael Glazier, Inc., 1985.

Garr, Arnold K. "A History of Brigham Young College, Logan, Utah." Master's thesis, Utah State University, 1973.

Garr, Arnold K., Donald Q. Cannon, and Richard O. Cowan, eds. *Encyclopedia of Latter-day Saint History*. Salt Lake City: Deseret Book, 2000.

Gaustad, Edwin Scott, and Philip L. Barlow. *New Historical Atlas of Religion in America*. New York: Oxford University Press, 2001.

Geertz, Clifford. *The Interpretation of Cultures*. New York: Basic Books, 2000.

Goodstein, Laurie. "A Leader's Admission of 'Mistakes' Heartens Some Doubting Mormons." *New York Times*, October 9, 2013.

Gordon, Lynn D. "From Seminary to University: An Overview of Women's Higher Education, 1870–1920." In *The History of Higher Education*, 3rd ed., ASHE Reader Series, edited by Harold S. Wechsler, Lester F. Goodchild, and Linda Eisenmann, 529–53. Boston: Pearson, 2007.

Gordon, Sarah Barringer. *The Mormon Question: Polygamy and Constitutional Conflict in Nineteenth-Century America*. Chapel Hill: University of North Carolina Press, 2002.

Gould, Stephen Jay. *Rocks of Ages: Science and Religion in the Fullness of Life*. New York: Ballantine/Random House, 1999.

Griffiths, Casey P. "The Chicago Experiment: Finding the Voice and Charting the Course of Religious Education in the Church." *BYU Studies* 49:4 (2010): 91–130.

Gruber, Carol S. "Backdrop." In *The History of Higher Education*, 3rd ed., ASHE Reader Series, edited by Harold S. Wechsler, Lester F. Goodchild, and Linda Eisenmann, 260–77. Boston: Pearson, 2007.

Guion, Payton. "Mormon Church Has Asked the Supreme Court to Ban Gay Marriage." *The Independent*, April 11, 2015. Accessed April 30, 2015, http://www.independent.co.uk/news/world/americas/mormon-church-has-asked-the-us-supreme-court-to-ban-gay-marriage-10169763.html.

Hansen, Klaus J. *Mormonism and the American Experience*. Chicago: University of Chicago Press, 1981.

Hatch, Nathan O. *The Democratization of American Christianity*. New Haven, CT: Yale University Press, 1989.

——. "The Populist Vision of Joseph Smith." In *Mormons and Mormonism: An Introduction to an American World Religion*, edited by Eric A. Eliason, 123–36. Urbana: University of Illinois Press, 2001.

Herbst, Jurgen. "Rethinking American Professional Education." In *The History of Higher Education*, 3rd ed., ASHE Reader Series, edited by Harold S. Wechsler, Lester F. Goodchild, and Linda Eisenmann, 412–20. Boston: Pearson, 2007.

Hickman, Martin B. "Josiah Hickman: A Student Defends the Faith," *BYU Studies* 11:1 (Autumn 1970): 99–103.

Hill, Marvin S., and James B. Allen, eds. *Mormonism and American Culture.* New York: Harper and Row, 1972.

History of the Bench and Bar of Utah. Salt Lake City: Interstate Press Association, 1913.

A History of Columbia University, 1754–1904. New York: Columbia University Press, 1904.

Holifield, E. Brooks. *Theology in America: Christian Thought from the Age of the Puritans to the Civil War.* New Haven, CT: Yale University Press, 2003.

Hutchison, William R. *The Modernist Impulse in American Protestantism.* Cambridge, MA: Harvard University Press, 1976.

James, William. *The Varieties of Religious Experience.* New York: Modern Library, [n.d., originally published 1902].

Klingenstein, Susanne. *Jews in the American Academy, 1900–1940. The Dynamics of Intellectual Assimilation.* New Haven, CT: Yale University Press, 1991 (republished by Syracuse University Press in 1998).

Larson, T. A. "Woman Suffrage in Western America." *Utah Historical Quarterly* 38:1 (Winter 1970): 7–19.

Leone, Mark. *Roots of Modern Mormonism.* Cambridge, MA: Harvard University Press, 1979.

Levine, David O. "Discrimination in College Admissions." In *The History of Higher Education*, 3rd ed., ASHE Reader Series, edited by Harold S. Wechsler, Lester F. Goodchild, and Linda Eisenmann, 457–73. Boston: Pearson, 2007.

Limerick, Patty. "Peace Initiative: Using the Mormons to Rethink Culture and Ethnicity in American History." *Journal of Mormon History* 21:2 (Fall 1995): 1–29.

Lyman, Edward Leo. *Political Deliverance: The Mormon Quest for Utah Statehood.* Urbana: University of Illinois Press, 1986.

MacDonald, Victoria-María, and García, Teresa. "Historical Perspectives on Latino Access to Higher Education." In *The History of Higher Education*, 3rd ed., ASHE Reader Series, edited by Harold S. Wechsler, Lester F. Goodchild, and Linda Eisenmann, 757–74. Boston: Pearson, 2007.

Mahoney, Kathleen. *Catholic Higher Education in Protestant America: The Jesuits and Harvard in the Age of the University*. Baltimore: Johns Hopkins University Press, 2003.

Marsden, George M. *Fundamentalism and American Culture: The Shaping of Twentieth-Century Evangelicalism, 1870–1925*. Oxford: Oxford University Press, 1980.

——. *The Soul of the American University: From Protestant Establishment to Established Non-Belief*. New York: Oxford University Press, 1994.

Marty, Martin E. *Modern American Religion, Volume 1: The Irony of It All, 1893–1919*. Chicago: University of Chicago Press, 1986.

Mauss, Armand L. *All Abraham's Children: Changing Mormon Conceptions of Race and Lineage*. Urbana: University of Illinois Press, 2003.

——. *The Angel and the Beehive: The Mormon Struggle with Assimilation*. Urbana: University of Illinois Press, 1994.

——. "Seeing the Church as a Human Institution." *Sunstone* 128 (July 2003): 20–23.

Monnett, J. D., Jr. "The Mormon Church and Its Private School System in Utah: The Emergence of the Academies, 1880–1892." Dissertation, University of Utah, 1984.

Moore, R. Laurence. Religious Outsiders and the Making of America. New York: Oxford University Press, 1986.

Nash, Gerald. *The American West in the Twentieth Century; A Short History of Urban Oasis*. Englewood Cliffs, NJ: Prentice-Hall, 1973.

Newfield, Christopher. "The Rise of University Management." In *The History of Higher Education*, 3rd ed., ASHE Reader Series, edited by Harold S. Wechsler, Lester F. Goodchild, and Linda Eisenmann, 346–58. Boston: Pearson, 2007.

Noall, Claire. *Guardians of the Hearth: Utah's Pioneer Midwives and Women Doctors*. Bountiful, UT: Horizon Publishers, 1974.

——. "Utah's Pioneer Women Doctors." *The Improvement Era* 42 (June 1939): 332–33, 372.

Nussbaum, Martha C. *Cultivating Humanity: A Classical Defense of Reform in Liberal Education*. Cambridge, MA: Harvard University Press, 1997.

O'Donavan, Collen. "'The Abominable and Detestable Crime Against Humanity': A Revised History of Homosexuality and Mormonism, 1840–1980." In *Multiply and Replenish: Mormon Essays on Sex and Family*, edited by Brent Corcoran. Salt Lake City: Signature Books, 1994.

Pardoe, T. Earl. *The Sons of Brigham*. Provo: Brigham Young University Alumni Association, 1969.

Peckham, Howard H. *The Making of the University of Michigan, 1817–1992*. Edited by Margaret L. and Nicholas H. Steneck. Ann Arbor: University of Michigan Bentley Historical Library, 1994.

Peterson, Charles S. *Utah: A History*. New York: W. W. Norton & Co., 1984.

Potter, David M. "The Historian's Use of Nationalism and Vice Versa." *American Historical Review* 67:4 (July 1962): 924–50.

Quinn, D. Michael. *Elder Statesman: A Biography of J. Reuben Clark*. Salt Lake City: Signature Books, 2002.

———, ed. *The New Mormon History: Revisionist Essays on the Mormon Past*. Salt Lake City: Signature Books, 1992.

Reuben, Julie A. *The Making of the Modern University: Intellectual Transformation and the Marginalization of Morality*. Chicago: University of Chicago Press, 1996.

Ricks, Joel Edward. *The Utah State Agricultural College: A History of Fifty Years, 1888–1938*. Salt Lake City: The Deseret News Press, 1938.

Roediger, David R. *Working toward Whiteness: How America's Immigrants Became White; The Strange Journey from Ellis Island to the Suburbs*. New York: Basic Books, 2005.

Shipps, Jan. *Mormonism: The Story of a New Religious Tradition*. Urbana: University of Illinois Press, 1985.

———. *Sojourner in the Promised Land: Forty Years Among the Mormons*. Urbana: University of Illinois Press, 2000.

Singer, Merrill. "Nathaniel Baldwin, Utah Inventor and Patron of the Fundamentalist Movement." *Utah Historical Quarterly* 47:1 (Winter 1979): 42–53.

Strong, Josiah. *Our Country: Its Possible Future and Its Present Crisis*. Revised edition. New York: The American Home Missionary Society/The Caxton Press, 1891 (first edition published 1885).

Sweet, William Warren. *The Story of Religion in America*. New York: Harper & Brothers, 1939.

Swensen, Russell B. "Mormons at the University of Chicago Divinity School." *Dialogue* 7:2 (Summer 1972): 37–47.

Turner, John G. *Brigham Young: Pioneer Prophet*. Cambridge, MA: Belknap/ Harvard University Press, 2012.

———. "Why Race Is Still a Problem for Mormons." *New York Times*, August 19, 2012.

Tweed, Thomas A. *Crossing and Dwelling: A Theory of Religion*. Cambridge, MA: Harvard University Press, 2006.

Van Wagenen, Lola. *Sister-Wives and Suffragists: Polygamy and the Politics of Woman Suffrage, 1870–1896*. Provo: The Joseph Fielding Smith Institute for Latter-day Saint History and BYU Studies, 2003.

Veysey, Lawrence R. *The Emergence of the American University*. Chicago: University of Chicago Press, 1965.

Wang, L. Ling-Chi. "Asian Americans in Higher Education." In *The History of Higher Education*, 3rd ed., ASHE Reader Series, edited by Harold S. Wechsler, Lester F. Goodchild, and Linda Eisenmann, 751–56. Boston: Pearson, 2007.

Ward, Margery W. *A Life Divided: The Biography of Joseph Marion Tanner*. Salt Lake City: Publishers Press, 1980.

Wechsler, Harold S. "An Academic Gresham's Law: Group Repulsion as a Theme in American Higher Education." In *The History of Higher Education*, 3rd ed., ASHE Reader Series, edited by Harold S. Wechsler, Lester F. Goodchild, and Linda Eisenmann, 442–56. Boston: Pearson, 2007.

Wellhausen, Julius. *Prolegomena to the History of Israel*. Edinburgh: Adam & Charles Black, 1885.

Wellmon, Chad. "Twilight of an Idol." *Hedgehog Review* 17:1 (Spring 2015): 139–41.

West, Cornel. *The American Evasion of Philosophy: A Genealogy of Pragmatism*. Madison: University of Wisconsin Press, 1989.

Westwood, P. Bradford. "Administrative History of the Church Educational System (CES), 1888–1984, 1995." Lee Library (Special Collections). Brigham Young University. Provo, Utah.

Whittaker, David J., ed. *Mormon Americana: A Guide to Sources and Collections in the United States*. Provo: Brigham Young University Studies Monographs, 1995.

Wilcox, Miranda, and John D. Young, eds. *Standing Apart: Mormon Historical Consciousness and the Concept of Apostasy*. New York: Oxford University Press, 2014.

Wilkinson, Ernest L., ed. *Brigham Young University: The First One Hundred Years*. 4 vols. Provo: Brigham Young University Press, 1976.

Yates, W. Ross. *Lehigh University: A History of Education in Engineering, Business, and the Human Condition*. Bethlehem, PA: Lehigh University Press, 1992.

Yorgason, Ethan R. *Transformation of the Mormon Culture Region*. Urbana: University of Illinois Press, 2003.

Acknowledgments

This book would not have been possible without the support of countless people. I have to name just a few. To sustain my research, the University of Virginia's Faculty Senate awarded me a year-long fellowship, an exceedingly generous gift of funding and time. Two institutes at Brigham Young University—the Charles Redd Center for Western Studies and the former Joseph Fielding Smith Institute for Latter-day Saint History—also provided critical funding for the early stages of my work. These grants allowed me to spend weeks, even months, at a time in Utah's university, state, and church archives. Their support also brought me into contact with a talented cadre of Mormon historians, whose suggestions, in seminars and at conferences, have been invaluable.

Archivists and other library staff offered me tremendous help in identifying materials relevant to my research. The special collections staff at Brigham Young deserves special praise; they handled my rapid-fire, wide-ranging requests with remarkable grace and skill. The assistance of the staff at the archives of the Church of Jesus Christ of Latter-day Saints, the Utah State Historical Society, the University of Utah, Utah State University, and the Daughters of the Utah Pioneers was likewise indispensable.

I owe a debt that cannot be paid to my relatives in Utah, who opened their homes to me throughout this project's duration. I could not have spent so much time in the archives, or enjoyed such a sense of kinship with this pursuit, if it had not been for Ron, Maisa, Kendall, and Erlynne Simpson. Similarly, Enes and Mubera Huskić made a home for me to write in their downtown Salt Lake City café; time and again they offered me comfort food, and they have become like family.

I am profoundly grateful to my academic advisers and mentors, especially Heather Warren, E. Brooks Holifield, and Carlos Eire. Without their encouragement and expert instruction, I never would have conceived of this project, nor had a fraction of the skill to execute it.

In similar fashion, my editor Elaine Maisner and her colleagues at the University of North Carolina Press have been wonderfully steadfast in their support of my work. In combination with the two brilliant readers they secured for the manuscript—whom I thank profusely as well—they helped me fulfill my vision for this book.

Finally, I thank the friends and relatives who have offered me their steady encouragement and keen editorial eyes: Deb, Rick, Erik, and Kim Simpson;

Carolyn Jacobson and Todd Hearon; the Humanities Division research colloquium at Carthage College; and the faculty and staff book club at Phillips Exeter Academy. Most of all, I thank my wife, Alexis, and our sons, Blake and Will, for knowing how much it would mean to me to see this project through.

Index

Page numbers in *italic* type indicate illustrations.

Anti-intellectualism, 6, 7, 83, 111–13, 122, 173 (n. 15)

Apostles (Mormon), 9, 29, 33, 34, 60, 73, 75, 81, 109, 123, 177 (n. 62); Council of Twelve, 172 (n. 5); PhDs named as, 84, 92, 95, 184 (n. 45); questions of professors' faith and, 113, 115; University of Utah president and professor ordained as, 92

Articles of Faith (Mormon), 117

Articles of Faith, The (Talmage), 84

Art studies (Paris), 49, 180 (n. 94)

Aspen Grove speech (Clark, 1938), 117–20, 123, 124

Association of American Universities, 93

Astronomy, 65

Baldwin, James, 45, 46

Baldwin, Nathaniel, 62

Baptists, 6

Barney, Elvira Stevens, 11–12, 167 (n. 2)

Baskin, Robert N., 169 (n. 31)

Beeley, Arthur, 86

Bellevue Hospital Medical College (N.Y.C.), 14, 15, 17, 27

Bell Laboratories, 85, 95

Bennion, Adam S., 92, 97–98, 190 (n. 3)

Bennion, Lowell, 114; "The Methodology of Max Weber" (PhD thesis), 114

Bennion, Milton, 63, 80, 88, 89; "The Modern Skeptic," 68–69, 80

Bennion, M. Lynn, 120

Berger, Peter, *The Sacred Canopy*, 123

Berkeley. *See* University of California, Berkeley

Biblical authority, 54, 55, 70, 74, 83–84

Biblical studies, 5, 55, 63, 98, 100, 101, 178 (n. 85); German biblical criticism and, 66, 70, 75; liberal approach to, 72; *The Fundamentals*, 75–76

Binzel, Alma, 71

Biological evolution. *See* Evolutionary science

Bitton, Davis, *Guide to Mormon Diaries & Autobiographies*, 10

Book of Mormon, 59, 98; belief in veracity of, 117; biblical study and, 100; distrust of the "learned" and, 6, 83, 105; higher criticism analysis of, 76–77, 78, 107; historicity of, 70

Bordin, Ruth, 172 (n. 7)

Bourdieu, Pierre, 123

Bower, William C., 101

Bramwell, E. Ernest, 111

Brigham Young Academy (Provo), 58, 178 (n. 85); accreditation of, 93; charter (1875), 5; Cluff and, 36, 39, 40, 45, 46, 47, 48, 59, 60–61; "college" designation of, 40; Dewey visit to, 63, 81, 82; education courses, 46, 56; instability of, 41; land donation for, 26; map, *99*; student petition, 79–80; summer school guest lecturers, 45–46, 48

Brigham Young College (Logan), 26, 40, 41, 62, 71, 86, 183 (n. 28); plight and closure of, 41, 185 (n. 67)

Brigham Young University (Provo), 26, 182 (n. 19); academic freedom controversies, 80–89, 95, 96, 112, 123–24, 178 (n. 85); academic rigor of faculty, 71–72; biblical criticism and, 98; changed academic climate in 1930s of, 93–97, 108, 113, 123; consolidation with normal schools, 185 (n. 67); current official policy statement of, 123–24; education department, 71, 114–15; first PhD president, 93, 95; inception of, 59; map, *99*; modernist controversy (1911), 5, 69, 70–89, 91, 92; motto of, 87; PhD degrees and, 95, 195 (n. 15); presidents, 58, 71, 81, 82, 93, 94, 95, 97, 178 (n. 85); religion faculty, 120; religious education modernization, 110; sabbatical leaves and, 179 (n. 86); science-religion relationship and, 117; secularism and, 124; seminary summer school, 100–101; Tanner's evolution course, 97; tenure and, 123

Brimhall, George, 58, 71, 78, 79, 91, 112, 178 (n. 85), 179 (nn. 86, 89); academic freedom controversy and, 80–85, 87; R. Chamberlin characterization of, 96; disillusionment of, 82–84

Brimhall, George H., 186 (n. 83)

Brooks, Joanna, 196 (n. 19)

Brooks, Juanita, 121

Brown, Ella Larson, 71

Brown, James L., 53

Bullock, Newell, 56, 58

"Cactus" (female Mormon medical student), 37–38, 39, 50; unknown identity of, 176 (n. 47)

Cannon, Angus, 53

Cannon, George Q., 29, 49, 58, 174 (n. 22), 180 (n. 94)

Cannon, Lewis T., 49, 180 (n. 102)

Cannon, Lillian, 181 (n. 3)

Cannon, Martha Hughes, 52, 53, 174 (n. 23)

Capitalism, 26, 28

Carver, Thomas Nixon, 190 (n. 9)

Case, Shirley Jackson, 98–99, 101, 103

Catholicism, 55, 70, 124

Central and South America, 59

Chamberlin, Ralph, 106, 119; BYU attempted recruitment of, 95–96; as critic, 90; *Life and Philosophy of W. H. Chamberlin,* 96–97;

modernist controversy (1911) and, 71–76, 78, 79, 80, 82–86, 96; summer recruitment tour, 185 (n. 69)

Chamberlin, William H., 72, 74, 75, 79, 82, 84, 85, 97, 106, 108, 119; brother's biography of, 96–97; as critic, 90

Chase, Daryl, 101, 102–3, 110–11

Chicago. *See* University of Chicago

Christensen, D. H., 188 (n. 112)

Christian movements: American universities and, 49; basic beliefs of, 117, 119; Catholics and, 55, 70, 124; early nineteenth-century democratizing of, 6; fundamentalism and, 55, 70, 75–76, 92; history of, 98, 100; Mormons and, 60, 104; nineteenth-century American populism and, 29; nonsectarianism and, 30; twentieth century and, 55, 104. *See also* Protestantism

Church of Jesus Christ of Latter-day Saints. *See* Mormonism

Church-state separation, 55, 70

Claremont Graduate University, Mormon Studies chairs, 195 (n. 4)

Clark, J. Reuben, Jr., 6–7, 111–12, 113–14, 117–20, *118,* 122–23; powerful and enduring influence of, 120; "The Chartered Course of the Church in Education" (Aspen Grove speech), 117–20, 123, 124

Clark, Walter Ernest, 190 (n. 9)

Clark University, 45, 48

Clawson, Rodger, 174 (n. 22)

Clawson, Will, 180 (n. 94)

Cluff, Benjamin, Jr., 9, 36, 37, 39, 40–41, 46, 47, 51, 53, 55, 56, 57, 59–61, 69, 90–91, 175 (n. 39), 179 (nn. 86, 92), 180 (n. 100), 183 (n. 29); Brigham Young Academy summer schools and, 45, 46, 48;

Mormon identity conflict and, 53, 119–20. *See also* Academic migration; General Board of Education; Higher education; Teacher training

Education fund, 61–63

Egalitarianism, 29

Eliot, Charles, 2, 5, 8, 191 (n. 24); influence on Mormon students of, 42–43; Salt Lake City speech, 43, 44, 45

Ellsworth, German, 87

Engineering studies, 11, 15, 17, 18, 27, 36

Ericksen, Alma (E. E.'s brother), 97

Ericksen, Edna (E. E.'s wife), 89

Ericksen, E. E., 37, 86–87, 89, 97, 107; defense of non-Mormon professors, 103–4; dissertation on generational Mormon conflicts, 103; *The Psychological and Ethical Aspects of Mormon Group Life,* 89–90

Eternal progression (Mormon doctrine), 65

Ethics (Dewey and Tufts), 86

Ethnicity, evolution of Mormon, 7

Eugenics, 96

Evangelization, 56

Evans, David, 35, 174 (n. 29)

Evans, Edwin, 180 (n. 94)

Evolutionary science, 3, 5, 22, 26, 34, 51, 54, 55, 56, 70; Abbott's approach to, 73; BYU and, 72, 79–80, 178 (n. 85); BYU changed view of, 97; Mormon eternal progression doctrine and, 65; Mormon "modernism" debate and, 70, 78–79, 83, 84; Mormon rejection of, 58, 73–75, 78–79, 82, 188 (n. 118); H. Peterson's defense of, 83, 188 (n. 118); Scopes Trial (1925) and, 92, 96; traditional creationist belief vs., 57; University of Utah course on, 96

Evolution of Christianity, The (Abbott), 73

Excommunication, 60, 125

Fairbanks, John B., 180 (n. 94)

Faith, healing power of, 12, 31

Federal government: anti-Mormon activity by, 34, 37, 41, 174 (n. 22), 175 (n. 35); Mormon officeholders, 60; Mormon truce with, 3–4, 29

Feminism, 7, 54; twentieth-century Mormon recession of, 90, 125. *See also* Woman suffrage

First Presidency: admission of "past mistakes" by, 125; members of, 9, 16, 31 (*see also* Smith, Joseph F.); "Origin of Man" statement (1909), 73, 84; reorganization of, 172 (n. 5); student plural marriages and, 50; Talmage's scholarly background and, 84

Fletcher, Harvey, 85, 95

Folk wisdom, 6

Freedom of religion. *See* Religious liberty

Fundamentalism, 55; Mormon, 28, 62, 117, 119–20; Protestant, 70, 75–76, 84, 92, 117, 124, 186 (n. 87)

Fundamentals, The (twelve volumes, 1910–1915, 75–76

Furr, Carl J., 103, 111

Garden of Eden, 180 (n. 96)

Gates, Susa Young, 173 (n. 12)

Gender, 9, 19, 55. *See also* Feminism; Women

Genealogy, Mormon, 4, 166–67 (n. 24)

General Authorities of the Church, 116

General Board of Education, 39, 63, 65; ban on books by non-Mormons, 73–74; "circular of instructions" (1911), 84; Cummings report to, 72–75; doctrinal rigidity resolution, 81–82; education fund, 61–62, 71

General Conference (semiannual), 9, 125

Gentiles (non-Mormons), 2, 4, 9, 11, 15, 18, 36, 38–39, 40; condemnation of plural marriage by, 175 (n. 35); lawyers in Utah, 169 (n. 31); Mormon animosity and, 2, 28–29, 90, 109

German biblical criticism, 66, 70; Protestant fundamentalist rejection of, 75

Godbe, William, 172 (n. 67)

Goodspeed, Edgar J., 98, 101

Graham, William C., 101

Grant, Heber J., 93, 95, 111, 117, 186 (n. 83), 190 (nn. 3, 9); denunciation of secular learning, 112–13

"Great apostasy" conception, 100

Guide to Mormon Diaries & Autobiographies (Bitton), 10

Hafen, John, 180 (n. 94)

Hall, G. Stanley, 5, 45, 48

Harrington, Daniel, 42

Harris, Franklin S., 93, *94*, 95, 96, 97, 110, 111, 113

Harrison, Elias, 172 (n. 67)

Harvard University, 1, 88, 96, 188 (n. 112); chapel services, 49, 115; Lawrence Scientific School, 45; law school, 8, 41, 42–43; Mormon student colony, 41, 42–45, *44*, 46, 48, 49, 58–59, 61, 66, 71, 149–54; president, 2, 8, 42–43; religious liberty of, 42–43, 56; summer school, 54

Hatch, Nathan, 6

Healing, divine principles of, 12, 14, 31, 39. *See also* Medicine

Henderson, Martin P., 190 (n. 17)

Herbal medicine, 14

Herbst, Jurgen, 191 (n. 24)

Heresy trials, 5, 55, 111

Hickman, Josiah, 50–51, 53, 56, 87–88; plural wives of, 88, 183 (n. 28)

Hickman, Martha, 50

Higher criticism, 74, 75, 76–78, 82, 83, 107

"Higher Criticism and the Book of Mormon" (lecture), 77

Higher education, 1, 2, 11–27, 83; admissions quotas and, 8; American promise of, 10; changes in (1920s and 1930s), 92–93; Cluff's faith in, 46, *47*, 48; controversy (1911) and, 6–7, 8, 72–78; faculty insecurity and, 189 (n. 135); modernist controversy and, 5, 69, 70–80; Mormon ambivalence about, 7, 31, 33, 63, 65–69; Mormon respect for, 46–47; Mormon institutions of, 26; map, *99*; Mormon populist distrust of, 6, 31, 33; Mormon studies abroad and (*see* Academic migration); non-Mormon educators at LDS general conferences (1921 and 1922), 190 (n. 9); religious studies and, 97–114, 191 (n. 24); secularism and, 40, 111–12, 124; social mobility and, 83; "whiteness" and, 8

Hinckley, Edwin, 79

Hinsdale, Burke, 45, 46

Historicity, Mormon, 3, 107–8

Holden, Perry G., 190 (n. 9)

Home-making. *See* Domestic science

Homosexuality, 33. *See also* Same-sex marriage

Hot drinks, 65

"How Knowledge Comes" (West), 67, 69

Hutchison, William, 72–73

Huxley, Thomas, 22, 26

Idaho, 7, 26, 111

Idaho Southern Branch College (Pocatello), 98, 114

Improvement Era (magazine), 63, 65–66, 67, 69, 80; "Theory and Divine Revelation" editorial, 82

Intellectual life: anti-intellectualism and, 6, 7, 83, 111–13, 122, 173 (n. 15); dissidents and, 63, 172 (n. 67); Mormon quest and, 6–7; in twentieth century, 63–80, 92–125. *See also* Academic freedom; Academic migration; Higher education

Isaiah, Book of, authorship of, 77

Ivins, Anthony W., 186 (n. 83)

James, William, 5, 42, 48, 69, 179–80 (n. 92); *The Varieties of Religious Experience,* 179–80 (n. 92)

Jenson, Joseph, 177 (n. 62)

Jesus Christ, 8–9

Jewish students, 8

Johns Hopkins University, 1, 34, 84

Jordan, David Starr, 2, 56, 97

Joseph Smith as Scientist (J. Widtsoe), 63, 65–66

Joshua, Book of, interpretation of, 115–16

Juvenile Instructor (Mormon periodical), 48–49, 50; "Philosophy and Church Schools" editorial, 82, 83

Kaysville (Utah) seminary, 110–11

Keeler, J. B., 79, 179 (nn. 86, 89)

Kelly, Kate, 125

Kennedy, John F., 120

Kerr, W. J., 177 (n. 64)

King, William H., 174 (n. 29)

Kingdom of God, 100

Kingsbury, Joseph, 88, 89, 188 (n. 118)

Knowledge, nature of, 69

Laney, Hiram, 174 (n. 29)

Larsen, Vernon F., 120

Latter-Day Saints. *See* Mormonism

Latter-Day Saints' College (Salt Lake City), 40, 71, 182 (n. 19); map, *99*

Latter-Day Saints' University (Salt Lake City), 66; map, *99*

Law. *See* Legal profession

Law of Moses, 76

Lay bishop, 9

LDS Business College (Salt Lake City), map, *99*

LDS Church. *See* Mormonism

LDS Institutes, 98, 101, 110, 111, 114, 120

Learning. *See* Academic migration; Higher education; Intellectual life

Legal profession, 7, 11, 15, 17–18, 27, 169 (n. 31); Mormon careers in, 174–75 (n. 29); Mormon suspicion of, 18, 33

Lehigh University, 34, 84

Leone, Mark, 4

Liberalism: political, 70; theological, 117, 119

Life and Philosophy of W. H. Chamberlin (R. Chamberlin), 96–97

Linford, J. H., 177 (n. 64)

Liquor, 65, 66, 106, 108

Lloyd, Wesley, 120

Logan (Utah), map of colleges and universities, *99*

Lory, Charles A., 190 (n. 9)

Lyman, Francis M., 73

Lyman, Richard, 49, 51, 53, 95–96, 110, 190 (n. 3); apostle ordination of, 92

Lyon, T. Edgar, 103, 104–7, 108, 109, 110

MacDonald, Julia A., 176 (n. 47)

Maeser, Karl G., 36–40, 41, 45, 48, 56, 61

Manifesto of 1890, 51, 122, 177 (n. 61); continuance of plural marriage despite, 60, 61, 62, 88; effects on Mormonism of, 3–5; study abroad prior to, 129–36

Market economy. *See* Capitalism
Marriage. *See* Plural marriage;
  Same-sex marriage
Marshall, George M., 88
Martin, Thomas L., 96
Mathews, Shailer, 98, 103
Maw, Charles, 182 (n. 19)
McKay, David O., 113–14, 190 (n. 3)
McKean, James B., 165 (n. 3)
McMurrin, Sterling, 120, 121
McNeill, John T., 101
Mead, George Herbert, 46
*Medical Aspects of the Latter-day Saint
  Word of Wisdom* (Oaks), 108
Medicine, 7; first Mormon student of,
  11–12; first Mormon surgeon
  training, 14; Mormon divine
  healing principles and, 31, 39;
  Mormon doubts about, 12, 14, 18,
  30, 38–39; Mormon women doctors,
  17, 18–25, 24, 27, 29, 31, 32, 50, 52,
  53, 122, 172–73 (n. 7); Utah Mor-
  mons' needs and, 12, 15, 17, 18, 27
Merrill, Joseph F., 92, 98, 100–101, 102,
  108, 110, 111, 190 (n. 3), 191 (n. 26)
Methodists, 6
Michigan. *See* University of Michigan
Military Academy, U.S. *See* West Point
  military academy
Military service, 28
Mill, John Stuart, 26
Millennialism, 11, 26, 51
Millikan, Robert, 85
Mining industry, 169 (n. 31)
Missionaries, 70, 112–13; consecration
  rites, 14–15, 16
MIT (Massachusetts Institute of
  Technology), 1, 49, 180 (n. 102)
Modernist controversy (1911), 5, 55,
  69–80, 83, 85, 86, 91, 92, 96;
  imprecision of meaning of, 70
"Modern Skeptic, The" (M. Bennion),
  68–69, 80

Monogamy, 8, 28
Moody Bible Institute (Chicago), 76
Moore, R. Laurence, 4
"Mormon Boy at College, The" (O.
  Widtsoe), 66–67, 77
Mormon History Association, 195
  (n. 4)
Mormonism: alternate terms for, 8–9,
  American mainstream and, 3, 4–5,
  28–29; American universities'
  effects on (*see* Academic migration;
  Higher education); anti-
  intellectualism and, 6, 53, 70–91,
  96; Articles of Faith, 117 (see also
  Doctrine and Covenants); birth of
  modern, 28–29; church organization, 9; communitarian solidarity of, 8, 11–12; converts to, 6, 15, 27,
  38–39; cooperative economics
  (United Order), 26; dismantling of
  separatism of, 28–53; "eternal
  progression" concept of, 73;
  exaggerated historical claims of,
  107; external pressures on, 122–23;
  federal government activity
  against, 4, 34, 37, 41, 174 (n. 22);
  form of address within, 9; generational attitudes of, 90–91, 103;
  "great apostasy" conception of, 100;
  healing power of faith and, 12, 14,
  31; heresy trials, 5, 111; intellectual
  life (1920s and 1930s), 63–80,
  92–125; intellectual life (late
  nineteenth century), 28–29, 42–43;
  internal issues (1896–1920), 54–90;
  liquor and tobacco abstinence and,
  65, 66, 106, 108; "loyal to the
  cause" meaning to, 114; male
  definers of, 55; multiple wives and
  (*see* Plural marriage); non-Mormons
  and (*see* Gentiles); "Origin of Man"
  1909 statement, 73, 84; "perfect
  society" aspirations of, 11, 12;

populist strain in, 5–6, 29–36, 83; post–World War II developments in, 124–25; Protestant fundamentalist view of, 75–76; racial discrimination and, 121, 125; religious education revisions, 110, 119–20; Salt Lake Tabernacle, 45–46, 89; scholarly authorities on, 92; science studies and (*see* Science-religion conflict); Second Manifesto (1904), 60; secular education doubters, 40; seminary students' summer school, 100–101; separatism underpinnings of, 29; social position of, 125, 196 (nn. 18, 19); Sweet critique of, 102; university religious studies and, 97–114, 123; Utah statehood and, 90; Zion meaning to, 5

Mormon seminaries, 98, 100

Mormon studies (academic field), 123; chairs, 195 (n. 4)

"Mormon Woman's View of Marriage, A" (1877 article), 20

Moroni statue, 89

Moses, 76

Mountain Meadows Massacre (1857), 121

Moyle, James Henry, 33, 35, 174 (n. 29), 175 (n. 35)

Murdock Academy (Beaver), 87–88

National Education Association, 188 (n. 112)

National School of Elocution and Oratory, 53

Natural sciences, 63, 96. *See also* Science-religion conflict

Nauvoo City Council, 107–8

Nauvoo Expositor (newspaper), 107–8

Naval Academy, U. S., 17, 25, 49

Nelson, Lowry, 113

New York City, 15

Niebuhr, Reinhold, 104

19th Amendment, 19

Normal schools. *See* Teacher training

North Cache seminary (Utah), 111

Nursing, 18

Nuttall, L. John, Jr., 114–15, 189 (n. 123)

Oaks, Lewis Weston, *Medical Aspects of the Latter-day Saint Word of Wisdom,* 108

Obstetrics, 18, 29

Old Testament, 100

Ordination of women, 125, 196 (n. 19)

Original sin, 100

"Origin of Man" (First Presidency 1909 statement), 73, 84

Oswego State Normal School (N.Y.), 48, 54, 55, 181 (n. 3)

Papal authority, 70

Paris art studies, 49, 180 (n. 94)

Park, John R., 169 (n. 27)

Parker, Francis, 45–46

Patriarchy, 18

Paul, Martha Hughes (later Cannon), 29, 30

Penrose, Charles W., 73

Pensions, 61

Pentateuch, 76

Periodicals, 48–50, 69, 91. *See also specific names*

Peterson, Henry, 71–72, 73, 74, 75, 78–79, 82, 84, 85, 88, 96, 106, 119; academic freedom defense and, 80, 83; academic sabotage of, 188 (n. 118); as critic, 90; firing of, 79, 83

Peterson, Joseph, 71, 72, 74, 75, 78, 80, 82, 84, 85, 87, 96, 106, 119, 185 (n. 69); on W. H. Chamberlin, 97; as critic, 90; resignation from BYU, 79; University of Utah professorship, 88, 89

"Philosophy, True" (editorial), 76

Physicians. *See* Medicine

Pius X (Pope), 55, 70

Plural marriage, 16–17, 59, 78, 93; direct revelation of, 20; excommunication for, 60; exiles and, 174 (nn. 22, 23); fundamentalist clinging to, 28, 36, 53; legal pressure against, 174 (n. 22); Manifesto of 1890 against, 3–5; medical student sister wives and, 21, 22–23, 24; monogamy replacing, 8, 28; of Mormon academic migrants, 41, 42, 50–51; Mormon student critics of, 35; Mormon vow to cease (1890), 41, 43; number of Brigham Young's wives and children, 168 (n. 19); numbers estimated practicing, 171 (n. 54); official sanction for, 171 (n. 54); post-Manifesto continuation of, 60, 61, 62, 88; prosecution of, 3–4, 41, 53, 165 (n. 3), 174 (n. 22), 176 (n. 46); Republican Party rhetoric against, 172 (n. 1); Supreme Court ruling against, 175 (n. 35); teaching of divinity of, 22, 78, 177 (n. 65)

Pocatello (Idaho), 98, 114

Political parties, 28

Politics, 53, 70

Polygamy. *See* Plural marriage

Populism, 5–6, 29–36, 38–39, 40, 50, 83, 119–20; characterization of, 29; Grant educational position and, 112–13; Mormon professionals' critique of, 29, 30–31, 32, 34, 46, 122; Mormon student validation of, 34–35; resurgence (early twentieth-century) of, 53; science and, 63

Poulson, M. Wilford, 97, 108, 109

Powers, Orlando, 169 (n. 31)

Pragmatism, 5

Pratt, Lorus, 180 (n. 94)

Pratt, Orson, 107, 109

Pratt, Parley, 20–21, 23

Pratt, Romania, 13, 17, 18, 19, 20–21, 23, 29, 32, 34, 39; anti-populist rationale of, 30–31, 34, 122; Deseret Hospital and, 171 (n. 46)

Pratt Institute (Brooklyn, N.Y.), 54

Presbyterians, 34

Presidency. *See* First Presidency

Priesthood, 14; ranks of, 9; women's exclusion from, 9, 19, 125, 196 (n. 19)

Primary Association (women's organization), 9

Property rights, 43

Prophecy, transcendent character of, 77

Prophet, 4, 9, 12, 18, 31. *See also* Grant, Heber J.; Smith, Joseph; Smith, Joseph F.; Taylor, John; Woodruff, Wilford; Young, Brigham

Protestantism, 8, 55–58; Chicago "modernist" theology and, 80, 109; fundamentalism and, 70, 75–76, 84, 92, 117, 124, 186 (n. 87); modernism and, 70, 92; Mormon relations with, 6; 109

Provo, map of colleges and universities, 99. *See also* Brigham Young Academy; Brigham Young University

Psychological and Ethical Aspects of Mormon Group Life, The (Ericksen), 89–90

Psychology, 68, 89–90

Public schools, 5, 28, 63, 93, 178 (n. 78), 188 (n. 112)

Puritans, 43

Racial discrimination, 121, 125

Rasmussen, A. T., 85

Ray, Clinton, 56, 58, 178 (n. 85)

Relief Society, 9, 18–19, 20, 27, 171 (n. 46), 173 (n. 13)

Religion, academic study of, 97–114. *See also* Biblical studies; Catholicism; Christian movements; Mormonism; Protestantism; Science-religion conflict

Religious liberty, 30, 42–43, 56; American universities and, 49; church-state separation and, 55, 70; ruling against plural marriage and, 175 (n. 35)

Religious populism. *See* Populism

Rensselaer Polytechnic Institute, 17

Republican Party, 172 (n. 1)

Revelation, 5, 9, 69, 179–80 (n. 92); Mormon direct, 12, 14, 20, 30, 31, 39; nature of Joseph Smith's, 65, 105, 106, 117, 179–80 (n. 92), 184 (n. 61); subjectivism and, 70

Reynolds, Alice, 187 (n. 106)

Reynolds v. United States (1879), 175 (n. 35)

Richards, George F., 186 (n. 83)

Richards, Heber John, 14–15, 16, 17, 168 (n. 11)

Richards, Joseph, 17, 168 (n. 11)

Richards, Stephen L, 190 (nn. 1, 3)

Ricks College (Rexburg, Idaho), 110

Roberts, B. H., 77; *Comprehensive History of the Church of Jesus Christ of Latter-day Saints,* 107

Rolapp, Henry, 35, 174–75 (n. 29), 175 (n. 31)

Roman Catholicism. *See* Catholicism

Royal Geological Society, 84

Royal Microscopial Society, 84

Royal Society of Edinburgh, 84

Royce, Josiah, 42

Rugh, Charles Edward, 98

Sabbatical leave, 179 (n. 86)

Sacred Canopy, The (Berger), 123

Saints. *See* Mormonism

Salt Lake City, 17–18, 89; Deseret hospital, 31, 171 (n. 46), 173 (n. 13); general conference (semiannual), 9; map of colleges and universities, *99*; Mormon woman doctor expert practice in, 29; public schools, 178 (n. 78), 188 (n. 112); University of Deseret, 17, 169 (n. 27); visiting educators' speeches, 43, 45–46

Salt Lake Tabernacle, 45–46, 89

Salt Lake Tribune (newspaper), 75, 78, 79, 80

Same-sex marriage, 125, 196 (n. 18)

Sayre, Lewis A., 14

Schools. *See* Education; Public schools; *specific institutions*

Science-religion conflict, 10, 22, 34, 42, 57–58, 90; creation and, 57 (*see also* Evolutionary science); reconciliation and, 63–69; scientific disciplines and, 96, separate spheres of (1930s), 114–21

Scientific evolution. *See* Evolutionary science

Scopes Trial (1925), 92, 96

Scott, Charles B., 181 (n. 3)

Scottish Common Sense philosophy, 76

Scriptural authority. *See* Biblical authority

Second Manifesto (1904), 60

Secularism, 2, 4, 40, 41, 111–12, 122, 124, 166 (n. 5)

Seligman, E. R. A., 88–89

Senate, U.S., 60

Sexuality, 125

Shipp, Ellis R. (daughter), 71

Shipp, Ellis Reynolds, 21–22, 23, 24, 29, 39, 50, 121

Shipp, Margaret (Maggie) Curtis, 21, 22–23, 24, 29–30

Shipp, Mary Catherine (Smith), 24

Shipp, Mary Elizabeth Hillstead, 22, 23, 24

Shipp, Milford, 22

Shipps, Jan, 4

Singer, Merrill, 183–84 (n. 36)

Skepticism, 68–69
Smith, George A., 17
Smith, Hyrum M., 186 (n. 83)
Smith, John Henry, 84
Smith, Joseph (founder and prophet),
    4, 11, 69, 100, 107, 113, 121; credibil-
    ity of, 70, 106, 109, 117; *Doctrines
    and Covenants* and, 12, 14, 106;
    liquor and tobacco dangers and, 65,
    66, 106; plural marriage practice
    by, 171 (n. 54); science and teachings
    of, 63, 65, 66; simplicity of, 29, 39;
    visions of, 65, 105, 106, 117, 179–80
    (n. 92), 184 (n. 61); Word of Wisdom
    proclamation, 108
Smith, Joseph F. (nephew of Joseph
    Smith), 31, 33, 56, 61, 62, 63, 75, 90,
    116–17, 172 (n. 1); academic freedom
    controversy and, 82, 83–84, 112,
    122; anti-intellectualism of, 173
    (n. 15); cautions of, 5–6; Second
    Manifesto (1904) of, 60; "simplic-
    ity" of church authority and, 83
Smith, Joseph Fielding (son of
    Joseph F.), 115–17
Smoking. *See* Tobacco
Smoot, Reed, 60, 175 (n. 33), 187 (n. 106)
Snell, Heber C., 100, 114, 192 (n. 30)
Snow, Eliza R., 19, 171 (n. 46)
Social gospel, 55, 98, 100
Socialism, Christian, 104
Social mobility, 83
Social psychology, 46
Social sciences, 63, 72, 123
Sociology, 89
Sorenson, Hannah, 38–39, 40, 50, 122
South America, 59
Spencer, Herbert, 45–46
Sperry, Sidney, 100, 101, 102–3, 120
Spiritual progression, 11
Stake (Mormon regional unit), 8
Stanford University, 1, 45, 46, 53, 85,
    97, 121, 181–82 (n. 7); academic

environment of, 56; education
    studies, 182 (nn. 7, 17); Mormon
    students at, 56–58, 62; president,
    2, 56
Stevens, Jean, 125
Stewart, David M., 15
Story of Religion in America (Sweet),
    102
Strong, Joseph, 165 (n. 3)
Study abroad. *See* Academic migration
Subjectivism, 69, 70
Suffrage. *See* Woman suffrage
Summer schools, 45–46, 48
Supernaturalism, 104
Supreme Court, U.S., 175 (n. 35)
Surgery studies, 14–15, 29
Sweet, William Warren, 99, 102; *The
    Story of Religion in America,* 102
Swendsen, George, 177 (n. 62)
Swensen, Russel, 97–98, 100–101,
    102–4, 108, 110–11, 120; *The Story of
    Religion in America,* 102
Swenson, John C., 45, 53, 56–58

Talmage, James, 33, 34, 41, 51, 90, 115,
    190 (n. 1); influence as Mormon
    apologist, 84, 188 (n. 118); *The
    Articles of Faith,* 84
Talmage, Sterling B. (son), science vs.
    religion debate of, 115–17
Tanner, Annie Clark, 177 (nn. 61, 65)
Tanner, Caleb, 44–45
Tanner, George, 101, 102, 103, 106,
    108–9, 110, 191 (nn. 26, 30)
Tanner, Jennie, 42, 177 (nn. 61, 65)
Tanner, J. L. (misidentification), 44
Tanner, Josephine Snow, 177 (nn. 61, 65)
Tanner, Joseph Marion, 62, 70, 90–91,
    120–21; Harvard law studies of, 41,
    42, 44–45; plural wives of, 42, 88,
    177 (nn. 61, 65); resignation of, 61
Tanner, Obert (Joseph's son), 120–21
Tanner, Vasco, 97

womanhood and, 18, 19, 21; medical
care for, 18, 29; as Mormon doctors,
17, 18–25, 24, 27, 29–30, 31, 32,
37–38, 39, 50, 52, 53, 122, 172–73
(n. 7); Mormon feminism and, 7, 54,
90, 125; Mormon "firsts" and, 53;
Mormon roles of, 9, 18–20, 125; shift
in Mormon educational aims for,
54, 122; University of Michigan
admittance of, 8, 27, 30, 50, 172–73
(n. 7)
Women's Medical College of Philadelphia, 17, 21, 22, 23, 27, 29–30, 50
Woodruff, Wilford, 56, 177 (n. 58). *See
also* Manifesto of 1890
Woolley, Jed, 51
Word of Wisdom, 106, 108–9
Wyoming territory, woman suffrage,
170 (n. 36)

Young, Alfales (Brigham's son), 17, 25,
173 (n. 18)
Young, Aretta, 54–55, 71, 181 (n. 3)
Young, Brigham, 2, 4, 11, 12–26, 13,
60, 113, 121, 165 (n. 3); contempt for
lawyers, 18, 33; death of (1877), 26,
28, 29, 53; descendants of, 85; fears
of intellectual environment and,
25–26; as governor of Utah territory, 19; Mormon dissidents and, 172
(n. 67); Mormon academic migrants
and, 11, 12–22, 25–26, 27, 40, 168–69
(n. 25); number of wives and
children of, 168 (n. 19); plural
marriage official endorsement by,

171 (n. 54); racism and, 125; sons'
studies and, 15–17, 25–26; successor
to, 14, 172 (n. 5); women medical
studies and, 18–20, 21–22
Young, Brigham, Jr., 33
Young, Clarissa Ross (Brigham's
wife), 15
Young, Don Carlos (Brigham's son),
17, 25
Young, Feramorz ("Fera") (Brigham's
son), 17, 25
Young, Joseph Richards (Brigham's
son), 17
Young, Kimball, 85, 95
Young, LeGrand (Brigham's nephew),
17–18
Young, Levi Edgar, 58–59
Young, Richard W., 89, 174 (nn. 24, 25)
Young, Seymour B. (Brigham's
nephew), 130, 169 (n. 25)
Young, Willard (Brigham's son), 15–17,
25, 62
Young Ladies' Retrenchment Society,
18, 170 (n. 33)
Young Men's Mutual Improvement
Association, 63, 65
Young Woman's Journal (church
magazine), 38, 39, 48, 173 (n. 12),
176 (n. 47)
Young Women's Mutual Improvement
Association, 9, 170 (n. 33)

Zane, Charles, 169 (n. 31), 174 (n. 22)
Zion, 5, 11, 12, 15. *See also* Mormonism
Zoology, 97

CPSIA information can be obtained at www.ICGtesting.com
Printed in the USA
LVOW07*1630070916

503622LV00010B/104/P